International Business

International

Business PRINCIPLES

AND PROBLEMS

Howe Martyn
THE AMERICAN UNIVERSITY
WASHINGTON, D.C.

THE FREE PRESS, *New York*
COLLIER-MACMILLAN LIMITED, *London*

FOREWORD

TOMORROW is the child of today. It is a product not only of the actions of statesmen but also of the discoveries of scientists and the decisions of businessmen. Each advance in science opens new vistas. Men of business translate these advances into more and better products and more and better jobs. They have done so at home—and in foreign lands—for more than 2000 years. But one feature that distinguishes our contemporary life is the extent to which businessmen have expanded their horizons to take in more and more countries around the world.

Today, international business is growing with incredible speed, growing both in size and in opportunities to win rewards and to serve. One measure of its increasing importance is that the annual sales of foreign subsidiaries of United States firms are already double the total volume of United States yearly exports. These subsidiaries transfer abroad substantial amounts of capital and equipment and, of even greater importance, priceless technological "know how" and organizational and management skills, as well. Their factories, classrooms, and offices provide some of the finest facilities for training people in the emerging countries to become the future captains of industry and commerce.

In this way, international concerns have become pioneers, opening up new frontiers in the developing regions of the world. Through their enterprise, they have brought to new lands increased employment and higher incomes. But if these foreign

v

subsidiaries have the power to do immense good, they can, in the hands of unenlightened leaders, also do great harm.

In view of this power, it is all the more surprising that so little has been written about the objectives, the activities, the risks, and the benefits of international business in the modern community of nations. Professor Martyn, in publishing this book, helps to fill a void in economic literature. He provides, in the following chapters, a broad discussion of international business activity, which should be invaluable to students, to governments, to businessmen, and to the informed public as a whole.

Professor Martyn is well qualified to undertake this unique study. After having won top honors at the universities of Toronto and Oxford, he was for thirty years a businessman with extensive experience in North America and abroad. He was, at the same time, a guest lecturer and a frequent contributor to business and academic periodicals. At present, he is devoting his entire energies to teaching and research in the field that is the subject of this book.

With this background in business, it is not unexpected that the author takes a strongly practical approach. It is soundly based on an awareness of the fact that, in the world of today, good business lies in making the host country's larger interests one's own. Professor Martyn rightly concludes that prosperity must be universal if it is to be secure and that, when a business invests abroad, it is acquiring a stake in the prosperity of that country.

Finally, most welcome is Professor Martyn's vision of a world in which, through private investment abroad, people help each other directly, come to know each other personally, and thus bring into being—at the grass roots—that practice of international cooperation which is a major contributor to international peace, harmony, and prosperity.

PAUL G. HOFFMAN
Managing Director
United Nations Special Fund

United Nations Headquarters
New York
December 1963

PREFACE

INTERNATIONAL business is attracting increasing interest as a field of concentration in schools of business administration at both undergraduate and graduate levels. This text describes, analyzes, and criticizes an important new economic and social development: the control and management by parent industrial corporations of large numbers of branches or subsidiaries in many foreign countries. As a result, a transformation has taken place in the structure, organization, and policies of international business—and of international trade in general. Sales from foreign subsidiaries have outgrown exports and direct foreign investments by corporations have outgrown international private portfolio investment. This text discusses the implications of this development on the composition of exports, the processes of international marketing, the terms of trade, and the determinants of payments and exchange-rate movements.

G. Keith Funston, President of the New York Stock Exchange, has said that "overseas plants, subsidiaries and other business installations . . . are the best way to transmit know-how." *(Saturday Review,* January 12, 1963, p. 48.)

What precisely are the distinctive contributions of the international business enterprise? Actual steps in the transmission of know-how by accounting practices, quality control, staff selection and training, use of patents, use of trademarks and advertising, are described and illustrated in this book on the basis of years of actual operating experience at senior management level in several international companies. Detailed information on profits, organization, personnel, advertising, and legal conditions are marshaled so as to show the significance to both management and economics.

Indeed, a distinctive feature of this book is that it provides an *international* view of international business. Even the most sheltered American businesses are no longer immune to world conditions, and no business manager or business student can be indifferent or ignorant regarding international business. This text seeks to answer the widely-felt need for material that transcends the clerical detail of import-export procedures and warrants international business as a required course for all business majors preparing to meet the conditions of the future.

Although international business is an extensive field embracing a great variety of industries and geographical situations, this book attempts to provide the student with a broad foundation for further study. It is hoped that the teacher using this book as a sole text will find that it gives students a many faceted vision of this complex subject.

HOWE MARTYN

Washington, D.C.
May 1963

ACKNOWLEDGMENTS

THE INITIAL suggestion that my international business experience could form the basis of a book came from Mr. J. R. M. Wilson, partner of Clarkson Gordon and past president of the Institute of Chartered Accountants of Ontario, who also read and criticized a draft. He deserves credit for what may be useful but he is not responsible for errors of fact or judgment.

Dr. N. A. Baily, Dean of the School of Business Administration, The American University, Washington, D.C., gave the invaluable encouragement and assistance of the academic appointment through which this work has been completed.

The expert editing of Mr. Martin Kessler has greatly improved the thought as well as the expression in this book.

Sir Roy Harrod and Professor Gilbert Ryle, my tutors at Oxford, made impressions that, after a long time and perhaps strange transformations, have found expression in this book. Also George A. S. Nairn, formerly president of Lever Brothers in Canada and chairman of Lever Brothers (Port Sunlight) Limited, my mentor in international business, gave an example of zest for the challenges of this field that I hope is reflected here.

Grateful acknowledgment is extended to Mr. Herman W. Bevis, senior partner, for granting the permission of his firm for quotation from the privately printed history of Price Waterhouse in America; to Professor and Ambassador John Kenneth Galbraith for permission to quote from *The Affluent Society;* and to the Stanford Research Institute for use of its report on investment in Latin America authorized for release by the Embassy of Japan.

The changes that occur when a business executive undertakes to do scholarly research and teach and write have been understood and accepted with good humor by my wife Marjorie, our daughters Nancy Chadwick and Sylvia Hubbard, and our son Peter.

CONTENTS

International Business

1

INTRODUCTION:
THE SIGNIFICANCE
OF INTERNATIONAL BUSINESS

INTERNATIONAL business is an urgent subject of study, particularly 'for businessmen and students seeking business careers and also for all who are concerned with international affairs. A questioning approach is required, not merely to answer the challenge of alternative systems but as a method for finding improvements. The business function may appear to be a conservative part of the Western social system, but business depends for success on innovation, in organization and policies as well as in products. Moreover international business has grown tremendously since World War II, creating new institutions and generating new forces. Nearly 3,000 American firms have foreign subsidiaries, and their sales are double what the United States exports. British, Dutch, Italian, Swiss, and other firms have also expanded internationally. Some American firms earn higher profits from their foreign operations than from their domestic business. The same is true of companies that originate in Britain and Western Europe. These profits and the increases in production and employment through which they are earned are in jeopardy, however, mainly because of misunderstandings and

1

confusion about the relations of business to political principles and social values. This confusion exists in the advanced countries as well as in the less developed nations where subsidiaries have been established. International business therefore requires the attention of political scientists, economic theorists, officials, and journalists as well as of businessmen.

There is confusion about the power that business generates. Politically, Western Europe and North America profess belief in self-determination and self-government, as the best means of ensuring the greatest long-term benefit to the greatest number. Today any population sufficiently homogeneous to elect a government by a democratic majority and occupying a definable geographical area is automatically regarded as a nation-state. Rousseau and Woodrow Wilson are long dead and buried but their ideas reverberate under remote seas and throw up new volcanic islands. Java, Sumatra, and the Celebes emerge from political colonialism and become the uneasy Republic of Indonesia.

Political theory has logical extensions in the field of business. As Senator Sherman observed more than seventy years ago, "If we will not endure a king as a political power, we should not endure a king over the production, transportation and sale of any of the necessities of life." (Quoted in Neale, 1960, p. 25.) Senator Sherman was, of course, the father of United States antitrust legislation, which is designed to limit the concentration of business power.

In reality, however, Western economic practice largely ignores democracy and self-government. Our industries are imperial in scope and autocratic in their government, despite Senator Sherman's efforts. A Tennessee Valley Authority is organized on the same hierarchical plan as the United States Steel Corporation. Colgate subsidiaries from Australia to Venezuela are under control and direction from United States headquarters. And, of course, such corporations are growing, while the proportion of the self-employed is declining.

The daily business of production and distribution, of earning a living, is at least as important in the lives of most people as politics. Most people in the industrially advanced countries have uncritically accepted inconsistencies between political theory and business practice for pragmatic reasons. Democratically conducted businesses fail. The British Cooperative Societies and the Swedish Konsums have had exceptional success, but they have employed conventional autocratic forms of management. There are some forms of democracy in business, the ballots issued to the shareholders of companies, for example, but even then money votes, not men. The election of a pope is more democratic than that of a company president because at least all the cardinals are equal.

Inconsistencies between political principles and business practices do not disturb an American or European company whose profits are increasing. Nor do they often bother those to whom companies are able to pay increasing wages, dividends, and public contributions through taxes. Logic is, however, a more important subject than business administration among the students at the growing universities in Calcutta and Caracas. They want to know how the advanced countries have attained their position. But they want reasons, not examples, and they have been alerted by suspicion of exploitation to look for fallacies in the reasoning of businessmen and their supporters. Furthermore it is unfortunately a fact that the logical structure of empiricism on which business operates is more complex, more advanced, and more difficult to understand than the false dogma of dialectical materialism.

The opinion-makers in Chile, Ghana, and even such industrially advanced countries as Canada are growing critical of dominating foreign businesses and the sale of their countries' assets to absentee capitalists. Business efficiency and productivity are not accepted as ends in themselves. Questions are asked about how the benefits are distributed and how they are related to ultimate human values.

International Business and International Relations

Foreign policies of the Western governments have been ambivalent toward the foreign operations of their corporate nationals.

On the one hand, they claim that business is a private rather than a public activity; on the other hand, they use business as an instrument of national policy whenever possible. While producing goods to make profits, companies also exert social influence that has political effects, and they may even render military services or disservices. The United States government had the most benign intentions toward Cuba all the while that foreign ownership of Cuban industries, including agriculture, was turning the local population into a proletariat with nothing to lose but its chains. At the other extreme, in the war for the survival of political freedom against German National Socialism, the representatives of American-owned Colgate and British Lever acted jointly, on their own initiative, to distribute radio transmitters through neutral Sweden to the underground in occupied Norway. Business activities are continually impinging on foreign relations, though seldom so dramatically.

Adolph Berle has predicted that "the time will come when any purely national organization of economics will be regarded as a quaint antiquity." (Berle, 1959, p. 119.) There is little evidence so far of movement in that direction, despite an immense increase in direct investment in foreign subsidiaries. One of the most progressive companies, judged by the products and services it offers as well as by its name—International Business Machines World Trade Corporation—rejects foreign participation in financial control or local profits so that it can "be free to make any decisions for any given company, on manufacturing policy and the like, that are in the interests of World Trade Corp. as a whole." (Sheehan, 1960, p. 236.)

Of course, the opportunities for any single enterprise to become truly international have been limited by the slow development of international cooperation in general. All businesses with any aspirations toward permanence must avoid breaking the law. There is, however, little applicable international law beyond the International Conventions on patents and postal rates. International business is not responsible for the narrow nationalism of the legal structure under which it still must operate. It can, however, help bring about improvements in the legal framework, mainly by encouraging public recognition and discussion of the problems involved. A notable contribution is the speech in New York on September 27, 1962, by Frederick G. Donner, Chairman of General Motors, in which he asked an International Congress of Accountants to consider how *international* ownership of international companies can be increased.

There is a new trend in a number of regions toward the merging of national authority into larger groupings—like the European "Six"—partly for economic benefits. This trend may appear to counter movements for wider and more effective self-government, including the authority of the governments of formerly autonomous states over such business functions as production, distribution, research, employment, and the rate of capital investment. But the trend to united economic "states" merely lifts the conflict between political sovereignty and international commercial power from the level of individual countries to that of the new regional blocs.

Common market movements gather impetus from expectations of benefits, which include increased protection for the rights and opportunities of the nationals of the participating countries. The citizens of the new Europe anticipate that they will be in a stronger economic position, for instance in tariff bargaining, than they were as Belgians, Dutchmen, Frenchmen, Germans, Luxembourgers, and Italians. Their united political powers are exerted over internal business such as the members of the prewar cartels as well as against foreign competition. The European Coal and Steel Authority, which was specifically created to assert public control over these influential industries, was a necessary precedent for the European Economic Community.

At the same time, movements for political independence continue to be so widespread and so strong that traditional economic entities like the British Commonwealth are disintegrating. They have failed to harmonize the increasingly divergent interests, economic and political, of their members. Indeed, one of the attractions of political self-government for the proliferating small new countries like Ghana and Guiana is that they gain a means of making themselves heard by large industrial corporations controlled far away in London or New York.

Regression can also occur. As more of the public in more countries becomes conscious of the scope and power of international enterprises, stronger assurances regarding the protection of their interests will probably be required. These requirements may deter foreign investment and delay development. Progress requires that industrial efficiency be reconciled with political responsibility. But nationalization of industries by smaller countries is no more effective in this respect than pressure by the foreign companies on their own governments to send in marines.

Business Power and Political Structure

The people in most of the countries of Western Europe, North America, Australasia, and Latin America—as well as in India, Ceylon, Japan, the Philippines, and some of the new African nations—rely on democracy to secure *responsible* government. That is why the future of international business enterprise is not enhanced by the appearance of irresponsibility in the supreme command of modern corporations. This appearance need not reflect on the rulers of business personally. Although autocrats, they may also be, as they are increasingly reported as being, conscientious family men who read books and work in their gardens. The frightening power of the old German General Staff and the modern Pentagon, however, was not built by a Nero or a Caligula. Both military and business organization have grown so large and complex that communications are difficult. The system encourages formulation of decisions and actions with far-reaching effects on the public interest without the public or its responsible representatives being consulted or even informed. This danger is the same as that so widely recognized and criticized in the "apparatus" of communist organization. The danger is compounded when political and military or military and business powers are combined. President Eisenhower, in his farewell address, warned of an unbalancing new influence on the government of the United States arising from an association of military and business interests.

The power of a company in a foreign country exerted through

a foreign subsidiary there may be greater than is the power of the parent company in its home country. In fact, it usually is greater. Business in the United States is regulated in the public interest by the Antitrust Division of the Department of Justice and by the Federal Trade Commission. Similar regulation is achieved in Britain by the traditionally powerful and independent upper Civil Service, especially the Treasury, which is able to exert informal control over business and commerce.

American antitrust concepts and methods do not answer worldwide needs. They are unilateral and nationalistic. They are designed for economic structures that are completely different from those of the smaller developing countries. Most important, they are merely negative, proscribing what business must *not* do. Only businessmen themselves can take the positive actions that will maintain and extend public acceptance of their power and the economic efficiency it promotes.

Companies with subsidiaries operating in countries like Mexico and South Africa no longer claim extraterritorial rights as they formerly did in China. They obey the local laws and regulations for the most part, and do not go looking for trouble. Compliance with weak laws and easy regulations is not enough, and companies can expect further regulation as host countries try to develop their legal frameworks to levels comparable to those achieved in the more advanced countries. The host countries have the right and the responsibility to make such efforts. Businesses of all kinds are granted their charters, licenses, patents, trademarks, and other legal privileges, including land titles, by the governments of the countries where they operate, in the public interest of the people of those countries.

Furthermore, the public has a right to be informed which is basic to the effective working of our western social systems. This right in itself is an important means of making authorities responsible, and it is essential for exposing when and where new or amended laws may be required. For international business to disclaim responsibility for public information is to invite intervention, of which an extreme example is the Cuban expropriation decrees.

The purpose of this book is to provide the student of business and the general public with information and to provoke discussion about the scope and organization of international business. Obtaining accurate and up-to-date information is difficult, and it is not made easier by the mistaken opinion of some businessmen that it is safe and sound for them to make profits out of international operations in secret. Modern business should have nothing to hide. On the contrary, educating the public (beginning with self-education) may be an essential component in the future success of international businesses.

The Productivity of International Enterprise

Despite the questions for the political scientist that have been raised in the preceding pargraphs, there can be no doubt among economists that international businesses are creating wealth, a large part of which remains in the countries where it is created. The evidence is the success and prosperity of companies with foreign subsidiaries and the recent goldrush of others to join them—a current so strong that it contributed to the crisis in the United States balance of payments and the drain on United States reserves in 1960.

Figures on the growth of international companies and the profits of foreign subsidiaries, even when they can be obtained, are only indirect measures of the contributions of international enterprise to the creation of wealth. They should be complemented with analyses of the contribution of direct foreign investment to increases in gross national product in a large enough number and range of countries to yield reliable generalizations. For the present, for most countries the facts are restricted mainly to the success stories of particular companies.

The available information provides grounds for the belief, strong among businessmen and accepted by many western governments, that international enterprise makes a net contribution to wealth and welfare. But much more work will be required to prove this proposition. Here is a productive field for future research. This is not to be confused with propaganda such as some of the training offered by business schools to foreign students which is based on the assumption that what is best for American subsidiaries is best for the economies of Pakistan and Peru. The inspiration and the financing of such programs have been generous but they need to put more emphasis on objective research and less on preaching a gospel. Research in which people of different nationalities work together on jointly-acknowledged problems avoids the superior-inferior relationship which offends people in developing countries. Research also provides a form in which new ideas are communicable to important groups of people such as those trained in the strict and narrow law-school logic that is the traditional education in the Latin world. In most countries there are more lawyers elected to congresses and parliaments than economists or businessmen. Their training has been concentrated on deductive reasoning from concepts like sovereignty and on legislating and regulating. This training has not made them sympathetic toward business pragmatism, but they can be led toward this through the respect which they give to the intellectual content of science.

Business Responsibility for Information

The onus for supplying information and supporting objective research falls inescapably on international companies. Whether or not they stand to gain from critical examination cannot be known in advance, any more than all the effects of a nuclear detonation in the Van Allen Belt can be predicted, but without research on their economic and social effects international companies certainly stand to lose because they will have no defences against attacks on grounds of nationalism and self-determination.

National governments are in equal need of comprehensive information about international enterprise. E. J. Kahn, Jr., has reported that "for the last ten years or so, our foreign critics have taken to identifying the policies of our State Department with those of the Coca-Cola Company." (Kahn, 1960, p. 4.) The governments of rich and advanced countries need more information about the activities of companies that, intentionally or not, are factors in their foreign policy. As recently as April, 1962, the United States government moved to require reports on the financial transactions of "U.S. businesses and persons holding interests of 10 per cent or more in foreign concerns." (*The New York Times*, April 24, 1962, p. 54.) While this step should result in some useful information, it will provide answers only to some questions. Organization and methods are also significant. In addition, the governments of other countries where foreign companies have extensive operations also urgently need more information before they can assess whether or not the changes suggested by nationalist sentiment will better serve their interests.

All concerned may happily discover that the tested power of publicity to engender public responsibility is sufficient to harmonize international business efficiency and progressiveness with the objectives of political nationalism. The first J. P. Morgan stated that "business must now be done in glass pockets." (Quoted in DeMond, 1951, p. 59.) Morgan's warning is equally valid today—and tomorrow.

2

NEW FORMS AND METHODS
IN INTERNATIONAL BUSINESS

THE WEALTH of nations is the historic field of the economist. National governments have given him materials to work with—population estimates, currency in circulation, exchange rates and, more recently, elaborate indices and composite figures on employment, prices, savings and investment, productivity, and gross national product. National governments have also given the economist the encouragement of attention and even occasional public employment. But economics has not yet become a science of control, either within nations or in their international relations, as official economic forecasts unintentionally reveal.

The economics of the firm developed later and here an elaborate body of theory still lags behind the facts. Private enterprise is understandably reluctant to disclose the activities from which it anticipates profits. Apparent exceptions sometimes occur when a company receives good publicity and makes profitable connections by participating in conferences, for which a popular location is Boston with its scholarly associations, or by supplying case-study material. American firms especially can afford to be quite open about their current methods because these methods are under constant revision and the important

11

profit potentials are hidden in plans for the future, which are
not divulged. Thus the large-scale adoption of a new variant
on a traditional technique, house-to-house distribution—as practiced by the Avon cosmetics and toiletries company—seeped into
the American economy. This firm's business rose to 25 per
cent of the volume of some classes of trade because of unortho-
dox methods that for years escaped the notice even of the
competition, including other manufacturers and the drug and
department stores. Such changes have to be looked for very
conscientiously and shrewdly by scholars and students involved
in truly empirical study of dynamic economics.

Business has also evolved a new institution, new in scope
and demanding new policies, methods and, probably, new social
orientations. This institution is the international firm, operating
a chain of foreign subsidiaries. Although it is likely to trade
under names that are becoming literally household words for
people of many languages and in far parts of the world, this
institution has as yet received scant attention in classrooms or
in the literature on international economics. As a result, it has
been left largely to the very tender mercy of its own public
relations department, which may hire a company historian or
provide publicity material to *Fortune* or *Business Week*. The
strength of this form of business suggests, however, that it
should be studied in its own right and not merely as a variant
of the firm in orthodox microeconomics. One reason is that such
studies may indicate a tendency for profits, the supposed catalyst
of western progress, to be concentrated more and more in international operations.

The most readily available material for the study of international economics has so far consisted of international financial
data and of statistics that attempt to compare standards of living
and rates of economic growth among various nations. The
comparisons of country levels with growth histories yield analogies as to the complicated and time-consuming stages through
which economies have moved. These are unreliable indicators,
however, because of the determination of many nations to pull
themselves up by their own bootstraps. They are doing this
by forcing the pace of industrialization which they can do by

making their own shoes, for example, with an assist from the Bata Shoe Company, despite the traditional British advantage in the export of leather goods and the American advantage in shoe machinery.

International finance, the other area of open information, has been interpreted from concealed premises. It suited nineteenth-century British thinkers to conceptualize an international financial mechanism that would regulate exchange rates, money movements, and consequently national interest rates, exports, investment, wages, and employment. For a while the Bank of England succeeded in accomplishing all that. But those theories were proved useless even to Britain in 1926, the year when the General Strike demonstrated that wage deflation was no longer a politically feasible means of stabilizing the business cycle. Money movements interact, of course, with other forces, but people are not willing to allow them to be the governing factors over trade and employment. The heads of the Bank of England and other central or reserve banks continue to use the title of Governor but they have had to give up forming their policies independently in favor of close consultation with government departments concerned with industry, trade, and employment as well as finance.

The Changed Basis of International Trade

Historically, international trade, which involves the organization, management, and finance of the movement of goods and services among countries, has called forth some remarkable institutions—the trading communities of the Phoenicians and the Venetians, the British East India Company, the Matheson-Jardine operations on the China Coast. The evolution which affected them has been seen at work more recently on the great importing houses like Jacobsen and Van den Bergh in the former Dutch East Indies and the Woolworth subchain and the Sears stores, which contributed such efficient retail distribution to Cuba.

International trade, viewed solely as the physical movement

of goods, has been a distracting influence for the understanding
of recent developments. It has limited observation of the facts
and permitted oversimplified theorizing. During the period
when cheap energy from freshly opened coal mines gave Britain
dominion over the value created by processing and transporting
other nations' raw materials, it seemed to British political economists that wealth flourished through the international division
of labor. That thinking is still current, despite the contrary
example of industrialization in the United States.

People in the industrially advanced countries, which now
include the United States, Germany, and others beside Britain,
are inclined to attach importance to what is called "the law
of comparative advantage" in international trade. But citizens
of former colonies and other less developed countries are becoming aware that it carries none of the certainty of a "law" of
physics. Furthermore, the advantage is frequently one-sided,
as in the case where both Brazil and the United States will
get more cars and more coffee if Brazilians stay bent over their
hoes, but the Brazilian share of the combined value produced
shrinks steadily. Within the United States farmers have found
that market prices are affected by other influences beside the
law of supply and demand which generally favor the food
processors, but they can successfully mobilize political influence
to improve their position.

It is now beginning to look as if the future of international
trade will be most promising if attention and effort are concentrated on products in which there is actual scarcity rather
than differences in price assumed to be derived from differences
in cost which may be historic or temporary or which may be
equalized by government action for reasons of policy. These
scarce products may be naturally scarce, like asbestos, or newly-
invented, like nylon, for which time is needed to assess markets
and build foreign factories. There is still an export trade in
heavy, bulky coal out of West Virginia, through the famous
old ports of Hampton Roads, because of the unique advantages
of this coal for steel production, which is becoming widely
internationalized under the influence of national government
policies. The importance of the former staples of international

trade has, however, declined relatively, and in some cases absolutely. Examples are rubber, cotton, wool because of synthetics; wheat because of nationalistic agricultural protection; oil, and even uranium, because of new sources of supply resulting from better prospecting. Northern countries used to be large importers of vegetable oils, including American cottonseed oil. Now synthetics have sharply reduced the demand for oils for soap, and the soya bean has been acclimated and deodorized to provide margarine. The nylon stockings from the United States that helped Americans to make friends with the best-looking girls all over the world right after World War II are no longer effective international currency, being manufactured and easily available in dozens of countries.

International activity is prominent in the extractive industries, although the modern trend is toward more local processing. International firms dominate the long-established Canadian nickel-mining and forest-products industries and the newer oil and iron-ore industries, the South African diamond mines, and the Congo copper mines. British firms were once as important in Argentine cattle ranching as American firms in Cuban sugar plantations until recently and Central American banana plantations. These firms are international, however, only in the sense that some of the capital and some of the know-how have been supplied from a nation other than the one in which the natural monopoly happens to be located—and that the firms have insisted on retaining domiciliary relationships with the countries from which the capital originated.

The geographical location of raw materials still attracts foreign investment in extractive industries, but not invariably. Canada has an oil industry, new since World War II, which dramatically stimulated all sectors of the economy for several years. Brazil, on the other hand, still imports oil, despite favorable geological indications. The reason for this difference seems to be that Canada's policies encouraged the peculiar stage in the development of an oil industry called wild-catting, in which Texans seem to be peculiarly adept. Brazil remained fearful that if a foreign Aladdin released the oil genie, Brazilians would never be able to control it. Mexico had nationalized its oil industry which had been largely foreign controlled. Argentina shared the Brazilian attitude for many years, and imports of oil were the heaviest charge on Argentine foreign exchange. Exploration was opened to foreigners in 1958, however, and production of oil in Argentina has increased so rapidly in the years since that almost all her requirements are now supplied domestically.

Companies that are widely international in operation are comparatively recent in the extraction field. An example is Rio Tinto mining. The managing director, Val Duncan, reported that "it was not until the early 1950s that we embarked seriously upon a programme of development of operational activities outside Spain." (Duncan, 1960, p. xxi.) The International Nickel Company of Canada, with its head office in New York, was exclusively concerned for many years with the exploitation of its deposits in the Sudbury area, and it has only recently moved into nickel-working in another part of Canada. A press report early in 1961 indicated that International Nickel was at last becoming operationally as well as financially international through the purchase of a mine in Greece.

Shell, New Jersey Standard, and their largest competitors pursue oil internationally and market their products and by-products internationally. Aluminium Limited is also widely international. Its raw material, bauxite, is common and widely distributed. The know-how for converting bauxite to commercial aluminum profitably, which includes the economic management of the necessarily large capital investment and the development of markets, has evidently been scarce, however, and for a long time almost exclusively the property of this one company. The larger companies in oil and metals are increasingly integrating their production and marketing activities and finding new markets internationally.

The typical international enterprise is no longer drawn to foreign parts solely in search of scarce natural resources. Even in the extractive industries, new technology in exploration and processing has widened the possible sources of supply. In their search for raw materials for import to their home countries, the entrepreneurs, assisted by mining engineers and technicians and backed by financiers, have created surpluses in many of the traditional markets—both geographical markets like the United States and Europe and such commodity markets as copper and cotton. The causes include more efficient exploration and production and the invention of synthetic substitutes. The effect is to change the emphasis from searching for supplies to cultivating demand.

The New Emphasis on Markets

The great international expansion of industry since World War II has been in pursuit of markets—populations with purchasing power. One of the revelations of the period has been the amount of purchasing power that could be called forth from apparent deserts of poverty. Customers, not raw materials, have been the attraction, and local manufacture is often the surest way to reach them. This situation is due partly to the multiplication of politically independent countries—which has increased the number of tariffs, quotas, and similar trade barriers—and partly to the need for local packaging and labeling, stocks, parts, service, and the like.

The magnitude of this new development cannot be easily determined. The lagging state of knowledge and the belated official interest are clear in the scarcity and the continuing upward revisions of the figures. Pizer and Cutler estimated that in 1959 the sales of United States-controlled foreign companies amounted to $35 billion. (Pizer and Cutler, 1960, p. 34.) Former Attorney General Herbert Brownell, however, has stated that "in 1960 there were 43 billion dollars of sales of products manufactured by U.S. business abroad." (Brownell, 1962, p. 1.) Thus foreign sales are at least 50 per cent and possibly even 100 per cent greater than the total exports from the United States, which were approximately $19 billion in 1959.

This development was foreshadowed more than a quarter of a century ago in the report of the Balfour Committee on Britain's Industry and Trade, which recognized the significance of British exports of machinery for the manufacture of textiles.

Those exports equipped the textile industries in Brazil, China, India, and Japan, thereby reducing British exports of finished goods and contributing to the depressions in Lancashire and other textile-manufacturing areas, which have been a nightmare to labor unionists ever since.

British manufacturing know-how went abroad with the machines, in the persons of British technical experts—the machinists who were the engineers of that period. There was also some capital export in the form of long-term credit, including debentures. There were also substantial international investments, primarily in the purchase of bonds by individuals. The British, however, did not make a practice of exporting marketing or general management or seeking permanent control over the use of their machines abroad.

Today, as a result of developments in marketing, it often happens that the home country of a company that achieves a technological advance finds itself the prosperous foster-parent of subsidiaries in many other countries. These subsidiaries are owned and managed by the parent companies. In the rapidly and widely internationalized drug business, the magnet is clearly markets, consumers, population—mainly human beings but also including domestic animals like the sheep of Australia, the beef cattle of Argentina, and the pet dogs of Britain. Pfizer sales of medical items in Denmark, for example, are exceeded by their veterinarian business. The experience of the drug industry also illustrates the particular attractiveness of direct foreign investment that consists largely of know-how. This term includes such intangible property as international patent rights and trademarks. The profits of most of these companies have been gained from comparatively small cash investments.

The difference between the foreign investment of the postwar years and the British investment of previous periods lies in the amount of control that has accompanied machines and money on their travels into foreign markets. The parent companies establish wholly-owned branches or subsidiary companies and thus obtain the power to run them efficiently. This arrangement appears to be more efficient than more primitive forms of inter-

national business like simple export of products and the selling
or licensing of machines and processes.

The heavy postwar expansion has taken the form of direct
foreign investment, the creation or purchase of local companies
as foreign subsidiaries. The investor is a corporation rather than
a private individual, and the investor obtains control of foreign
operations instead of mere claims for interest on borrowed
money. Direct ownership gives rights to profits, including stock
bonuses, which usually yield much higher returns than the fixed
rates on bonds and preferred stocks. The Canadian government's Bureau of Statistics has reported that "direct investments
in foreign-controlled enterprises . . . make up more than half
of the total . . . of foreign long-term investment in Canada . . .
and have been growing more rapidly than portfolio investments." (Dominion Bureau of Statistics, 1962, p. 47.) Approximately one-third of all American foreign investment is, of course,
in Canada.

The largest influence on the modern form of international investment has been the United States. The Swedish economist
Gunnar Myrdal has pointed out that "there has been a strong
bias in favor of direct investment through either the establishment or the development of United States enterprises abroad."
(Myrdal, 1956, p. 105.) Direct investment, meaning complete
control, has long been the fashion in the United States. There
are a number of circumstances which will be discussed in
following chapters that have encouraged direct foreign investment. Some of them are financial, some psychological. In American business, the important considerations include what the
business press purports to reveal as the secrets behind the success of such international firms as Colgate, Gillette, and I.B.M.
In *Sears Roebuck de Mexico, S.A.*, the first case study (1953)
in a series called "United States Business Performance Abroad,"
issued by the National Planning Association, Richardson Wood
and Virginia Keyser advised that "you will do better for your-
self and the country that receives you when you send abroad
not just capital but the methods and the management that are
your most valuable stock in trade." (Wood and Keyser, 1953,

p. 52.) The subsequent experience of many companies has demonstrated that they can develop in foreign countries with comparatively little outside capital, provided that they can supply new methods and enterprising management.

The various guidelines laid down by these companies have been followed by so many other American companies with such success that a new pattern of international business has been formed. In addition to American expansion, which has been the largest and most conspicuous, British, Canadian, Dutch, Italian, Swedish, and Swiss companies have quietly moved along parallel lines. German and Japanese companies were delayed by postwar reconstruction problems and by foreign mistrust, but they are now rapidly following up and consolidating their export marketing successes by forming new subsidiaries abroad, particularly in Latin America. They may be able to take competitive advantage of any slackening of American activity resulting from political confusion and uncertainty in the United States.

The Impact of International Firms on International Finance

The striking proliferation of international firms on the contemporary economic scene may prove to be second only to Keynesian national monetary and fiscal policies in influence over general economic conditions. Indeed James Coyne, former Governor of the Bank of Canada, has said that the power and activities of international firms have inhibited the effectiveness of national monetary policies. (Coyne, 1960, p. 23.) How it can happen is revealed perhaps unintentionally in another National Planning Association study: "In periods when the Brazilian government's inflation control policy restricts commercial bank facilities, the flow of credit has to be reduced and (electric) appliance sales decline. At such times the manufacturers generally try to offset in part these restrictive effects by lengthening their credit terms to distributors and retail dealers." (Geiger, 1961, p. 47.) Credit allowed by manufacturers and wholesalers and by retailers like Sears is an important part of the modern financial mechanism. In Britain, the home of Keynesianism, credit control has been extended by law and regulation to cover the field of consumer credit since the old bank interest-rate method of restraining credit had proved inadequate. In countries without British laws and discipline, it is easy and almost natural for companies with the financial strength provided by their international affiliations to "offset" local government policies that could reduce their profits. The basic problem is that neither the governments nor the companies are as yet fully aware of the powers and effects of the new forms and methods of international business.

Company decisions on investment in foreign operations, including reinvestment of foreign profits, affect the monetary situation in both the home and foreign countries. The problems arising from the flow and—even more important—the ebb of foreign investment in recipient countries, are discussed in Chapter 15. A number of countries have brought the outward movement of investment under control of their domestic monetary policies. The Capital Issues Committee of the British Treasury and similar agencies in European countries keep internal investment by foreigners, as well as external investment, under surveillance and control.

In the United States, the dollar crisis, on the one hand, and a belief that the rate of reinvestment at home has not been adequate to maintain growth, on the other, aroused concern among the monetary authorities early in the 1960's. The use of fiscal regulators, specifically taxation on profits as they are earned in certain foreign countries rather than as they are remitted, was proposed. Tariff reductions were also viewed as a possible means of restraining investment in foreign manufacturing. Such indirect methods are difficult to administer and often have political effects outside the area of financial policy. Serious disagreements about the facts in this complex situation —particularly the arithmetic of the effects of foreign investments on the balance of payments—were illustrated by a statement filed with the Finance Committee of the United States Senate on April 26, 1962. In this statement, the Standard Oil

Company of New Jersey boldly challenged the official calculations by the United States Treasury of the rate and amount
of the net return to the United States from foreign investments.
Clearly, governments have the authority and the responsibility
to establish and enforce policies on foreign investment. It seems
probable, however, that existing national financial policies and
methods will require serious revision to meet the new conditions that have arisen in international business. The first requirement is for more information and better appreciation
of the problems by all the governments concerned.

Political and Economic Effects
of Direct Investment

From his vantage point in independent and prosperous Sweden, Myrdal sees "an explosive issue" developing in many
countries and involving "final authority, including economic
policy and commercial relations with the outside world." (Myrdal, 1956, pp. 286-87.) Companies like General Electric undoubtedly are willing to face that issue—perhaps more coolly
than the government of Brazil, for example. That does not mean
that either side, international company or national government,
fully understands the issue.

The influence of international enterprise is so great and so
complex that it requires wide discussion. Shell Oil, one of the
largest international firms, presents an example of the problems that can arise. What will happen if another Labor government is elected in Britain and attempts to nationalize the British
wing of this Anglo-Dutch complex, either outright or by purchase of controlling shares? Shell has large interests in Venezuela.
W. C. Taylor and his colleagues have pointed out that "the
government (of Venezuela) grants oil concessions to private
companies which, by law, cannot be under the control of any
other government." (Taylor, Lindeman, and Lopez, 1955, p. 3.)
Incidentally the British Labor Party can properly talk only of
nationalizing—not of socializing—the large British industries that

have operations abroad, because the British have no intention of losing foreign earnings by turning over foreign subsidiaries to the people of the countries in which they operate.

In another example, the American government classifies as secret significant defense research carried on in the American laboratories of companies like General Electric. What is the position of General Electric's wholly-owned Brazilian subsidiary? It will not receive United States government contracts or information in sensitive fields from the United States parent company. But even so, discoveries may be made. Could the Brazilian government retain them exclusively or sell them to other governments? Could GE which is the largest electrical concern in Brazil accept defence research contracts from the Brazilian government, or alternatively could it refuse?

Canada is commonly pictured as a country richly endowed with natural resources—indeed with more than her sparse population could hope to develop without recourse to foreign capital. It is not surprising, therefore, that the Dominion Bureau of Statistics reported that in 1958, 60 per cent of mining and smelting and 80 per cent of petroleum and natural gas were under foreign control. International enterprise had, however, created a new situation and one that spread from business into politics when, in 1958, 51 per cent of all manufacturing in Canada had passed into foreign ownership and fifty-seven per cent into foreign control. As James Coyne added, "in many important types of manufacturing the foreign predominance runs from 75 per cent to 100 per cent." (Coyne, 1960, p. 22.)

Canada may seem to be a unique case, since its geographical proximity would naturally tend to make it an economic appendage of its industrially more powerful neighbor, unless it were to adopt such artificial means as high tariffs to stimulate its own domestic manufacturing. This book will show, however, that American companies that are predominant in Canada are also extending their operations to more and more countries (see Chapter 4). Some of them made their first foreign venture into Canada because it is easy to reach, its people speak English, and its currency is in dollars. But most of those companies, having tasted foreign success, are roaming farther afield. Canada's special significance in the spread of international enterprise has been as a training-ground for many companies, British as well as American, in the techniques and the profits of foreign operations. This trend has already gone so far that it has compromised the capability of Canadians to determine independently not only their economic policy but also their political and cultural future.

The recent return to foreign control of a national economy may look like a reversion to economic colonialism in a new form. This result was not intended or anticipated by the particular corporations that made the investments—or by the people and governments who encouraged them. The diversity of companies involved makes concerted economic or political pressure unlikely, except in the subtle but powerful trend of their reinvestment policies. A dilemma is created, however, for governments and for enlightened corporation managements. Do they allow business to transcend national authority, as well as national boundaries? Or do they allow narrow jurisdictions and national vanity or conservatism to delay economic development and keep people poor and hungry? The Russians adopted the negative solution of complete nationalization of industry, which cut them off from the advantages of direct association with western industrial progress. Cuba has done the same. There are indications, fortunately, that other radical new nationalist regimes like those in Guinea, Ghana and Guiana are still open to any solution that can harmonize development by international enterprise with their national aspirations.

3

HISTORICAL INFLUENCES

THE COMPANY of Adventurers Trading into Hudson's Bay, founded in 1670, invested British capital and Scottish skill in a chain of retail outlets on the northern fringes of America. These outlets sold blankets, tobacco, fishhooks, cooking pots, guns, and other hardware to Eskimos and Indians for payment in the local currency, beaver pelts. In its early years, the Company made fabulous profits on foreign exchange. The beaver pelts commanded a wide premium in London, where the currency of the Indians was a scarce luxury commodity.

The Hudson's Bay Company has survived, and it continues to pay dividends, though at relatively lower rates, as a chain of retail stores. While it never actually encouraged economic development through local manufacturing in its area of influence —and though it actively discouraged agriculture to save the hunting grounds—it pioneered in transportation. It was also at times the sole provider, over wide areas, of what is now called social capital—law and order, surveys and maps, the layout of town sites, community buildings, education and entertainment, these last in the form of the Factor's bookshelf and the Factor's Christmas party. The Company always managed, however, to avoid becoming inextricably involved in politics and to concentrate on commercial activities.

The Hudson's Bay Company, a British corporation still directed from London, had enough vitality in 1960 to be able to take over a chain of department stores in eastern Canada. By this extension from its western Canadian stronghold, it became one of three national department store chains in Canada, the others being one entirely Canadian firm, the T. Eaton Co., and a company associated with the American Sears Roebuck.

The long slow development of the Hudson's Bay Company gives perspective to the trend that has been conspicuous in recent economic history, direct foreign investment. That history also illuminates the possibilities of foreign investment, because the contribution of capital by the original shareholders was a token compared with the returns. Annual dividends often exceeded 100 per cent in the early years. The Company financed its growth entirely out of profits. The 1960 valuation of assets was $115 million. The Hudson's Bay Company invested working capital plus the technical know-how of retail trade, much of which consisted in the early days of working long hours, honesty, a knowledge of bookkeeping, and the ability to survive wilderness food and weather with no help from home except Scotch whisky.

Even earlier in history, the Medici established foreign branches of their Florentine banking enterprise in Rome, Lyons, Bruges, London, and elsewhere. These branches acted as more than mere correspondents. They did local banking, accepting deposits from the early traders and manufacturers and risking them in loans to princes. Although founded on Medici capital, the branches owed their development to the pioneer knowledge of banking that the Medici family had built up at home in Florence. They provided an early instance of how practical and profitable it can be for a business to spread internationally on a basis of exclusive but easily transported know-how. When this know-how of the Medici declined, perhaps because the head office management became too involved in affairs of state and church—first governing Florence and then ascending to the papacy in Rome —their international business disappeared.

In the sixteenth century another family, the Fuggers of Augsburg, became prominent in international finance. "About 1525 . . . their business relations reached from Hungary and Poland to Spain, from Antwerp to Naples." (Ehrenberg, 1928, p. 83.)

Here too, politics, in the form of too close an identification with the House of Hapsburg, contributed to their decline.

The Lombard bankers who laid the permanent foundations of British banking had moved in person to London along with their money rather than attempting to operate internationally. British banking eventually developed provincial branches, but even at the height of British international commercial influence, the usual British procedure was to found the Hong Kong & Shanghai Bank, the Bank of Australasia, or the Union Bank of South Africa as separate corporations designed to give local banking service in those regions, rather than to establish subsidiaries of Lloyds, Martins, or the Midland.

The international banking business created by the Rothschilds in the nineteenth century and still in operation today anticipated the organization of the modern international corporation in some respects. The Rothschild family provided a cadre of international executives with family loyalty, confidence, and know-how. They kept in touch with one another. They were, however, free from ties to place and to various nationalisms, and they branched out from Frankfurt to Vienna, Naples, Paris, and London. There are reported to be Rothschilds now resident in New York and Toronto, personally extending the family business still further. The Rothschilds have also shown exceptional skill and foresight in reconciling the family internationalism with individual service to their adopted countries, for which they have been rewarded with titles of nobility in Britain and France.

National Policies and International Business

The direct effects on international business of the advantages Britain obtained through the Industrial Revolution in the first half of the nineteenth century are described in all the economic histories, and they also provide the basis of much of economic theory. The immediate consequences—those that occurred in the stronger countries like the United States and Germany, on the one hand, and in the weaker countries of Africa, Asia, and Latin America, on the other hand—are familiar. Further consequences, especially in the second group of countries, are still unfolding.

Colonialism extended commerce, widening the area of movement of goods, as well as of people and money. It increased the sources of materials and expanded markets, also stimulating greater production of commodities in the colonies. But colonialism also concentrated the profits and other benefits of processing, insurance, banking, and even higher education, in Paris and London and their environs. The so-called free trade of the nineteenth century gave the British manufacturer and merchant access to many markets throughout the world but kept the primary products exporter largely dependent on one market in Britain. True, the British and subsequently the Americans (but no one else) incorporated free competition into the legal framework operative throughout the areas they controlled, but there could never be equal competition between the conquerors and the colonies.

It is not necessary to go to the colonies of the European countries for examples. "Free trade" with the United States gave Americans a monopoly of the Philippine market, and was imposed on the Philippines, over the protests of the National Assembly of the Philippines, in 1909. Shirley Jenkins has stated that "by the time the United States was ready to act on the question of political independence for the Philippines, twenty-five years of free trade (with the United States) had tailored the economy of the islands to fit the American market." (Jenkins, 1954, p. 34.)

Canada had ceased to be a British colony, in the political sense, in 1867. Subsequent developments in Canadian economic policy have current significance for the numerous countries that have recently obtained political independence. In 1879, a "National Policy" of fostering Canadian industry by protective tariffs was introduced. This policy represented a political departure from British free-trade views and was in line with the German "infant industry" theories that Bismarck found so useful and that had also been adopted by the United States. Today, a national policy on trade, including a tariff policy, be it high or moderate, accompanies the emergence into nationhood of every new country.

It is extremely important to notice, however, that tariff protection did not work in precisely the same way in Canada as it did in Germany or in the United States. The aim in those countries was to strengthen their new political nationalism with national industries. In Canada, as demonstrated by the research of Herbert Marshall and Kenneth Taylor, a few manufacturing industries had been started before the National Policy of protective tariffs was introduced. These were independent Canadian businesses even though several of them were founded on the "importation of (American) enterprise and skill." (Marshall and Taylor, 1936, p. 11.) An immigrant named Gurney from the United States started a foundry and stove factory in Hamilton in 1842 and his descendants continued this business for more than a hundred years. Daniel Massey who began the now-international Massey-Ferguson farm equipment business in Canada in 1847 was the son of an American who emigrated to Canada to farm. The purpose of the Canadian tariff of 1879 was to stimulate this kind of development. The actual result was an influx of branch plants with nonresident ownership. The new path was blazed in Canada by the du Ponts. In 1876, in astute anticipation of the new tariff laws, their American gunpowder trust went international by purchasing two existing Canadian powder mills. The du Pont case supplies the first important American branch plant operation that Marshall and Taylor could uncover. An Edison branch, which later became the Canadian General Electric company was opened in 1883. Incidentally there was substantial Canadian investment in CGE for a number of years, but most of this stock was bought up by the parent American company in 1925.

It was possible for the Canadian protective tariff to produce du Pont and General Electric subsidiaries instead of more Canadian firms with resident owners and managers like the Massey family, who became leaders in education and the arts and contributed the first Canadian-born Governor-Generals because of a great extension of the rights of foreigners in Canada. By the legal device of incorporation, foreigners could obtain the same rights as residents, wherever they chose to invest their money. Foreign investors found that they did not require resident partners.

This keystone of modern international economic development slipped into the legal structure of many countries without discussion and without being presented to the public for approval even to this day.

Curiously, du Pont and General Electric did not follow up their early start in international enterprise, made in Canada, on any considerable scale. Until very recently, they lagged noticeably behind companies like Colgate and Coca-Cola in the extent of their international operations, despite the greater relative importance of technical know-how in their industries. This lag raises the question of the historical importance of American antitrust laws, which will be explored in a later paragraph.

Alfred Nobel of Sweden, who invented dynamite, blasting gelatin, and smokeless gunpowder, founded his first branch plant in Hamburg, Germany, in 1866. The obvious problems involved in transporting explosives stimulated local manufacture. His specialized personal know-how in the chemistry, production, and handling of explosives, supported in some countries by patents, was used to establish a worldwide chain of factories. Nobel provided an early example of an international manufacturing business founded on technological advances. The business grew, however, without any central organization except Alfred Nobel's personal financial and managerial interest in the various companies. The only over-all management instrument evolved by Nobel for his companies was a scientific advisory board of which he was, of course, the moving spirit. Regional corporate groupings were formed, however, in 1886-87, when the Nobel Dynamite Trust Company, Limited, of London embraced the British and German factories and the Société Centrale de la Dynamite took over the Belgian, French, Italian, Swiss, and South African operations. (Halasz, 1959, p. 141.) The Russian, Swedish, and a few other national companies were not grouped. Nobel sold his interests in the United States in 1885, because of his difficulty in getting the courts to recognize his patents. He died in 1896, leaving the Nobel Prizes but no comprehensive international organization corresponding to the international market that his inventions had created.

William Lever of Britain, founder of Lever Brothers, the soap

company that later adopted the name "Unilever" upon amalga-
mation with a European group of margarine companies called
the "Margarine Unie," was, like Nobel, an innovator who found
a worldwide response to his ideas. The first Lever soap factory
outside Britain was opened in 1899 in Toronto. This was the
beginning of an international chain that now operates in fifty
countries.

Lever, unlike Nobel, was truly a pioneer of modern international industrial methods and organization. He developed soap
for suds rather than economy and cut it up into convenient
tablets in the factory, the historic Sunlight Soap. His innovations
in proprietary marketing, particularly in labeling and advertising, were even more far-reaching. A famous Lever advertisement asked, "Why does a woman grow old quicker than a man?"
Lever's dramatic marketing techniques were so profitable that
he acquired a dominant position in the domestic British market,
while he still had the personal energy and ambition to carry his
operations abroad. He found that foreign markets were respon-
sive, wherever they were accessible. Bismarckian protectionism
had, however, already been adopted by many countries, and
Lever marketing ideas could function in those countries only
when backed up by local production. Lever proceeded to buy
and build factories to give scope to his talents for salesmanship
and advertising. As a result, the housewives of the world benefited. The idea of labor-saving in household tasks, which Lever
helped to disseminate by advertising the ease and convenience
of his products, may be connected with the fact that the life
expectancy of women in the advanced countries is now actually
longer than that of men, a full five years in the United States.

The centrifugal force of Lever's marketing innovations placed
great stress on the financial structure of his company and the
prevailing forms of administrative organization. Eventually Vis-
count Leverhulme, as he was by then called, had to delegate
much of his personal control. Internal reorganization became so
important that the succession to Lever fell on Sir D'Arcy Cooper,
previously head of the firm of professional accountants that
audited the Lever companies. Methods were evolved for holding
together a diversified and widespread complex of marketing and

production operations. A hierarchy of managers and a uniform system of accounts proved to be the organizational essentials.

The foreign operations of Colgate, another pioneering international manufacturing enterprise, evolved gradually out of its manufacture of toothpaste and toilet preparations. Here again was a business in which a large number of customers and effective methods of reaching them through salesmanship and advertising were more important than the size or location of factories. Procter & Gamble, on the other hand, went widely international only after World War II. At that time, P & G had the great advantage of being able to exploit new processes for making synthetic detergents that their American laboratories had perfected during the war and that proved applicable to a wide range of products. These processes were protected by patents, which many countries allowed under the International Patents Convention. Similar circumstances encouraged many other American industries to branch out into foreign operations.

The Political Climate

A circumstance that has affected the recent history of international business is a climate of opinion among many American businessmen and a relatively few British and Europeans (mostly those who already had connections with America) that, given the proper approach, money could be made in foreign operations. This approach might be described as parlaying one's bets. If only one or two countries were entered, those countries might happen to go communist or might impose exchange restrictions or devalue their currency, and then the whole of a company's foreign operations would be operated at a loss. Dispersed among a large number of countries, however, a company's branches would have opportunities to counterbalance losses with windfall profits. Taxes would fall only on the net profits taken home after transfers from one foreign country to another to build new subsidiaries. This approach was mapped out, in full color, in a timely series of articles on Unilever in *Fortune* in the issues of December, 1947, and January and February, 1948.

Some of the biggest and most progressive companies found an easier way than going abroad themselves. They simply made arrangements with foreign companies doing similar business to lease patents and other know-how, including trademarks, on a royalty or exchange basis. This method yielded revenue without cash investment and prevented patents from lapsing through lack of prompt use and prevented knowledge from being pirated. In some instances this method fostered the development in foreign countries of national industries using the capital of people in those countries and under native management, thus avoiding the conflict of interests and loyalties between the nation and the international firm that is emerging as a serious problem today. Some critics of recurrent economic colonization are now advocating precisely this pattern of international business. However, there are serious difficulties in the management of operations based on licensing or "joint ventures." Also, this form of development has been restricted because the Antitrust Division of the United States Department of Justice has taken a negative view and has made it operative internationally.

The first du Pont move abroad in 1876 was the purchase of a powder mill. When the du Ponts widened their interest in chemicals after World War I, they encountered the well-developed German I. G. Farben chemical combine and Imperial Chemical Industries, which enjoyed the determined support of the British government. In Canada, a company was formed jointly by du Pont and I.C.I., called Canadian Industries Limited, in reference to its location rather than its ownership, which was divided between the two foreign parent companies. General Electric, Radio Corporation of America, and others faced similar well-developed foreign companies, government-backed Marconi in Britain, Philips in Holland, Siemens in Germany. They made arrangements, which included the pooling of patent rights extended by foreign governments to the several electrical groups under the International Patent Convention.

The legality of cooperation by American companies with foreigners, in ways that could be construed as market sharing, was in doubt for many years. This doubt was strong enough to keep many companies at home and to make others go abroad

entirely on their own. Soon after World War II, the Antitrust
Division of the United States Department of Justice secured con-
firmation from American courts that the actions of American
corporations and of the foreign companies they control are subject to American laws and regulations. Cooperative sharing of
the American market had been determined to be illegal *per se*
under the Sherman Act by the Addyston Pipe case as early as
1898, but the Act's application abroad remained in doubt for
many years, partly because of the difficulties with foreign governments that attempts to enforce the Act on foreign subsidiary
companies might create. Then in the Alcoa case in 1945, Judge
Learned Hand of the United States Court of Appeals expressed
the opinion that "any State may impose liabilities even upon
persons not within its allegiance for conduct outside its borders
that has consequences within its borders which the State repre-
hends." (Quoted in Neale, 1960, p. 324.) As Neale points out,
"Judge Hand's view . . . has been influential . . . and has been
reflected in a number of actions and decrees of American courts."
(p. 325.) Judgments were given against Minnesota Mining and
Manufacturing in 1950, against Timken Bearings in 1951, and
against du Pont and British I.C.I. in 1952, for Sherman Act
violations abroad.

As a matter of fact, the power of the United States government
to enforce American policy is far-reaching. In addition to the
financial penalties it can impose on companies, it can fine individuals, and it can jail them as common criminals. These penalties
can be imposed on directors of foreign companies who are
American citizens.

Du Pont and Imperial Chemicals operated Canadian Industries Limited, not as a partnership but as Siamese twins. C.I.L.
was born that way and had grown up very large indeed. The
United States courts did not follow the judgment of Solomon—
an operation was performed. It appears to be successful. Imperial
Chemicals took the established Canadian Industries Limited
name, while the du Pont Canadian subsidiary uses the du Pont
name and receives the benefit of heavy overflow advertising
from du Pont in the United States. The competition of two
foreign giants instead of one makes the outlook for an indigen-

ous Canadian chemicals industry even bleaker than previously.

Even before the final drastic court decisions about the foreign relations of American companies, there had been enough risk of legal troubles to discourage American international enterprise. Any agreement with foreigners for exclusive use of American know-how might be construed as a conspiracy to restrain competition. This view might even apply to an American company participating with native businessmen in the formation of a national company in a foreign country. A number of American companies did take the risk of legal trouble at home in order to go into business with foreign partners in the period between the wars. Some of them did so because otherwise they risked the loss of valuable patent rights abroad through nonuse. Other prominent American companies stayed home safely cultivating the rich and growing domestic market—Campbell Soups and General Foods for example. They were less dependent on patents and more interested in advertised trademarks—which would have to be adapted to foreign languages, advertising media, and other complicating conditions. Dramatic evidence of how profitably such foreign adaptation could be accomplished began to come in at about the same time that the significance of the legal decisions began to be realized.

United States court decisions in the 1950's appear to Neale and apparently to the legal advisers of many American companies to hinge on "combined operations." Neale notes that "a foreign branch that was actually part of an American company or even a wholly-owned subsidiary would incur practically no legal risk from the mere fact that it was directed exclusively to supplying its local market, for no restrictive agreements would be required in such a case." (P. 311.)

United States national policy, as interpreted—or created—by the extension of the authority of the Antitrust Division and the Federal Trade Commission into foreign operations, put pressure on American companies to go abroad on an exclusively American basis. A totally American subsidiary avoids the automatic suspicion of restraining trade by market sharing that attaches to any agreements with foreign companies or even individual foreign businessmen.

Zealousness for American interests has, however, exceeded the bounds of logic or consistency. The Antitrust Division and the F.T.C. have actually attempted to enforce their rules over parent companies in Britain through subsidiaries incorporated in the United States and, in the peat moss case, through American customers with whom a Canadian exporter was doing business. (Brewster, 1960, p. 19.) At the same time, the Webb-Pomerene Act had, ever since 1918, allowed "American exporters to act together in export markets in ways that would otherwise violate the Sherman Act." (Neale, p. 9.) It will be noticed that this reference is to exporters as distinct from overseas subsidiaries. There has been an effort by the Antitrust Division of the administrative branch of the American government to guide the development of international business by unilateral action in some of the Sherman Act prosecutions. This influence has not been consistent with the Webb-Pomerene Act and it has not recognized that the sovereignty of other nations may be involved.

Some countries, for instance Norway and Japan, have had laws requiring companies incorporated in those countries to have a certain proportion of local shareholders. Japan was persuaded to reduce her requirement of this kind and she liberalized her foreign investment regulations as recently as May 1, 1961. An issue had been made of this matter in 1960 by the I.B.M. World Trade Corporation, which, as mentioned earlier, has a policy of complete control over all its subsidiaries.

A pattern of development appears to be emerging, and it is far from one of free trade. Neither is it monopoly or autarchy. The United States demand competition, but it must be competition by American, British, and a few other international giants against national companies in smaller countries. There is little awareness that the exclusiveness of the operations of American companies abroad, the total Americanism necessary to satisfy the antitrust laws, can have monopolistic effects by inhibiting the sharing of know-how with national companies abroad.

United States Treasury rulings on taxation have also contributed to the historical growth of the present form of international enterprise. Substantial tax privileges, such as allowing international firms to offset losses in one foreign country against profits in others, have been available only in the cases of foreign branches or wholly-owned subsidiaries.

The British attitude toward trade agreements with foreign companies remains tolerant, despite increased activity against restrictive practices internally. The British Treasury relentlessly pursues profits for taxation, whether they are earned by wholly-owned subsidiaries or minority interests. There is a withholding tax but only for declared dividends. The Swiss deliberately encourage holding companies by their generous treatment of profits that are collected in Switzerland for later remission abroad. The Swiss themselves also control two of the most successful international business enterprises, Ciba (drugs) and Nestlé (foods), the latter now controlling Crosse & Blackwell of Britain, the United States, Canada, et al., and Raleigh of Australia. Canada has similar tax law provisions. A popular tax-haven is provided by the Republic of Panama. This haven was certainly established with the knowledge and probably with the advice of the United States government, in view of the special relations it has with the Panamanian government.

In summary, it is clear that companies with international operations, except for the exploitation of natural monopolies, were rare until comparatively recently. Previously, capital flowed internationally through loans, and know-how traveled separately and comparatively slowly. The establishment in many nations of property rights for foreigners in the form of patents, trademarks, and corporation voting stock opened new opportunities. Many national governments, led by Germany and the United States, also adopted protectionism to encourage industrialization. Owners and managers had, however, to learn how to use these opportunities. American antitrust regulations appeared at first to be an obstacle, but later were discovered to permit and require completely controlled foreign operations.

4

THE EXTENT OF
INTERNATIONAL ENTERPRISE

THE ANALYSIS and evaluation of foreign operations in this book are based mainly on information available through the year 1960, which may stand as the peak year, unless new policy developments occur. More companies will undoubtedly go abroad, despite the inhibiting influence of proposals by some governments to increase taxes on foreign profits. The number of countries that are open to international enterprise is more likely to decrease for a while. The lessons of Ceylon and Cuba cannot be applied fast enough—even with deeper understanding and a greater willingness to apply such understanding than have so far been shown—to forestall nationalization of foreign companies in some additional countries. Western economic influence may, indeed, prove to have been already on the ebb in 1960, despite the flood of foreign enterprise into areas like Western Europe, in order to participate in the Common Market. In Latin America and Africa, the government-to-government loans that had been generously made by the United States, Britain, France, and others were based on some economists' assumptions that private enterprise would automatically follow, as it had in the more advanced economies of Western Europe after the Marshall Plan. This follow-up has not occurred.

The 1960's are seeing a belated effort by economic planners and other officials to acquire practical knowledge about how and why business enterprises actually do appear and develop. It has become evident that more than bank rate and "infrastructure"—power and transportation—are involved. A new and higher tide of widespread prosperity may eventually arise, however, through the deliberately combined influence of national governments and international firms.

The first requisite for more effective national policies is to get more facts, especially facts about the extent of the activities in which international firms have already become engaged and the results that they have achieved. There are obstacles, in both attitudes and methods. Existing information services are mostly the creations of national governments, compiling statistics obtainable under national authority, in national terms. This national information also remains the source material for most of the apparently broader reports of the United Nations. The International Monetary Fund can add little more than the often distorted reflections of business activity in the international financial transfers entering national balance of payments statements. Analysis is handicapped by these limitations of material, which would often show up startlingly if allowances made for errors and omissions in the data had to be indicated in all tables by black-face type.

Some of the missing information exists, notably in the account books of international companies. Many of these companies also have detailed information about their competitors, customers, and suppliers. Private research organizations like Business International and A. C. Nielsen in the United States, the Economist Intelligence Unit in England, and numerous industry or trade associations have a wealth of information in their strictly confidential files. Publication of this information would permit the updating of a good deal of currently accepted thinking on international economics. An important contribution has been made by Professor Emile Benoit of Columbia University in a paper on "The Balance of Payments Payoff of Direct Foreign Investments." (*Michigan Business Review*, July, 1962, p. 9.) This article carried acknowledgments to the H. J. Heinz Company and the Industry Committee on Foreign Investments. It appeared, however, only after threatening new foreign tax proposals had been sent to Congress by the Administration.

American business has nevertheless progressed far ahead of British and European companies in its attitudes toward public information. American companies do not delude themselves that they are hiding profit secrets from their competitors. Americans still fear, however, that their information may be misunderstood or misinterpreted by journalists and politicians, not recognizing that the only assurance against those dangers is more public education.

Apart from the lack of information arising from the shortsightedness of national governments and private business, there are also technical difficulties in designing a yardstick to measure the extent of international business. An important indicator would be the proportions of gross national product (in a significant number and range of countries) attributable to foreign-controlled companies over a period of several years. Not enough countries have the records or the trained personnel for such an exercise. Only recently have the United States, the largest source of international investment, and Canada, the largest recipient, begun to compile and issue statistics on this subject. *U.S. Business Investments in Foreign Countries*, by Samuel Pizer and Frederick Cutler, issued by the United States Department of Commerce in 1960, and *The Canadian Balance of International Payments, 1959, and International Investment Position*, containing a supplement on foreign ownership and control of Canadian industry, issued by the Dominion Bureau of Statistics also in 1960, through the initiative of Douglas Blyth, are landmarks in the official recognition of the importance of international business enterprise.

A number of figures are quoted below, and they are described as indicators of the extent of international business, but they are incomplete, as well as indirect. It is, moreover, unfortunate and indeed misleading that most of the figures being published come from United States sources and deal with United States investments. This situation may give a false impression that international business is an almost exclusively American development, which could be harmful to the position of all foreign subsidiaries in some countries. Governments and companies in other countries, specifically Switzerland, a small, politically independent country, can therefore make a contribution to their own and the general interest by adopting more complete information policies.

The few available government figures on international business —other than exports and imports, which are readily obtained from customs declarations—are mostly estimates. When these purport to show the value of foreign subsidiaries, they are certain to be artificial and arbitrary. Obviously, most subsidiaries are worth more than the money paid out to establish or buy them, and therefore international investment transfers are not a dependable guide. Government statisticians attempt to take account of accumulated reserves and other increased assets by using reported book values, but company accountants have produced those figures mainly to reflect earning capacity after periodic revaluations and write-offs. In some countries, the figures are adjusted by companies to influence future profit repatriation privileges.

A supplement to the few available figures on foreign operations is provided by lists of countries in which the more important companies have operations. Most American companies are happy and indeed proud to give the number and names of the countries in which they have subsidiaries, but the secretiveness of European companies is an obstacle here also.

National Aggregate Figures on International Business

The book value of American-owned foreign affiliates was estimated at $30 billion by the United States Department of Commerce at the end of 1959. For 1961, the figure was $34.7 billion after adjustments to eliminate investments in Cuba, which were expropriated in 1960. (Pizer and Cutler, 1962, p. 19.) At the end of 1959, more than one-third of United States foreign holdings were reported to be in Canada and slightly less than one-third in Latin America. The values of investments increased in both these areas in 1960 and 1961, but the rate of growth was greater in Europe. The proportion of American foreign investments located in Canada at the end of 1961 was slightly less than one-third of the total and in Latin America about one-quarter. The figure for United States direct investment in Britain was less than $2.5 billion in 1959 but had jumped to $3.5 billion by the end of 1961. The total book value of American investments in Britain by this time was greater than in all six European Economic Community countries, despite increases there; the amount of increase in Britain from 1959 to 1961 was also greater, exceeding $1 billion.

International investment originates from several other countries besides the United States though evidence in the form of official statistics is scarce. The British *Board of Trade Journal* is now publishing figures on the investments which British companies are making abroad but only the increases and excluding the important categories of oil and insurance. The British increases in 1958, 1959, and 1960 amounted to the equivalent of $400, $550, and $700 million. (*Board of Trade Journal*, October 6, 1961, p. 715.) Other countries, like the Netherlands and Switzerland, house companies with large and numerous foreign subsidiaries, but no figures have been located. For West Germany, one indicator is the estimate that the German investment in Latin America, up to the end of 1959, was $198 million, while that of Britain was $800 million and of the United States $8,990 million. (Benveniste, et al., 1961, p. 78.)

While the early lead of Britain in international business gained by industrial inventiveness and commercial enterprise has evidently been overtaken by the United States, the British contribution continues to be important. It appears from the estimate given above to be nearly 10 per cent of that of the United States even in Latin America, an area of special interest and convenient access for the United States, and the British share could stand much higher in Africa, Australasia, and India. British holdings in some countries, like the United States, had to be sold during

World War II, but government policy has generally recognized that the earnings and influence of foreign subsidiaries are worth more than their cash sale value and subsidiaries have been retained or re-established whenever possible. The British recovery since the war, which is remarkable in view of the scarcity in Britain of the natural resources for modern industry, has included invisible exports obtained by enlarging foreign operations. Leading British profit-earners, listed by *Fortune* in July, 1961, include British-American Tobacco, Coats Patons and Baldwins, Courtaulds, Dunlop, and Imperial Chemicals, all of which have extensive foreign operations, and two other firms, Shell and Unilever, which own many subsidiaries in other countries and are themselves owned partly in Britain, partly in the Netherlands.

Profits earned abroad are another indicator of the extent of international business and a more direct one than book values, which, as mentioned, are apt to be derivative. But profits are not a perfect measure either, since they are affected by corporate decisions on such matters as prices and advertising expenditures, which may be set low and high, respectively, to promote business growth. Pizer and Cutler gave $3.9 billion as the earnings of American direct overseas investment in 1957. They reported a decline in 1958 but a return to the 1957 level in 1959. The published figures for 1960 and 1961 are not directly comparable because they give only the American share of the earnings of foreign subsidiaries. These figures were $3,556 million for 1960 and $3,700 million for 1961. (Pizer and Cutler, 1962, p. 23.) If we add 10 per cent for foreign minority interests, a figure that Pizer and Cutler used in their earlier study, the total would appear to have reached $4 billion by 1961. This figure would constitute an increase of 100 per cent over the estimated $2 billion in 1950.

The profits on foreign investments by British companies, including earnings retained abroad as reserves or for reinvestment (but again excluding the important oil and insurance businesses), were equivalent to approximately $550 million in 1958, $670 million in 1959, and $725 million in 1960.

Company Earnings as an Index

Some indications of the extent of international business are also given by an analysis of foreign operations based on the profits reported by specific companies. The following figures are mostly for the year 1960. These figures were obtained by independent investigation but they will be found in line with the results of a survey of a number of companies listed on the New York Stock Exchange conducted by *The Exchange Magazine* and published by that organ of the New York Stock Exchange in the issue of January, 1963, thereby making an important contribution to the information on international business available from official sources.

The American Radiator-Standard Sanitary company, purveyor of world-famous American central heating and American plumbing, made $8.7 million abroad, 66 per cent of its aggregate profit. Black & Decker, leader in small power tools, made $1.1 million, 34 per cent of its total, abroad. In the burgeoning business machines industry, Burroughs, IBM and National Cash Register earned 54, 30, and 60 per cent of their profits from foreign operations.

In another field of American leadership, the manufacturing and marketing of medicines, the Pfizer chain of companies made $9 million, 40 per cent of its profits, outside the United States. Schering drugs made the same percentage of its profits abroad. Foreign operations contributed 67 per cent of Sterling Products' profits. In cosmetic and toilet preparations, Cheseborough-Ponds received 57 per cent of its profits from foreign subsidiaries, Gillette 40 per cent (amounting to $14 million, not including profits from Canada), and Colgate-Palmolive 60 per cent ($16 million).

Foreign profits in the basic and competitive food processing industry are an even more remarkable measure of the extent of international business activity. Heinz's foreign profits of $8.7 million in 1960 constituted 80 per cent of its total. Corn Products, expanding rapidly, earned 41 per cent of its profits abroad. National Dairy (Kraft products) made $6 million abroad, excluding Canada, although this figure represents only 11 per cent of the total profits for this company. Coca-Cola profits of $7.6 million abroad (excluding Canada) came to 40 per cent of the total. Nestlé of Switzerland and British-Dutch Unilever are also very large and very active in the food processing business, and, although they have not disclosed their profits from different kinds of business or parts of the world, the share of turnover attributed to foods in the Unilever Annual Report for 1961 was 14 per cent.

In motor cars and trucks, another basic and influential industry, Ford reported foreign profits of $72 million or 16 per cent of total profits. General Motors' earnings from "operations overseas," presumably excluding Canada, were 14 per cent of the total in 1960, compared with an average of 10 per cent in the preceding five years. The Goodyear business, mainly in tires for motor vehicles, earned foreign profits of $22 million or 30 per cent of total profits in 1960. Standard Oil of New Jersey made $455 million and 66 per cent of its profits from international operations.

Another large American earner of profits abroad, International Telegraph and Telephone, made $168 million in 1960, constituting 66 per cent of the total.

As already mentioned, policies of secrecy cloud the operations of companies originating in the older countries. There are, however, a few indicators. British-American Tobacco, a British corporation, earned the equivalent of $184 million entirely from outside Britain, since this company was organized to take over foreign operations, leaving the British home market to Imperial Tobacco. The Metal Box company, the British associate of Continental Can of the United States, made $56 million abroad, one-third of its profits. Bowaters (paper), with large American and Canadian operations, earned 70 per cent of its total profits outside Britain. According to the *Fortune* survey (August, 1961), the largest European profit-earner in 1960 was the Dutch Philips complex of electrical companies. Though figures are not available, the profits earned outside the small Dutch home market must have been very high. The same is true of the Ciba drug business, originating in Switzerland but challenging American

Pfizer's position as the largest in the world, and of another large Swiss drug company, Hoffman-LaRoche. Italian Necchi sewing machines can be compared with American Singer, which has not published foreign profits but reports 61 per cent of sales through its foreign subsidiaries. Cinzano, originating in Italy but now using a holding company located in Montreal, Canada, is estimated to make 66 per cent of its profits outside Italy.

Sales by foreign subsidiaries reveal the extent of international business more accurately, more clearly, and also more dramatically than do foreign profits. Though nothing that even approximates a world picture has been developed, the dimensions are indicated by American figures. Aggregate United States foreign subsidiary sales for the year 1960 were estimated at $43 billion by former Attorney General Brownell. This figure compares with United States physical exports of approximately $20 billion during the same period. Although Brownell's figure exceeds Pizer and Cutler's estimate of only 35 billion for 1959, either set of figures justifies the conclusion that American foreign subsidiary sales have grown much more rapidly than exports and that they are now far greater.

Measures of the extent of international business are afforded by the values of the foreign sales of a number of companies. The companies for which figures have been located are all American except Dutch Philips, with foreign sales of $100 million, and Massey-Ferguson of Canada, with foreign sales of $428 million, 87 per cent of its total. Among the American companies for which information has been obtained, Ford's foreign subsidiary sales were given as $1,800 million in 1960 or 25 per cent of the total. General Electric's foreign sales were $386 million in 1960 but this figure came to only 9 per cent of total because of GE's huge domestic business. The du Pont position was similar, foreign sales of $363 million amounting to 12 per cent of total sales. International Business Machines reported $300 million of sales abroad, compared with $1,436 million at home. The $363 million foreign subsidiary sales of Singer Sewing Machine came to 61 per cent of that company's total business. Caterpillar Tractor's foreign sales were $274 million or 37 per cent, Kodak's $252 million or 20 per cent and Corn Products' $250 million or

26 per cent. International Harvester's foreign sales were $239 million and 30 per cent of the total. Other American companies with foreign subsidiary sales in excess of $100 million in 1960 include American Radiator-Standard Sanitary ($139 million, 40 per cent), Coca-Cola ($100 million, 35 per cent), and National Dairy ($120 million, 7 per cent).

General Motors has released figures on sales in units in 1960 for several countries: United States—3,681,377; Germany—366,817; Britain—245,981; Canada—208,357; Australia—140,336; and Brazil—18,128.

A few comparisons of proportionate foreign profits to proportionate foreign sales are possible. Black & Decker made 34 per cent of profits on 20 per cent of sales; Cheseborough-Ponds, 57 per cent on 40 per cent; Coca-Cola 40 per cent on 35 per cent; Corn Products, 41 per cent on 26 per cent; Goodyear, 30 per cent on 20 per cent; Heinz, 80 per cent on 50 per cent; National Dairy, 11 per cent on 7 per cent; Procter & Gamble, 22 per cent on 15 per cent; Schering, 40 per cent on 22 per cent.

International operations through foreign subsidiaries have extended from primarily manufacturing firms to those whose primary function is retail distribution, as exemplified by Sears Roebuck, whose foreign sales came to $100 million in 1960. J. Walter Thompson, the largest advertising agency in the world, places 35 per cent of its advertising billing volume outside the United States. There are Thompson offices in twenty-two foreign countries.

The number of countries in which particular international firms operate provides another indication of the extent of international business. The highest published figure is that of Pepsi-Cola, which operates in eighty-four countries. Other widely extended businesses are Bata (shoes), formerly of Czechoslovakia and now of Canada, which operates in seventy-three countries, and Philips of the Netherlands, which operates in fifty-five countries. Unilever has subsidiaries in fifty countries; I.B.M. in thirty-six countries; Colgate in thirty; Standard Oil of New Jersey, British-American Tobacco, and Swiss Ciba in twenty-eight. The following companies have branches in twenty-five foreign countries: Abbott (drugs), General Electric, Kodak,

Pfizer, British Coats Patons and Baldwins, and British Dunlop. Italian Cinzano operates in fifteen countries and Olivetti in eighteen. *Reader's Digest* is published in sixteen countries outside the United States.

The Location of International Business

It is difficult to relate official figures to the new facts of international business organization because the information is compiled by broad geographical regions rather than by companies and countries, the way the investments are actually made. The exceptions are Canada and Britain. The reported number of American investments in Canada is much higher than in older and longer-industrialized Britain, and the figure of 2,700 for Canada is very close to the total of 2,800 for the number of American companies that have foreign investments anywhere, thus confirming the observation that a large majority of American companies making foreign investments have included this neighboring and comparatively less-developed country. The total number of 2,800 companies was given in the Department of Commerce Survey of U.S. Business Investments in Foreign Countries, for the year 1957 (Pizer and Cutler, 1960, p. 6.) The figure of 10,272 was given for the total of direct foreign investments, all of these 50 per cent or more American-owned except for 600, these representing only about 5 per cent of the total by value. By area, in 1957, there were 2,700 direct investments in Canada, 800 in Britain, 1500 in Europe, and 3,000 in Latin America. Unfortunately the number of companies and the location of investments are not related and the survey does not give any indications regarding multiple ownership, exemplified by the W. R. Grace enterprise which operates in textiles, sugar, paper and paint, as well as shipping, and in at least ten different countries all in Latin America, or regarding concentration of investments in particular countries within a region.

Foreign subsidiaries have become clustered in particular countries, but there does not seem to have been the degree of deliberate concentration in the more advanced countries that some critics assume. More probably, those countries that exhibit high degrees of economic development and foreign investment owe their advanced position to the intensity of internationally aided industrialization. Canada is a significant example. During the 1920's and the early 1930's when the Great Depression was as severe in Canada as anywhere in the world, that country was a backward, underdeveloped economic colony. Its transformation into a country with the second highest standard of living in the world was due primarily to the peculiar circumstances that made it strategic and economical to process Canadian raw materials at home during World War II—and to manufacture in Canada as much as possible of the required capital equipment and consumer goods for the labor force.

There are many causes for the clustering of foreign subsidiaries. There is, for instance, a highly successful concentration of British subsidiaries in India, while a much lower proportion of American international firms have subsidiaries there. Connections surviving from colonialism are not sufficient explanation, for today there are practically no Dutch businesses in Indonesia, formerly the Netherlands East Indies. The British position in India reflects not only the long colonial connection but also British policies toward Indian independence. In another example, there are many subsidiaries of both British and American firms in Australia. There are proportionately more international firms of American than of British origin in Brazil, Mexico, and Venezuela. In fact, study of available information on the distribution of foreign subsidiaries indicates that the British have not fully utilized their century-long connections with Latin America to establish subsidiaries, perhaps because of London's known discouragement with defaulting on South American bonds.

The lists of subsidiaries abroad of sixty-one leading American companies have been examined by the writer in company annual reports, press releases and similar documents. The companies ranged from Abbott drugs to Yale & Towne builders' hardware, covering a wide range of industries and size of companies. This study shows that more subsidiaries are located in Australia and Mexico than in either France or Germany. There are also numer-

ous American subsidiaries in the Philippines—far more than in
Sweden, for example. These figures provide further evidence
that subsidiaries are not concentrated mainly in the older and
more developed countries. One of the most remarkable indicators of the extent of international business is the following
partial list of countries where the Bata shoe firm operates:
Algeria, Australia, Bolivia, Brazil, Britain, Cameroons, Canada,
Chile, Congo, Cyprus, Egypt, France, Germany, India, Indonesia, Iraq, Jamaica, Jordan, Kenya, Lebanon, Libya, Mada-
gascar, Malaya, Mexico, Morocco, Netherlands, New Zealand,
Nigeria, Pakistan, Peru, Rhodesia, Senegal, South Africa, Sudan,
Switzerland, Tanganyika, Thailand, Tunisia, United States, and
Vietnam.

A very important indicator of the extent of international business would be the relative shares of national markets obtained
by a number of companies in a variety of countries. Market
shares of the major companies in important industries are
becoming recognized as information that has official, professional, and public interest in the United States, but comparable
figures for foreign markets are very rare, even for American
companies. Many companies possess this information, obtained
from their own records, from competitors directly or through
trade associations, from customers, or from private research
organizations like A. C. Nielsen. But few companies release
such figures. The most cooperative organization in this respect
is Ford. In 1960, Ford claimed 23 per cent of the market for
trucks in Argentina and 21 per cent in Brazil. It also supplied
28 per cent of the market for all motor vehicles in Britain, 22
per cent in Canada, and 10 per cent in Germany. Singer Sewing
Machine controlled 33 per cent of the market in Brazil, 66 per
cent in Britain, 30 per cent in Canada, 33 per cent in Italy and
50 per cent in Mexico. The Canadian firm, Seagrams, is reported
to control 24 per cent of the liquor market in the United States.
There are not enough figures of this kind to give a general
picture, yet it is widely known among company executives,
government officials, and leaders of the press (who can judge
from advertising revenues) that foreign subsidiaries are the
leaders in national industries in many countries. Furthermore,

there are often two or more foreign companies competing for and dividing the biggest part of the market, relegating national companies to minor positions.

A final measurement of the extent of international business is the extent of foreign control of the industry and trade of various nations. The most complete and perhaps the most extreme figures are those for Canada. Nonresident control at the end of 1958, based on estimated book value, was 57 per cent in Canadian manufacturing of all kinds, 75 per cent in petroleum and natural gas, and 61 per cent in mining and smelting. (Dominion Bureau of Statistics, 1902, p. 59.) The proportional profits ao cruing to the foreign-controlled companies and the shares of the Canadian market controlled by these companies could well be higher than the book-value ratios, because of more productive employment of their assets. The extension of international business in other countries could also be revealed through the use of the same measure. Inspection of the lists of foreign subsidiaries of leading companies in a wide variety of industries shows Australia, Mexico, and South Africa listed nearly as frequently as Canada. International business may have extended into these countries to the point where foreigners have the majority control of all major forms of productive activity except agriculture, utilities (including transportation), construction, and services.

Firm conclusions about the extent of international business must obviously await the publication of more information by governments and companies. Large contributions to knowledge can easily be provided by release in more countries of national data on the numbers of subsidiaries and where they are located, the levels of profits and where obtained, absolute and relative sales by markets, and the proportions of foreign control in each industry. The indications already provided—that sales from American subsidiaries abroad far exceed American exports and that foreign subsidiaries dominate most important industries in Canada, for example—reveal that very large operations are going on behind the velvet curtains of corporation conservatism and strongly suggest that these curtains should be drawn back.

5

THE PATTERN OF
INTERNATIONAL INVESTMENT

THE TYPICAL contemporary international enterprise comprises a chain of companies or branches, engaged in parallel manufacturing and/or distributive operations in a number of countries, owned and controlled by a parent company with its head office in the country where the business was founded. Bayer of Germany, Procter & Gamble of the United States, Nestlé of Switzerland, Philips of the Netherlands, Reckitt & Colman of Britain, and many other widespread and profitable companies conform to this pattern.

A variant that helps to highlight the essential pattern is Aluminium Limited of Montreal, Canada. This company now holds the shares of the original Pittsburgh company and many other subsidiaries throughout the world. The shares of the relatively new Canadian holding company, formed in 1928, are largely in the hands of American citizens, including the descendants of the founding Mellon family. Another special situation exists in Unilever, which consists of two holding companies, one British and one Dutch, joined by a profit-equalizing agreement. The ownership of subsidiaries is divided between the two Unilever parents according to political and tax considerations. Directors are members of both boards, but the top management is now located in London. In any case, management control of the subsidiaries of these two holding companies in foreign countries is based on concepts of efficiency rather than legal ownership. Thus both the Lever and the Lipton subsidiaries in the United States report to London, although they are legally controlled by Rotterdam.

It is common in international firms for one subsidiary in its turn to own and control others. This arrangement does not break the line of ultimate ownership and control from the original parent. The A. C. Nielsen market research company, a dynamic and profitable modern American specialist business, owns a subsidiary in Oxford, England, which in turn owns and supervises operations in Australia and several European countries. This pattern is also followed by the Hoover electric appliance business. Pizer and Cutler report that the book value of American investment in Swiss companies rose to $408 million in 1961 from only $68 million in 1957. They comment that "a considerable part of these investments is ultimately invested in other countries." (Pizer and Cutler, 1962, p. 19.)

Foreign subsidiaries are commonly created both by the purchase of existing companies and by new incorporations. In manufacturing, some companies have been drawn into international operations after discovering foreign markets for their products through the success of exports arranged by an export broker or a local import merchant without encouragement or even prior knowledge on the part of the manufacturer. There is a story that the homely remedy, Eno Fruit Salt, was taken around the world by British sea captains, whose resilience to the climate and other hazards of shore leave inspired a worldwide demand. Somewhat better authenticated is the story of the famous salesman "Carload" Ritchie who controlled the Eno business. Ritchie was one of the first to take advantage of air routes that had opened new vistas to the commercial traveler, when he flew to South America and the Orient looking for new markets. Today, when enterprising businessmen take tours abroad to enable their wives to view the cathedrals, they often see possible new markets, shops, and customers, and ask themselves, Why aren't our products on sale here?

After World War II, competition intensified in the American home market. The volume of business grew, but profit margins did not. Increased American attention to foreign affairs, reflected in the Marshall Plan and in subsequent foreign aid programs, revealed other markets to American business. There was also a supply of potential sales managers, young Americans who had become acquainted with many foreign countries during the war and were not averse to returning for a while as a means of getting established in business.

Customers had been recognized as the prime movers of business, but for many firms customers were more difficult to obtain than raw materials, efficient production, or capital. The physical power plant was no longer dependent on heavy, bulky coal and was therefore emancipated from water or rail transport and given more freedom as to location. Oil for diesel engines could be pumped through pipelines. Mass production had been so thoroughly mastered that many of its economies could be achieved on comparatively small runs. During this postwar period also many industries discovered that economies in the stock room and the warehouse, due to improved materials handling and inventory control, could be as important as production economies. Machinery was lighter and could be more readily transported by trucks or by air, even into rough country. Quality control was so refined that a girl in Caracas, Venezuela, could be taught checks that would guarantee the same standard product as that produced in Jersey City or Los Angeles. In fact, the new production package designed to decentralize American industry into strategic locations in new suburban developments was ideal for Caracas, Frankfurt, Milan, and Melbourne. The international conditions guiding the recent pattern of private foreign investment included, therefore, the intensified search for markets coupled with the transportability of production.

The influence of markets on the present flowering of international enterprise warrants further attention. The experienced traveler will remember the black markets in nylons, Parker pens, Swiss watches, and Nescafé in London, Hamburg, Rome and Rio de Janeiro in the years after the war and lasting, in some cases, for a whole decade. In Brazil and India, the black market for diplomatic motor cars continued into 1960. That kind of demand, however, can be quickly satisfied by exports, as soon as foreign exchange becomes available. Such markets are ephemeral.

The markets that have provided the stable and continuous volume of business required for and developed by manufacturing by subsidiary plants in foreign countries have been a function of rising national incomes combined with wider distribution of purchasing power in many countries. Purchasing power and new products have appeared together in former commercial deserts since World War II. Markets involve the inducement of demand—in its simplest form, the creation of knowledge that a product is available. Sterling Products, for example, discovered that headaches are as common in Mexico City as in Chicago— and perhaps more so because of the altitude and the rough quality of some Mexican liquor. One marketing genius, taking advantage of Latin American ignorance or laxity regarding the appropriation of descriptive words, secured trademark registration for "Mejoral" which is Spanish for "better." The Latin Americans are told to take a Mejoral and feel better. Selling a headache tablet under that name has given Sterling a gold mine as lucrative as any discovered by the conquistadores. It was necessary, however, to send production men, advertising men, and sales managers into every Latin American country to realize its full potential. Sterling also had the tact to work through an old company, Sydney Ross, which Latin Americans think of as their own.

Direct foreign investment to meet the new market opportunities in foreign countries has been the dominant pattern primarily because it is more profitable. In the case of American firms, it has also been the necessary result of national policy, as expressed by the Federal Trade Commission and the Treasury Department in their respective rulings against combinations with foreign firms and in favor of wholly-owned subsidiaries. For British, Dutch, Italian, and Swiss firms, profits have been motivation enough.

The Crucial Role of Management Techniques

Direct foreign investment usually involves corporate risk capital rather than strictly individual private investment. A corporation can get market information that is not available to private individuals because they cannot afford it or do not know how to obtain it. The international firm can buy enough of the shares of a business to obtain control. Armed with this authority it can send its expert staff to supervise its investment. The assets used in obtaining controlling interests in foreign subsidiaries often consist mainly of patents, trademarks, and know-how, with comparatively little cash. The private investor does not control such assets. Where money is required to buy land and build a plant, the international firm can borrow from local banks against those fixed assets and repay out of profits before taxes. Interest rates in Brazil can be more than 12 per cent, but profits can be more than double that rate.

The bargains in foreign investment that were picked up during the 1950's, mainly by American firms, are only now beginning to be appreciated. The Committee for Economic Development has shown that "in 1957 United States companies in Latin America . . . spent about $1.7 billion for property, plant and equipment, about $900 million for additions to inventories and other assets. A billion dollars of this amount came from United States sources, $700 million from retained earnings, $400 million from depreciation charges and $400 million from local capital." (Cabot, et al., 1961, p. 40.) Retained earnings and depreciation together contributed more than new investment from American sources, which probably included transfers out of subsidiaries in Canada and Europe. In the case of Black & Decker, the inventive producers and marketers of small power tools, "equity in the net assets of foreign subsidiaries included in the consolidated balance-sheet as of September 30, 1958, amounted to $6,507,765 in excess of its $1,051,347 investment in such subsidiaries." (Moody, 1960, p. 633.)

At the Ford Motors shareholders' meeting on May 18, 1961, John Bugas, Vice-President of Ford International Group, stated that foreign investments in the decade 1951-1961 had been nearly $600 million and "it is important to note that in most instances, investment in these facilities has been financed almost entirely from retained earnings and other resources of the affiliated companies." (Bugas, 1961, p. 30.) Kodak has reported that "the $31 million which we have invested in new and replaced capital assets since 1945 (and prior to 1957) has all come from retained earnings." (D. McMaster, Vice-President and General Manager of Kodak, quoted in Fenn, 1957, p. 101.) These indications have been confirmed in recent studies by Frederick Cutler, who reports that "foreign capital outlays and working capital in mining, manufacturing and petroleum required total financing of $5.6 billion in 1961," but of this sum "the capital flow from the United States supplied only a little over $1.2 billion. The remaining $4.4 billion came from internal funds generated by the operations of the companies abroad, or was obtained from foreign external sources." (Cutler, 1962, p. 17.)

An extreme instance of the use of local capital by companies under international control, that is, with more than half of their shares owned by nonresidents, was given by Donald Gordon, President of Canadian National Railways. He said that "in the mining and smelting industry, more than half of which is controlled by U.S. interests, only 2 per cent of all the capital required by the U.S. part of the industry came from the U.S. in 1957 while practically all of the remainder came from Canadian sources." (Gordon, 1960, p. 8.) Those Canadian sources include loans from banks, insurance companies, and private investors, and reinvested profits and depreciation and depletion allowances against profit taxes. Gordon also noted that the total American investment in Canada was $16 billion by the end of 1957 but that United States Department of Commerce showed that only 31 per cent of this total had ever actually been transferred from the United States into Canada.

A policy of direct foreign investment and complete control is logical for the international firm. If the capital required for a profitable subsidiary consists mainly of patent rights, interna-

tional brand names, production and marketing skill, and bank
credit, what reason is there to offer shares to the natives?

Direct investment in outright ownership also saves the international firm from pressure by native shareholders for dividends.
Without this pressure from native partners, the international
firm is free to expand by unlimited reinvestment of profits,
including making transfers to other countries. The international
firm may also forego short-run profits in order to expand the
market through low prices or heavy advertising, to assure higher
profits later. The international firm may use the profits from one
foreign subsidiary to buy or build another foreign subsidiary.
There may also be simple addition to the local capitalization
from retained earnings to improve the base for future claims for
profit remission, in the event that there are government-controlled profit rates.

These various influences affecting the pattern of international
investment are now so strong that companies that went international earlier have taken expensive steps to obtain complete
control. Abbott Laboratories (drugs) had owned 51 per cent
of a Canadian subsidiary since 1930 and bought up the remaining shares as early as 1937. Ford of Detroit bought out Canadian
shareholders in Ford of Canada in 1959 and British shareholders
in Ford of Britain in 1961, in spite of public criticism in both
the United States and Britain. In 1959, International Business
Machines bought up the outside holdings (38 per cent) in
their British subsidiary. As already mentioned, General Electric
bought out a Canadian minority in 1925, and in 1961 they increased their interest in an Italian associated firm in order to
obtain control.

For all these reasons, neither foreign investment by actual
transfer of funds nor nominal capitalization provides adequate
indication of the scope of international enterprise in the contemporary economies of western countries or of the pattern that
foreign investment has followed. Nor do disclosed profits. The
degree of a company's participation in the industry of a particular country and the dependence of the country on that firm
are most clearly shown by the proportion of the total sales of an
industry that the firm controls in that country. Both percentages
and total sales need to be viewed over a period of years in order

to judge the real influence of the forms of investment characteristically made by international enterprise.

Few governments obtain this information. Where they do,
they have concentrated mainly on questions of possible monopoly. The market percentages controlled by firms engaged
in particular industries are not regularly published anywhere,
except in the case of a few commodities like beer, cigarettes,
motor cars, and chain-store goods, in the United States. The
A. C. Nielsen company, however, has extended its systematic
research into sales of drug and grocery products to twelve
countries outside the United States. Other products, like motor
cars and TV sets, are licensed by many governments and figures
could be developed. In most countries, the larger companies
use one means or another to learn their competitors' sales. The
public and professional economists are the only ones left in
ignorance.

In countries where foreign economic penetration is a direct
question of public policy, the figures on market percentages may
soon be declared to be of public interest and disclosure may be
made compulsory. Many critics will argue that private enterprise needs privacy for this kind of information. That argument
used to be applied to all business figures. Profits of incorporated
companies are now generally published, and in the United
States, a free enterprise country, aggregate sales are also easily
available. Nothing could be more candid and complete than
sales figures and market percentages of retail chains in the food,
drug, variety, shoe, department, and mail order businesses, reported by G. M. Lebhar in the trade paper he edits and in *Chain
Stores in America, 1859-1959* (1960). The annual breakdown of
figures on the drug and grocery trades by classes of product, in
Drug Topics and *Grocery Topics,* is another example.

The Productivity
of Private Foreign Investment

Until international sales figures become more generally available, speculation and controversy will continue to surround the
crucial question of foreign investment: How much does direct

private foreign investment contribute to increasing gross national product? Up to now, economic studies have concentrated mainly on the economic development directly attributable to foreign investment by governments through American foreign aid, the Colombo Plan, and French assistance in Africa—and, for earlier periods, on investment that could be traced through bond issues. Much of the capital transferred by international bond issues and by government-to-government loans and grants has gone into railways and more recently into such public works as roads, dams, and atomic reactors. These investments have attracted academic attention for the familiar reason that the figures are available. Actually, the amounts that have been charged to the taxpayers of the contributing countries are probably as poor a measure of true assets created as are actual transfers of liquid capital in the private sector.

Government grants and loans can easily lead to overestimation of assets created, while private transfers of capital lead to underestimation of them. Government investment is diluted by wastage from high administration expenses, beginning with cost-plus feasibility studies at home and continuing abroad. At the level of the contractor supplying gravel, wastage often includes graft, which cannot easily be eliminated. Companies also occasionally make excessive expenditures, but they can terminate them and write them off, while governments are under political pressure to justify all their actions and may spend extra money for this purpose. The figures for foreign investment by governments are misleading on another score. Airstrips, harbor installations, and connecting roads that are of more obvious relevance to military strategy than to the local economy are included in the foreign aid section of foreign investment figures for some countries, including the United States.

What are the true values of assets? Certainly, they are not equivalent to the money that has been paid for them, as many investors in penny gold stocks have learned. As applied to fixed investments, the notion of assets is an accounting convenience. They seldom remain on company books at cost value but are written up or down according to their earning power. The money that companies spend abroad has been known to bring annual returns of 100 per cent—not only in the historic example of the Hudson's Bay Company. Government loans are, of course, subject to other criteria, frequently being intended to provide needed assets like schools and harbors, the income from which is not immediate and not calculable in money alone. Monetary values attributed to those investments are, therefore, arbitrary and can be exaggerated, and there is no earnings yardstick to show up excessive initial expenses or subsequent changes in their usefulness—when air transport reduces not only the commercial but also the strategic importance of ships and harbors, for example. This problem is further complicated when overlapping services, such as sea and air transport, on the one hand, and road and rail facilities, on the other, are both subsidized.

In summary, it is clear that investment in public utilities and similar assets now comes mainly from governments and, in the less developed countries, from loans from foreign governments. These investments are often characterized by high initial costs and low annual rates of return. Meanwhile, a form of private investment has been found that brings high returns, and this kind of investment has often been made on a sort of installment plan that enables payments to be made out of profits obtained from the very assets being paid for. During the 1950's, a great number of firms that had been successful in the industrialized countries, especially the United States, sought to maximize profits by extending their markets through subsidiaries in many other countries. This process has displaced in importance the investment that used to be made through the money markets of London and New York. The activities of international firms have generally been accepted or positively encouraged by governments and public at home and abroad, in the more advanced and in many of the less advanced countries, for their assumed contributions to economic development.

The typical international firm of today is, however, built on outside control of its subsidiaries based on majority ownership of the voting stock and often total ownership. It is therefore an empire in its organization, as well as in its scope. This pattern is not necessarily permanent. It may be—and may have to be—a transitional stage toward forms of organization that provide more native participation in management and investment. To permit this evolution, the United States may have to modify its antitrust and tax regulations. Investors and corporate management in the United States and other advanced countries may have to change their policies to allow sharing of investment opportunities with the people of the countries where their subsidiaries are earning profits.

6

THE LEGAL FRAMEWORK
AFFECTING INTERNATIONAL
BUSINESS

THE UNITED NATIONS has not yet made any provisions for allowing the incorporation of companies directly under its authority. Every company is therefore dependent on a charter granted by a national government or, as in the United States, by a state government.

As long as business remains confined to the area controlled by the government granting the charter, it need observe only the laws of that government. National company law in the industrialized countries has, of course, become very complicated, very expensive, and very powerful in its influence over business. In Buenos Aires and Mexico City as well as on Wall Street, the most opulent office suites in the high rent districts are occupied by the experts in company law.

There are a few among those corporation lawyers who are represented to be experts in international law. Their practices have grown up through two main types of case: actions between governments and actions affecting shipping companies and airlines that operate internationally. These so-called international lawyers are specialists in specific branches of the law of the several nations with which their clients have contact. There are now also lawyers in the advanced countries who have acquired knowledge of many different countries' *national* laws affecting business in order to advise clients about operations within those countries, and in that special sense they are international lawyers. But there is no international law, applicable to business, because there is no supranational authority to issue and enforce it. The World Court at The Hague is an international body of arbitration. Its findings have been ignored even by countries that have petitioned for them.

The nearest approximation to international law in operation today is the International Conventions. They must be ratified by national governments to become effective, and they have no effect in countries where they have not been incorporated into the national law by enactments of the governments. In addition to a Convention that provides for extradition of criminals from one national jurisdiction to another—which applies to commercial crimes only in the extreme case of embezzlement —there are Conventions on labor, postal rates, and patents and trademarks. The International Labor Convention has been widely adopted, and it has probably helped to restrain extreme forms of exploitation, especially of female and child labor. It has not, however, had any traceable effect on international enterprise. The International Patent Convention, on the other hand, is extremely influential. The International Postage Convention also helps international firms—magazine publishers directly and indirectly those firms that advertise in media with international circulation. The Havana Charter of 1948, intended to provide an International Trade Organization and a code for international business, has not been ratified by the United States or any significant number of other countries.

Before the International Conventions are considered in further detail, notice must be taken of the position of international firms in relation to national laws. Companies are subject to the laws of the countries where they operate—the legal tradition of "the king's brief." The brief runs wherever the king's officers can travel, but no farther. If they attempt to enter the territory of another sovereign without permission, they commit a serious offence that may require an apology and payment of damages, to avoid a breach of diplomatic relations. The sovereign government of each country controls everything within its borders. On the open seas, national sovereignty applies in peacetime only to ships and planes that fly the national flag, signifying their national allegiance. A Convention among Belgium, Britain, Denmark, France, Germany, and the Netherlands in 1882 extended the jurisdiction of those countries to three miles off their shores in order to protect fishing rights. The "three mile limit" concept, which played so large a part in international trade during the Prohibition Era in the United States, was based on the effective range of cannons mounted on the shore. More recent international discussions aimed at increasing the extent of territorial waters to twelve miles have so far been fruitless.

National sovereignty covers corporations as well as people, and corporations are required to have domiciles as are people. When persons or businesses become resident in a country, they become subject to that country's laws.

There have been promulgations of the doctrine that domain follows property. This doctrine has been used to excuse interference by strong nations in the internal affairs of weaker countries, mainly during times of imperialist expansion. The doctrine is not accepted today by any of the smaller countries or by any substantial body of opinion in the larger countries. There have nevertheless been suggestions that countries can and should be required to sign treaties that bind their governments to maintain indefinitely the terms and privileges granted at any time to foreign investors. The United States has what are called Treaties of Friendship, Commerce and Navigation with a number of countries. These treaties include pledges that American property will not be expropriated without due legal process and fair compensation and, in some cases, that capital may be repatriated at any time. Treaties between countries have proved, however, to be much less binding than laws. There is no power of enforcement superior to that of the parties. A government can therefore be expected to protect foreign investments only so long as they serve its interests. When they no longer do, the treaty is likely to be denounced. Attempts to maintain by

military force or economic pressure arrangements that have
clearly become one-sided have been made in the not-distant
past and in some cases the strong have successfully imposed
on the weak, but in other cases they have failed—when the
United States and Britain attempted to prevent the nationalization of the Mexican oil industry, for example. Under present-
day conditions, especially the glare of publicity that can develop even in a dark area of Africa like the former Belgian
Congo, intervention by one nation in the economic affairs of
another is very difficult. Realistic investors avoid leaning on
such broken reeds as treaties negotiated with unpopular political
regimes.

Businesses acknowledge national sovereignty by paying taxes,
obtaining licenses, and reporting required statistics, as well as
by incorporation under the company laws of the host country.
The legal recognition governments give to corporations in
return, however, has permitted nonresident owners to obtain
most of the privileges of citizens in many Western countries.
Some of these countries generously give all companies incorporated under national laws the same privileges, no matter
whether the investors, directors, and management are native
or foreign. In other cases, such privileges result only from
mutual arrangements between governments.

The Legal Framework in Advanced Countries

The business laws of the advanced countries, in which most
international companies originate, are, as one would expect,
more comprehensive than the laws of new governments in less
developed areas. Commercial regulations in the United States,
issued by government agencies like the Securities and Exchange
Commission, the Federal Trade Commission, the Interstate Commerce Commission, the Federal Drug Administration and the
Federal Communications Commission, are specific, detailed, and
strictly enforced. The power of these agencies is augmented by
the publicity the news services give to their investigations of
business activities.

Additional power over business is generated by the news coverage of Congressional investigations. Public hearings ordered by Congressional committees are an almost unique and extremely significant mechanism for harmonizing the activities of large, powerful modern companies and the public interest. This fact needs to be appreciated by other countries that seek the advantages of private enterprise while trying to maintain effective control over their economies. A somewhat similar mechanism operates in countries that follow British Parliamentary practice, where Royal Commissions are occasionally instructed to make public inquiries into specific areas of business—the Pilkington Commission on Broadcasting, for example, which investigated British television advertising. Congress has standing committees, however, that provide continuous watch-dog service. The life-appointed Senators in the Canadian Parliament have indicated growing awareness of the possibility of finding a useful function for themselves in the hearings they have held on unemployment and manpower and on the policy of the Bank of Canada.

The gap between the laws and regulations applied to business in the United States and legal controls in many other countries where American branches or subsidiary companies now operate is so great as to create a vacuum from the point of view of American legislators and enforcement agencies. There has been a natural temptation to intervene and make American laws applicable in other countries, which naturally sharpens the issue of national sovereignty. Thus American law enforcement agencies have frequently provoked government reactions in other countries—for example, in Britain over demands made on British members of the North Atlantic Steamship Conference and in Canada over demands for the record books of Canadian pulp and paper companies accused of collusion in their export policies. The United States government has also angered Canadians by attempts to restrict the exports of Canadian companies in accordance with American foreign policy. Again, when the government of India allowed Mobil Oil and Standard Oil of New Jersey to form a joint Indian subsidiary and the Canadian government allowed du Pont and Imperial Chemicals to do the same in Canada, these joint subsidiaries were broken up on American government orders. The National Labor Relations Board has assumed the right to hold hearings on union certification on the ships of foreign countries. In 1962, however, the Department of Justice and the governments of Britain, Colombia, and Panama pointed out to the American Court reviewing an N.L.R.B. case on unionization of foreign seamen on a foreign ship that attempts to extend United States jurisdiction were damaging American foreign relations.

Britain's sovereignty over companies operating within its territory and colonies is not so fully defined as American sovereignty. It is operative, however, to much the same extent although in different ways. British trade associations like the Federation of British Industries exercise tacitly delegated authority in some directions; the headquarters staff of British labor unions in Transport House, London, influences the formation and enforcement of national policy on such business matters as the perennial British export drive. In addition, the power of British professional accountants and of the banking community to induce conformity with the broad purposes of the British Treasury can scarcely be exaggerated.

Trade associations in the leading industrial nations of Europe have legal authority to regulate various aspects of commerce and industry. In Germany, membership in such associations is compulsory. The Australian and Japanese governments participate in producers' organizations that control the quality and quantity of the vital exports of those countries. Sweden, which wrote a new law on industrial combinations after the Second World War, adopted the Sherman Act principle that collusion among companies is likely to constitute conspiracy against the public. It allowed, however, for exceptions and provided means for proving public benefit (for example in contracts between manufacturers and dealers that require after-sales service).

Differences in National Corporation Laws

The laws of many countries provide advantages to foreign companies. Tax concessions given by the less developed countries, which are seeking industrialization, are the most important kind. These concessions may apply specifically to companies that invest scarce foreign currency or equipment and materials that would cost foreign currency, or they may be given to all companies that introduce new industries and are thus likely to be foreign. A subsidiary may also obtain the services of head-office experts partially remunerated by tax-free fees and traveling allowances. Some countries, however, charge high fees for visas for business visitors, and the Philippines has attempted to collect tax on the total income of business visitors. Tax provisions may also allow substantial indirect advantages to foreign companies without specifically favoring them. Depreciation allowances, for example, offer most benefit to companies that make the fullest use of labor-saving machinery: usually the international companies.

Peculiar legal situations are found in some countries. In Mexico, foreigners may not own any land within 100 kilometres of the coasts and borders. Neither foreigners nor Mexicans may obtain large holdings of agricultural land. The original intention was to prevent the removal of this prime natural resource from the control of the native population and particularly to maintain a class of farming proprietors, thus preventing plantation agriculture from creating a rural proletariat. An incidental outcome is that a foreign manufacturer wanting to build a new suburban plant may encounter what seems like needless red tape, but it is significant that no such laws existed in Cuba where 40 per cent of the sugar lands had passed into foreign ownership prior to the Castro expropriations. Land reform is now regarded by Alliance for Progress and other experts as an urgent necessity in several Latin American countries.

Foreigners are denied entry to certain industries in a number of countries. Argentina, Brazil, and Mexico do not allow oil wells to be privately owned in order to prevent foreign control. Argentina now allows private exploration but not ownership. The United States refuses radio or television broadcasting licenses to foreigners. In Brazil, magazine publishing enterprises must be wholly owned by citizens of that country, and in Mexico they must be more than 50 per cent owned by Mexicans. Britain acted to enable the American Astors, now British citizens, to put the semi-official newspaper, *The Times* of London, out of the reach of foreign investors by establishing a trust. Canada refuses licenses for radio or television broadcasting to private companies that have more than a minority of foreign shareholders, on the ground that public communications are of national concern.

Public utilities are increasingly being operated at uneconomic rates, supplemented by subsidies, in order to encourage other industries and secure greater benefits for the general public. The national railways in Britain, and, indeed, the railways in most countries of the world today are subsidized. Public power developments receive cheap government credit in the United States as well as in many foreign countries. In some countries, notably Brazil, expropriation of private utilities in favor of public ownership involves foreign companies. This problem, however, is not new. As far back as 1906, a Conservative government in the Canadian province of Ontario formed a Hydro-Electric Power Commission under public ownership to forestall American control of the distribution of electricity in that part of Canada, and in 1917 the generation of power on the Canadian side at Niagara Falls was put under public ownership.

In all of these cases the sovereign power of the state has been invoked for reasons of national security rather than on doctrinaire socialist grounds. The objection is to alienation of resources or to economic colonization rather than to capitalism. The backbone of the moderate socialism of Sweden has been the "K. F." Cooperative Union and its "Konsum" stores, which have been thoroughly practical and businesslike and whose origins can be traced directly to reaction against foreign cartels. The question arises: To what extent does socialization in other countries have the same roots? The possibility exists that foreign economic penetration may arouse a socialistic or even communistic reaction when it fails to involve local partners. Ceylon, Egypt, Indonesia, Burma and Algeria formerly were host to large foreign agricultural estates, and practically all the mining and manufacturing was owned by foreigners. When these countries expropriated foreign investments and expelled the foreigners who managed them, there was nobody except the government to take over because foreigners—including not only Europeans and Americans but also Indians in Burma and Ceylon, Chinese in Indonesia, and Levantines in North Africa—had monopolized most of the industry and trade. In India, however, there were some progressive Indian-controlled industries like Birla textiles. The first socialistic Indian economic plan left the door ajar for private industry. The second plan opened wider opportunities, perhaps partially because of Indianization policies adopted by Lever and other foreign firms.

The Special Problems
of American Antitrust Policy

Business problems stemming from differences in national laws are not new, but they are increasing as more companies form foreign subsidiaries at a time when more countries are becoming politically independent. The economic penetration of China during the nineteenth century was accompanied by the doctrine of extraterritoriality, whereby the Great Powers of that time claimed that their citizens were subject only to their laws, even while resident within the territory of the Chinese government.

Whether or not because of the obvious gap between the regulations applied to companies in the United States and those applied elsewhere, a new American doctrine of extraterritoriality has appeared. A small example is the dying Eisenhower Administration's order on Friday, January 13, 1961, that any American controlled company that held gold in any other country must sell it regardless of the laws of that country. The American government had previously extended its regulations against trading in specified goods with nations it regarded as unfriendly—China, for example—to foreign subsidiaries. There is also a long list of interventions by the Federal Trade Commission, the Antitrust Division, and the Maritime Commission outside American borders. Efforts by the Maritime Commission to exercise jurisdiction over British shipping companies have been so persistent as to provoke denunciation in the House of Commons by the British Prime Minister.

These American regulations have teeth. The government can penalize American citizens who are directors of foreign subsidiaries. There is even a question about the legal position of a citizen of a foreign country who becomes a director of a subsidiary or affiliate of an American company. Neale has pointed out that "the [United States] Courts have asserted *in personam* jurisdiction over officers of foreign companies when they have appeared in the United States on business or personal visits." (Neale, 1960, p. 326.) This behavior of the American government can be interpreted abroad to mean that any government that grants a charter to a company with American directors is also granting powers to the agents of a foreign government, friendly perhaps, but still foreign. American directors have been discreetly reluctant to bring to a head this issue of extraterritorial control but it requires public acknowledgment and discussion in the United States. To gloss it over is to attempt to plaster over a crack in the foundations of Western alliances. Until this situation is corrected, suspicion shadows even the most constructive efforts of American business in other countries.

The uncertain legal position of the international company reflects the absence of international law in the field of business. This absence will continue until political organization catches up with economic developments. Industrial organization is now widely international, for economic efficiency transcends national frontiers. The proof is abundantly clear in the profit statements of companies that have gone abroad. Also, gross national product in many countries has been greatly augmented by the activities of international firms. Pointing to increased economic efficiency of firms and nations, however, does not answer all the political questions that are being raised in countries like Brazil and Canada, which find large segments of their social organization under the active control of foreigners.

Serious conflicts may be avoided if true international law develops far and fast enough to provide economic justice. The ultimate ideal is a code for business under a world government. This ideal is even more remote than agreement on armaments because of the fundamental differences in the economic organization of the West and the East. Regional development is possible through the British Commonwealth, the European Economic Community, and the Organization of American States. The North Atlantic Treaty Organization periodically includes economic affairs on the agenda for its meetings, and the Organization for Economic Cooperation and Development, created in 1961, includes European neutrals beside the United States, Canada, and the other NATO countries. None of these organizations, however, has yet adopted a code of the rights and obligations of private firms that could operate throughout the territories of its member states.

There remains the possibility of further development of international commercial law on an *ad hoc* basis. Such law could be modeled after the International Patent Convention. The United States has attempted unilaterally to prevent restraint of trade and to encourage competition. More progress might have been made, in the long run, by calling conferences like those that led up to the Patent Convention, and carrying on missionary work among the delegates—for the promulgation of international industrial conventions containing regulations similar to those of the United States and for adherence to such conventions by other countries. International conventions could cover competitive practices, as well as patents, and they could also be extended to accounting practices, allowances for research, withdrawal of capital, publication of annual reports, and protection of national industries and the rights of national investors.

The General Agreement on Tariffs and Trade, sometimes referred to as the Geneva Convention, has not fulfilled its original purpose of achieving a general reduction of tariffs. In the area of tariff regulations and their administration, however, it is conceded to have brought about substantial improvement. Importers and exporters now receive uniform treatment, and there are established channels for explanation and review of decisions in most of the participating countries. These examples provide clear evidence that international conventions can extend the rule of law over international business.

The International Patent Convention and International Business

To gain wide acceptance, international conventions will have to be fair to both rich and poor countries. The International Patent Convention does not seem to ensure such fairness. Professor Corwin Edwards, an authority on restrictive business practices, has noted, on the basis of averages for 1930-37, that "Canada is an extreme case, her nationals receiving only one per cent of United States patents issued while United States residents receive 66 per cent of total Canadian patents issued." (Edwards, 1945, p. 66.) In the Annual Report of the United States Commissioner of Patents for fiscal 1960, the patents issued to residents of Canada had fallen to .7 per cent. The share of Canadian patents issued to Americans in 1960 reached 68.2 per cent. This spread cannot be explained by differences in population, talent, or education. It derives, instead, from legal and economic influences that concentrate research activities in the United States.

The International Convention for the Protection of Industrial Property (patents)was adopted in 1884. It has been widely accepted by Western governments, except in Latin America. It operates through recognition by member governments of patents filed with other members and through accordance of the same rights to foreign patentholders as to natives. Most countries do require, however, that the patent be exercised by the owner or his licensee within a reasonable time.

The ostensible purpose of this Convention was to encourage invention by ensuring rewards for inventors from all countries in which their inventions were used. Originally Britain, France, Germany, and the United States were relatively equal sources of new inventions, which were still largely the work of individuals.

The conditions that existed when the International Patent Convention was drawn up have changed. Commercially applicable invention or the development of ideas into practical and patentable form now frequently require heavy investment in laboratory facilities—in industrial laboratories and at universities and government research stations—and in the training and time of teams of research workers. The royalties on many patents go to companies rather than to individuals as rewards and encouragement. Most companies undertake research to meet competition in their home markets and are not directly influenced by the incentive of foreign royalties, which are windfall profits. Procter & Gamble embarked on its great international safari after its wartime discoveries in synthetic detergents had been patented and fully exploited at home. It entered the international market with exclusive and tested competitive weapons.

Only recently have the aspirations of countries like Australia, Brazil, and Italy for industrialization been recognized, even by their own governments. All the implications and conditions have not yet been examined. Professor Penrose has concluded, however, that "the idea of an individual inventor rewarded by a monopoly patent in his invention is an anachronism in modern cooperative research" (Penrose, 1951, p. 191), and, furthermore, that "most countries have little if anything to gain economically from granting patents to foreign firms." (P. 141.)

The British have had a dramatic experience with the workings of the International Patent Convention. The pure research that provided the background for the discovery of penicillin was done in England by Sir Alexander Fleming, and the actual preparation of the drug was also done there by Sir Howard Florey and E. B. Chain. The wartime importance of this discovery led to sharing of this information with the United States. Technicians in American pharmaceutical companies worked out mass production processes, which were patented, while the original discovery was not. As a result, the profits went to the American companies, not only in the United States but in many other countries where the International Convention enabled them to obtain exclusive manufacturing privileges.

Professor Penrose has pointed out that patents encourage exploitation rather than fundamental research—working to the advantage of international firms through the International Convention which enables and encourages them to exploit widely the monopolies afforded by the control of inventions. Thus a foreign country may get a new product or a whole new industry much faster because an international firm can profit by exercising a patent than by depending on local enterprise. While it is compulsory to publish in the country of origin in order to secure a patent and while full disclosure is intended by the law to enable another company to use the new knowledge if the patent is not exercised, in fact there is undisclosed know-how in most modern cases. And a foreign country is dependent for know-how on the international firm that has developed the invention.

Research appears to have outgrown the patent laws. It is no longer primarily the search for a single invention. Instead, it is an elaborate process designed to ensure a continuous flow of new products and product improvements and more efficient methods. It is a new monopoly open only to very large firms like du Pont, General Electric, General Foods, General Motors, Procter & Gamble, Philips in the Netherlands, and Ciba in Switzerland.

There is another effect of the patent system that favors international firms by giving them a basis for securing tax advantages. The revenue departments of many governments can still be persuaded, on the strength of an international patent granted by another department, that payment for its use by a local subsidiary to a foreign owner is a business expense chargeable before profits tax. Fees are a frequent and important international financial transfer. A prospectus issued by Gairdner & Company Limited in Toronto on January 9, 1961, stated that "a fee equal to 12½ per cent of the annual net profit before taxes or 3 per cent of the net sales, whichever is the lesser" is paid by Exquisite Form Brassieres (Canada) Limited to the American parent for "exclusive rights to sell in the Company's operating areas all products designed by the American corporation. The Canadian company also benefits from the American company's market research, advertising campaigns, technological developments and methods." An agreement made in December, 1960, between the government of Mexico and the Scott Paper firm of the United States made a point of including a 3 per cent limit on royalties and technical service payments. (*Business Week,* March 4, 1961, p. 87.) The Beecham Group of London charges foreign subsidiaries a percentage of sales for research in lieu of royalties. Foreign tax authorities often allow such charges without receiving any accounting of the actual costs to the local company.

International Trademarks

The fundamental research by advertising pioneers like Lord Leverhulme in England and Albert Lasker of the Lord & Thomas advertising agency in Chicago has been used by the Madison Avenue agencies to create a new form of international industrial property that also enjoys international protection. This property consists of the familiarity of the public with distinctive words and designs registered as trademarks.

Trademark law originated as protection for the public, so that purchasers would not be deceived about the makers of products. The use of brand names and designs was therefore restricted to the manufacturers or distributors who originated them. The original hallmark of quality was the maker's mark on sterling silver. The right to use names and designs was confirmed by registration of trademarks. Proof of use is still a condition of registration in many countries.

Names and marks became valuable when the public learned through experience to show preference for certain ones in their purchases. The president of the MacGregor Instrument Company of Needham, Massachusetts, has given an illuminating modern example. "Our experience has been that a trademark in foreign countries is much more valuable [than a patent]. We do business with medical men, and they care nothing about patents. To a doctor, a patent is anathema, but he will respect a trademark, and he will see to it that his nurse or associate orders your merchandise by your trademark. He knows the goods we make by the trademark we use." (Quoted in Fenn, 1957, p. 91.)

The followers of Lasker and Leverhulme have learned how to induce artificially public acceptance of brands, how to use advertising as a substitute in the consumer's mind for buying experience. This modern technique is ingenious and usually very expensive, but it is correspondingly profitable. Advertised trademarks enable one manufacturer to obtain a large proportion of the sales of a class or several classes of product over very wide geographical areas. The resulting economies in production, distribution, and even advertising, per capita or per unit of sale yield immense profits.

International protection for trademarks is available. The advantages afforded to the international firm, however, are less obvious than the advantages of a patent. Trademarks have to be made known, which takes either a very long time or a great deal of money. Coined words and designs encounter difficulties of pronunciation and other meanings *sous-entendus* among people with different customs and languages. Colgate made an expensive mistake by introducing its trademark "Cue" into French-speaking districts, where the word is pornographic. Trademarks also have to be policed. Before General Foods, the proprietors of "Jello," became active in Australia, a competitor had registered the name "Mello" without arousing protest.

Despite such pitfalls, international trademarks provide real advantages for the advertising experts employed by international firms. In the new jargon of operations research, a "model" of a successful advertising campaign in one country can be constructed to facilitate and expedite the planning and execution of a campaign in another country. For instance, consumer research in the country of origin of Exquisite Form Brassieres can be confirmed or modified on a much smaller sample in another country. Human nature and the human figure are fundamentally the same. If a product designed to serve certain wants or needs in the home country will not fill such wants or needs in another country, properly described in the language of that country, the company concerned may decide that it is not likely to sell for any other readily discovered reason either and that the profitable policy would be to try another market. The psychological structure of an effective advertising campaign is as useful internationally as a blueprint for a building or a machine and quite as profitable. The advertising earns profits, of course, by directing demand to the exclusive, registered brand.

The protection available for international advertising under the present legal framework is effectively limited to brand names and designs. Plagiarism of advertising ideas is widespread but difficult to prove. The only worthwhile protection is widespread prior use. Modern companies built on advertising are therefore encouraged to secure the benefits of their ideas in as many countries as possible.

Advertising also spreads internationally through overflow circulation of publications and of radio and television in certain areas. Parts of Canada and Mexico are within reach of American broadcasting stations, and parts of Britain can hear Radio Luxembourg. Some stations are located where there is no local market to sustain them, but they can reach Britain or Canada with advertising that is forbidden there.

The International Convention on Postal Rates increases the value of the advertised brands of companies in countries that have a powerful press. British brands used to receive a bonus of foreign exposure from the wide international circulation of *Punch* and the *London Illustrated News.* Now *Life,* the *New Yorker,* and the superior American trade and technical journals have that kind of circulation. They are distributed by post in countries that have signed the International Convention on the postage paid in the United States. Their subscription campaign letters receive the same privileges. The United States Post Office receives the revenue, such as it is. In fact, American rates on those classes of mail are uneconomic, a subsidy to the American press. Smaller countries bear the cost of dragging into their territories these modern economic Trojan horses. Reciprocity in postal privileges is purely theoretical because only the aggressive publications of the largest countries are able to obtain worthwhile volume of foreign subscriptions.

In summary, it is clear that the law affecting international enterprise, little as there is, favors large companies originating in economically strong and advanced countries by giving them competitive advantages over companies originating in smaller and weaker countries.

7

INTERNATIONAL ENTERPRISE

AND ECONOMIC GROWTH

THE PURPOSE of this chapter is to define and illus-
trate two persistent problems of economic growth rather than
to propound any new theory or to survey the theories that
already abound. The first problem is that adequate growth
to meet present needs, which include rapid population growth
and large political aspirations, is not being obtained by present
methods, doctrines, and policies in any country—and the prospects of the advanced countries are actually dimmer than those
of many less developed countries.

The second problem is that only empirical methods can yield
useful knowledge about real growth. Observations have to be
extended in great detail and on a continuing basis to include
not only national aggregates but also the growth of companies,
in which inheres a large part of the growth of modern noncommunist national economies. International companies appear to
offer especially important material because of their recent
growth record and because of the ways in which their growth
appears to affect the many countries in which they operate.
Such companies are promising sources of evidence in support
of the statement made by an outstanding authority on economic
growth, W. W. Rostow, that "the rapid growth of one or more

new manufacturing sectors is a powerful and essential engine
of economic transformation. Its power derives from the multi-
plicity of its forms of impact." (Rostow, 1960, p. 58.)

Economic growth has become a question of intense interest
to the general public in many parts of the world. The evidence
of public interest includes the frequency of references to growth
in political speeches, usually in association with promises to
provide more growth. Americans have reason to feel a sort of
proprietary interest in growth. Beside enjoying great increases
in goods and services, they have appeared to find in substantial
and fairly continuous growth a way of transcending the more
serious conflicts about distribution of wealth that have disturbed
other countries. American production and employment have increased and so has productivity, permitting increases in both
profits and wages. If the American example or American aid
and advice could induce similar economic growth in other countries, it might offer some protection against the spread of
communism.

In many parts of the world, there is now strong hope for
economic growth among the local inhabitants and their leaders.
This hope is new and has the power to guide people's actions.
It is no longer a mere passive dream or envious wish, for growth
now appears attainable in those countries. The popular reasons
for this faith are primarily the examples of the United States
and subsequently Russia, the European Economic Community,
and Japan. Also included among the factors that bolster confidence in growth are the successes of companies like Ford,
General Motors, Nestlé, and Unilever, with their thriving subsidiaries in many countries. These companies appear to offer
transfusions of growth serum from advanced to less developed
countries. While international firms make contributions which
deserve increased recognition, the requirements should not be
oversimplified. There are social and political conditions of the
kinds that have been emphasized by Professor Rostow in his
historical analysis of economic growth. There are also the hard
work, sacrifices, and numerous frustrations and failures on
which, as businessmen know, growth is built. The significance
of the growing number and size of foreign subsidiary com-

panies in many countries is that they give substance to hopeful analogies between those countries and the advanced countries by increasing the number of points of similarity.

The demand for economic growth will be satisfied, however, only when growth spreads in certain directions that are not yet generally included among the growth objectives of the average corporation. One such direction is employment. The family business used to include among its other purposes providing secure employment for relatives first, of course, but often also for faithful employees. Now, however, many companies explicitly forbid the employment of relatives. Furthermore, provision of jobs is entirely subordinate and indeed quite incidental to earning profits. The normal basis for profit increases is rising output, part of which is expected to be achieved by higher productivity of labor, and the number of jobs may actually decrease through increased mechanization made practical by larger volume.

Here is, of course, the threat posed by automation. There is now a real possibility that more and more goods can be produced by fewer and fewer people, with doles to the rest to maintain purchasing power. Unemployed people are, however, wasted resources, and unemployment also puts people into an intolerable psychological and social position from which political turmoil is certain to arise. No definition of economic growth is politically acceptable if it allows for persistent unemployment. The public sector plays its part, especially in compensating for short-term fluctuations in employment, but to make full employment the responsibility of government alone is to invite creeping socialization. The alternative is for corporate management to think twice about every proposal involving displacement of labor and to allow full publicity to the problem so that the repercussions in other industries can be explored. There are rationalization programs in many businesses today which do not afford any significant early cost reductions. Such labor-saving programs seem advantageous in long-run projections, but they are bad business in the short-run, for costs of maintaining or retraining displaced labor have to be met. This burden will weigh so heavily on general business that even firms that initially seem able to shift their share to others may need to revise their calculations.

One way in which business can extend economic growth is by taking the jobs to the people instead of leaving the people to seek out the locations where new jobs are available. It is now common practice for American companies to try to locate where the employees want to live, in California or Arizona for example. New industries are now moving into southern Italy— branches of northern Italian companies, as well as subsidiaries of foreign firms. This development is particularly significant because the industrial possibilities of Italy were long considered to be very limited and because Italians were hard-working and adaptable immigrants. It generally took them only two generations to become good Americans, Argentinians, Australians, Canadians, or Venezuelans.

But the mobility of labor has been increasingly circumscribed by government action, notably by the United States. The annual quota for immigrants to the United States from the Philippines is only one hundred. These restrictive policies are based on common sense rather than on economic theory, but they also make economic sense when the full implications are recognized and accepted. Mass migrations of labor involve great costs, including the emotional costs of uprooting people and requiring them to learn new languages and social customs, in addition to new ways of work. Such costs are sometimes financially measurable in higher law-enforcement and social-work costs. There are good reasons for believing that it is better to develop more industries in Puerto Rico than to bring more Puerto Ricans to Harlem. Immediate costs are also heavy for new roads, houses, schools, and other utilities when large population transfers are made, especially when they are superimposed on the large natural population increases now occurring.

If people are not to be moved around the world like other factors of production, theory and policy on industry and trade must be adjusted. This necessity has been recognized in the protective external tariffs and the elaborate internal arrangements affecting the location of industries established by the European Economic Community, even though these countries have adopted greater freedom of labor movement among themselves than prevails among most other countries. It should be remembered that West Germany had severe problems in finding work for displaced persons from East Germany after the war. The Netherlands had its returning colonists from the East Indies and Belgium from the Congo, while Italy suffered from chronic unemployment. The demand for economic growth through industrialization—assisted by tariffs, quotas, and subsidies when necessary—is the response in many countries to the pressure of population. The participation in economic growth of this kind by companies with foreign subsidiaries is therefore more soundly based than is international trade in common commodities and manufactures relying on comparative advantage in natural resources and level of industrialization.

Economic Growth: The Facts

Anything that international business enterprise can do to assist economic growth deserves attention, in view of ambitious modern plans and aspirations, on the one hand, and of indifferent achievements so far, on the other. A compilation of average annual rates of growth of gross domestic product during the last decade appears in the United Nations *World Economic Survey* for 1961. The figures show wide differences, with Israel, Japan, Venezuela, and West Germany among the highest and Argentina, Belgium, and Britain among the lowest. The United Nations figures for a representative list of countries outside the communist bloc are given below.

The Alliance for Progress in Latin America exemplifies this general belief that economic growth is the paramount need of underdeveloped countries. Identification of this need has probably raised expectations greatly. Economic planning and massive public investment are being applied, but they have not, as yet, produced more private enterprise or counteracted dependence on commodity exports. The Alliance for Progress has predicted that a 6 per cent increase per year in gross national product throughout South and Central America and Mexico will be required to provide a 3 per cent increase in per capita income, because of the increasing population. Unless there are new industries in profuse variety, as well as expansion of existing businesses, this goal will remain mere wishful thinking.

The leaders in economic growth, first Britain and then for many years the United States, have slowed down. The United States is having difficulty absorbing additions to its domestic labor force. Both countries have responsibilities toward other countries that they can meet only if their economies are healthy —commitments made on the assumption that growth would be maintained. This assumption seemed reasonable on the basis of linear projections from past records. But such projections involve no certainties—only probabilities—and reasonable probabilities develop only when research demonstrates what John Stuart Mill called "a tissue of regularities." It is also necessary to watch for irregularities like the slow absorption of labor into the American labor force since 1958.

A probability of growth is more difficult to establish for the United States than for the less developed countries. In the latter, the search for facts and combinations of facts that yield probabilities of growth from their present low level is aided by comparisons with the earlier experiences of Britain, the United States, Japan, Canada, and the countries of the European Economic Community. W.W. Rostow has warned, however, that aggregates veil the complex conditions that have been present in those growth economies (Rostow, 1960, p. 21) and that ag-

Average Annual Rates of Growth of Gross Domestic Product (in percentages)

Argentina*	2	France	4.3	New Zealand	3.5
Australia	3.9	Germany, West	7.6	Norway	3.5
Austria	5.9	Greece*	6	Pakistan*	3
Belgium	2.9	India*	3	Peru*	4
Brazil*	6	Indonesia*	4	Philippines*	6
Britain	2.7	Israel	9	South Africa*	5
Canada	3.8	Italy	5.9	Sweden	3.2
Chile*	3	Japan	9.5	United States	3.3
Colombia*	5	Mexico*	5	Venezuela*	8
Denmark	3.4	Netherlands	4.7		

* 1950-1951 to 1958-1959; otherwise, 1950-1960.

gregative analysis does not solve this problem. These comments are applicable to the problem of growth in the United States today and particularly to the problem of identifying those growth situations in American industry that are numerous and strong enough to influence the level of the whole economy. Research on growth is currently more active for the less developed countries than for the countries from which leadership is expected and needed. The recent growth of companies with international connections that have given them new products for use in their home operations—most of the large drug companies and some food companies, for example—may have importance that goes beyond the profits of those particular companies by providing insights into how growth occurs.

Government Efforts to Stimulate Growth

American businessmen have always tended to believe that economic growth is created exclusively by private enterprise and, furthermore, that any form of government interference inhibits growth. The exclusive franchises, subsidies, and use of public property granted to railroad, power, telegraph, telephone, and broadcasting companies are overlooked. The argument is still sometimes heard that growth would be resumed with full nineteenth-century vigor if government would only get out of business. While some regulations may hamper growth, withdrawing all regulations would not necessarily increase growth. In fact, there is growth today in countries with active government participation in business—in moderate France, Italy, and Japan, for example—and, of course, there has been growth in completely state-administered economies like Russia. Complex modern businesses depend on government-managed currency and credit, government-imposed tariffs and government-negotiated trade agreements, government information and education, courts and rules and enforcement of decisions. All these services are continuously extended, as new knowledge about labor relations, drugs, air pollution, and water, soil, and forest conservation becomes available.

A version of the idea that growth can be increased by re-
moving government restrictions appears in the periodic proposals for general tariff reductions. There is, of course, strong
support for this idea in pure economic theory, but the assumptions on which it rests are unfortunately unrealistic. One such
assumption is that free movement of labor will accompany the
free movement of goods. Another is that only long-run effects
need be considered and that the costs of adaptation to free
international competition can be ignored. A third condition is
that truly general tariff reductions be in fact made without
special exceptions for industries essential for military advantage
—or for the re-election of senators, deputies and members of
Parliament.

It is unrealistic to look for extensive reductions in government
regulations on domestic business or foreign trade. On the contrary, public concern about economic growth is more likely to
increase government intervention. The practical question for
both businessmen and officials is how they can achieve knowledge of growth processes that will give them a basis for mutual
respect and cooperation.

The growth that has occurred in France, Italy, and West
Germany and, to a lesser extent, in Belgium and the Netherlands, since their governments began to organize an economic
community has suggested that regional customs unions would
have beneficial effects in other areas like South America. The
Europeans, however, describe their aim as establishment of an
economic community, rather than merely a common market.
The word "community" is a reminder of the underlying cultural
and religious similarities among the countries that have joined
and also of their physical proximity and their common network
of communications and transportation facilities. This conjunc-
tion of unifying influences is not often duplicated in the rest
of the world. Some of the credit for European progress is also
attributed by the economic planners to their combination of
strong programs in the public sector and better guidance toward
profit opportunities for private investment.

There has been, however, still another influence that deserves
recognition—Western European countries have received a bonus

of development from the backlog of innovations in both public and private sectors available from the United States, Britain, and other outsiders. They include improvements in housing, highways, and hospitals, and in cars, kitchen appliances, and mass entertainment (television and tourism). American, British, and Swiss firms built plants to obtain production inside the proposed new common tariff wall. This activity increased employment and provided a wide variety of new products that greatly strengthened consumer demand in Europe. These influences may have been quite as important in the recent economic development of "the Six" Common Market countries as the savings in costs from larger scale manufacturing for the wider new market. Moreover, the actual economic growth preceded the actual reductions of the internal tariffs of the European Community.

The economic growth of nations remains haphazard in its occurrence, and rates are variable, even while growth has become accepted as a major objective of national policy and while great institutional, financial, and intellectual resources are being applied to foster it. Although we have learned much, our knowledge has enabled us only to supply more favorable conditions for growth rather than the essential growth itself. Monetary measures—easy credit, for example—are very helpful when there are borrowers disposed to use credit productively; otherwise, they are inflationary. Fiscal measures, including accelerated depreciation allowances, are similarly dependent for their effects on the use made of them by business. Depreciation allowances do not automatically assure re-equipment of industry with improved machinery. A government may find itself giving large allowances to a steel industry that has done little recent research and made few technological improvements—and that may, indeed, have poor prospects for growth because customers are economizing in the use of steel and substituting other materials. Such government measures are blunt instruments difficult to use discriminatingly to promote growth, even when industries with growth potential are identifiable. They are most effective in the less developed countries, where almost any increase in industrialization constitutes growth.

Other economic tonics that have been widely prescribed to

stimulate growth include large doses of publicly financed transportation, power, essential materials production, irrigation and other aids to agriculture, and technical education. Such measures are desirable, and in many countries they are essential, but they still provide only the tinder. They do not strike the sparks.

The Contributions of International Firms to Economic Growth

The experience of international firms is not unimportant in relation to the complexities and difficulties of the growth of nations. A large part of economic growth is and must continue to be the growth of such firms. The records of some of the leaders suggest that they may have important contributions to make. International firms are oriented toward growth situations because they recognize the profit opportunities afforded by increased sales from new markets opened by introducing new products and services. The expression, "NEW from Procter & Gamble," frequently and of course blaringly repeated during the last fifteen years, may seem an overworked cliché, but it has proved a successful formula for the growth of the firm. This growth has been on a scale that suggests there must also have been positive effects on national growth, particularly in smaller countries like the Philippines and Venezuela.

The most promising markets for new products are to be found in the lesser developed countries, in which many products long established in the advanced countries are still new. The quickest means of introducing them are usually under the control of the firms that originated them. Many of these new or improved products are still capable of stimulating far-reaching growth effects in more primitive economies.

Meeting the basic conditions of economic growth—for example, obtaining a food supply sufficient to free at least part of a country's work force from scrabbling for daily existence and enable them to contribute their labor to achieving longer-term goals—requires introduction of new products. To help meet this need, countries with surpluses have made generous donations of food to underdeveloped countries. They have also contributed machines and skill for irrigation, land clearing, and reclamation, as well as fertilizer, seeds, breeding stock, insecticides, and even agricultural colleges. Some of the most effective development work has been done by international firms selling farm implements and chemicals. They know how to mobilize credit by encouraging farmers or groups of farmers to buy on the installment plan. Their salesmen also know how to educate customers to use their products.

Another aspect of the primary growth requirement for more food is the contribution, still inadequately recognized, that can be made by simple improvements in food processing. The waste of nutritional values in traditional methods of food handling, particularly in hot countries, is stupendous. Food spoils in vast quantities from the action of sun, air, water, and bacteria—or it is consumed by rodents and insects. The modern food-processing industry can transform a country's economic situation by introducing canning and bottling and the newer processes of freezing and drying. International firms have led and continue to enlarge this development. American firms like Heinz are prominent in this area, as are the British canned meat and the Swiss canned milk industries. The methods of these firms have been proved effective internationally, but they have not yet been applied as widely as they can be.

The impetus for growth from increasing food supplies by modern industrial methods needs to be considered when the question of land reform arises. Freedom from hunger has been achieved in the advanced countries by technology that is beyond the means of the peasant proprietor. The first industrial revolution in Britain was made possible by an agricultural revolution, led by Coke of Norfolk and other large British landowners, who disproved Adam Smith's claim that a large proprietor is seldom an improver (Smith, 1910, p. 343.) These large farmers made improvements in cultivation and stock-breeding methods, producing crops for sale rather than mere subsistence. When manufacturing subsequently created a large home market for labor and for agricultural produce, farming methods improved still further, and the food supply increased. Land reform, which is oversimplified to mean merely parceling out small holdings for the continuation of monoculture with less efficient organization or for subsistence farming is regressive.

As in many other fields, progress in realizing the benefits of food processing is slow because, while the economic indicators are favorable, psychological and social inhibitions remain in force. The important task is to win acceptance of food in new forms by consumers. Social changes, especially in such primeval customs as eating, do not come automatically. Tastes and prejudices permeate eating habits. Vitamin C, recognized as medically important only a generation ago and now provided by daily consumption of fruit or tomato juice, has become an integral part of the habitual diet in the United States. Its acceptance is the result of continuous educational and promotional activities during the last quarter-century. The processes through which the habit of including vitamin C became established were complex: the tomato, for example, was reclassified as a vegetable instead of a fruit. It changed from primarily a hot, cooked food to a cold, fresh one and from a summer specialty to a year-round staple. The tomato is one example of how new tastes are acquired and cultivated. The industries concerned with processed foods must win confidence in the safety of canned foods, especially for those with high acid contents, must convince housewives of the importance of vitamins, and finally must stimulate appreciation of new flavors among all consumers. In the example of the frozen foods that have brought about another major revolution in American food habits, new facilities and routines had to be established, not only in production but also in retail distribution, home storage, and meal preparation.

Changes corresponding with these revolutions in American food habits have still to be made in many parts of the world, in order to achieve the improvements in nutrition that production technology affords. International firms have already made substantial contributions to the spread of more efficient food processing, and they can do more. There have been patents that encouraged international enterprise in this field, but the greatest advantage of international firms has been their skill or know-how.

Techniques that are effective in producing even apparently minor changes in the behavior of great masses of people are not common and not simple. One factor in such techniques is product standardization, which is easier to seek than to achieve. When Unilever commenced manufacture in Britain of dry soup mixes, perfected by the Lipton subsidiary in the United States during the Second World War, one problem was to find suppliers of ingredients and container materials that would meet the narrow tolerance of moisture content. Such standards were previously unheard of in the damp British climate.

Another factor in the food industry, which may seem superficial but has proved to be extremely influential, is color, the precise color of the product and the exact and widespread representation of this color in advertising. Meticulous care about color in products and advertising is a long-standing policy of the highly successful Campbell Soup Company, pursued to such a point that they have paid bonuses for exact reproduction and have refused to pay for color work that deviated from their standards. The proliferation of new products in the American food industry has been accompanied by great improvements in the means available for acquainting large audiences with these developments, particularly color photography and color printing.

The spread—to many countries—of modern food industries using techniques of consumer and distributor education, as well as of production, is important for economic growth because an agriculturally-based economy is no longer a desirable end in itself. Farming as a self-sufficient way of life is anachronistic. Food production is both an industry itself and a basis for other industries. Exploitation of the soil for food or raw materials has been organized in Cuba, Kenya, the Philippines, and many other economic colonies to support manufacturing in other countries. But integration through the development of processing industries and services can take place where the food or other natural resources—and the people—are already located. This second alternative is illustrated by the case of Sweden, which has built up a well-rounded economy on a modest base of forest products, minerals, hydroelectric power, and a still more limited agriculture. The Swedish natural endowment is not any greater than that of Cuba, the Philippines, Nigeria, or Venezuela. Sweden's accomplishments underline, therefore, the conclusion of Gunnar Myrdal that "in all the underdeveloped countries the economic development problem is primarily a problem of seeking national integration in its necessary combination with economic progress, the one being both the result and the condition of the other." (Myrdal, 1956, p. 167.)

The Price of Industrialization

The rapid industrialization now being sought in many areas requires, however, machines, components, and know-how that are most easily obtained by importation. When governments or independent local companies seek to modernize production, they find the know-how elusive and the machines expensive. They may not realize the importance of know-how until after expensive failures, but the bill for industrialization has often been presented promptly—in the form of a balance-of-payments crisis caused by imports of machinery and materials. The fact is that the less developed countries are caught in a sort of quicksand. The harder they try to shovel themselves out by exporting their wheat or coffee or sugar, the deeper they sink. In the United Nations *World Economic Survey* for 1959, the need for exports to finance the means of development is related to the unfortunate fact that "world demand for most primary products upon which under-developed countries continue to depend has tended to lag behind the rate of growth of production in the developed countries." (United Nations, 1960, p. 8.) The Mexican economist, Victor Urquidi, has been more specific and emphatic. "The overall rate of growth has been declining, and this is true of all the major Latin American countries. An explanation can be found in large part in the fact that the expansion of exports since 1950 has slowed down and is actually below the rate of population growth. In addition, the terms of trade, which have declined over the last 70 years, and which only improved materially during the war and postwar decade have declined 10 per cent since 1950." He concludes that "what we need is industrialization in depth." (Quoted in Hamlin, 1960, p. 54.)

The Latin Americans are not alone in this predicament. All countries that rely on commodities as their main source of export income are affected, including Australia, Canada, India, Indonesia, and the emerging African nations. The problem is most acute in the countries most dependent on export income for investment funds. On the one hand, they need to import machinery and components for industrialization, factors that are growing steadily more complicated and expensive. The crisis of foreign exchange that accompanies efforts to reduce dependence on imports and to improve local employment by increasing local manufacturing has become a familiar experience. On the other hand, the prices of the commodities these countries export are being steadily pressed down by forces of growing strength.

The causes for this long-term trend in the terms of trade, favorable to manufactures and unfavorable to raw materials, deserve careful notice. They can be illustrated by the radical change that has taken place in the market for wheat in the advanced countries, now controlled by conditions that recall the remark attributed to Marie Antoinette, "Let them eat cake!" The American pioneers took their wheat to a mill and, after paying a fee, often in kind, received flour with which they baked their own bread. Sale of flour for home baking practically ceased, however, a couple of generations ago. Nowadays, the factory bakers are hard put even to sell a standard loaf of bread. They must restore the vitamins the millers took out by their patent flour processes; they add other ingredients to provide novelty and variety and justify a fancy name like "Hollywood" bread. They must also sell packaged and frozen oven-ready rolls, Danish pastry, and coffee cake. The fastest-growing market is for packaged cake mixes, in which the packaging materials alone cost more than the wheat used, not to mention the other ingredients and the costs of manufacturing and advertising. The constantly rising levels and costs of processing illustrated here are, of course, covered by higher consumer prices, justified by convenience and certainty of results. The ability of the higher-processed product to attract the consumer also assures that an increasing proportion of the price will go into processing, packaging, and advertising.

The need for growth through industrialization and the accompanying obstacles, especially rising costs of industrial requirements and falling income to primary producers, mean that international firms offer exceptional advantages to developing countries. Their investment often takes the form of machinery in return for which they accept equity rights that carry no claim on the foreign business until profits begin to be earned. Those profits, moreover, may be reinvested on the basis of estimates of the potentials for expansion of the business.

The growth of national economies through integrated industrialization need not result in any decline in physical international trade, but it will cause changes in the composition of such trade. Developing countries seek to reduce their dependence on commodity or one-product exports and to secure some of the benefits of processing—in more and better jobs and higher earnings. As a result, the composition of their imports and exports changes. The aggregate may grow because industrial development increases the demand for specialized imports, as well as the ability to pay for them, by raising the value of exports. Integration of industrialized economies has a similar effect. The increased tariff discrimination against outsiders that is part of the economic integration of the European Economic Community did not prevent an increase of 60 per cent in imports from the United States in the first three years—1958, 1959, and 1960 (E.E.C. Executive Commission, quoted in *The New York Times,* March 13, 1962, p. 11.) A large part of those imports were such materials of growth as machinery and chemicals.

Obstacles to Economic Growth
through International Business

Although factory equipment and patent rights may not cost any foreign exchange, at least until there are profits to remit, imported materials must be paid for. Even a plant to process local materials will almost certainly require some specialized imports like bottle caps, label paper, container board, essential oils for flavors, and so forth. There is some question whether or not the present policies of international firms make adequate contributions to the foreign-exchange earnings that developing countries need for these purposes.

The developing countries need processed exports from their new industries. International firms allocate markets among their foreign branches and do not tolerate poaching by one branch in the territories assigned to others. The international patent system and local registration of trademarks can be used to enforce this policy, since the law of one country can be invoked to exclude products made elsewhere under patent licenses or sold under brand names granted exclusively to the branch in that country. Indeed, the branch system has been organized to supersede physical exports and imports. Prof. J. J. Deutsch, Vice-Principal of Queen's University in Kingston, Canada, has stated that "in many cases . . . Canadian branch operations limit themselves to the Canadian market and possibly to certain specified markets abroad, leaving the remainder of the export possibilities to the parent concerns in the United States. This situation must, on the whole, have had the effect of limiting the size of a number of Canadian manufacturing operations." (Quoted in the *Toronto Globe & Mail*, Nov. 16, 1960, p. 7.) When physical movement of goods remains part of an operation, as with Campbell's importation of soup stock to Britain and California Packing Co.'s importation of Del Monte canned pineapple to various markets, the sources are determined by the importing branch. Orders for supplies may be switched from the United States to Italy and then to Spain, according to the prices of tomatoes and cannery labor, and from Hawaii to Australia to Singapore for pineapple.

The international firm also fails at present to make any long-term contribution to exports in countries where it sets up branches, since it makes the same standard products everywhere it goes. Indeed, for many branches, this standardization is their *raison d'être* and the secret of their success. American tourists increasingly complain that wherever they go they are offered the same goods that they find at home, even though the natives often think they are selling their own goods. Distinctiveness of product so essential for growing export trade is most likely to be supplied by independent indigenous manufacturers. International firms could, however, modify their policy and encourage more research and innovation by their subsidiaries. This contribution can be invaluable because it is clear that while low-priced manufactured exports like Indian textiles and Japanese radios have aided some developing economies, exports of such products soon clash with the industrializing purposes of the receiving countries. The importance of distinctiveness, which is fully appreciated in practical marketing, needs greater recognition among economic advisers and stronger support by national governments in their policies toward industry and toward such services as industrial design.

In summary, it is clear that the current emphasis on economic growth is hopeful. The established governments of advanced countries, the fledgling governments of new countries, the dictatorships as well as the democracies, are all promising growth and are all experimenting with new ways of attaining it. Growth is now understood to involve increased quality and variety of production, as well as increased quantity and increased wages to purchase more goods and services. It might be described as organic growth, to emphasize economic integration.

The focus is directly on business, where much of the growth must take place. The ability to provide growth is becoming an implied clause in company charters and franchises. The demand comes from shareholders and staff, as well as from governments. For business, the prospect of increasing profits is of course the prime incentive and criterion, but growth in volume of production provides the basis on which increased profits are commonly returned. An important number of companies have found growth in international operations and presumably have assisted growth in foreign economies. There is more to this contribution than simple investment of capital. For example, the introduction of advanced technology is also vital, and may require organized innovation to keep it productively employed. The essentials of economic growth in the less developed countries may prove significant for the advanced countries.

8

THE EXPENDITURES OF
INTERNATIONAL FIRMS

DISTINCTIVE, fertilizing characteristics are discernible in the expenditures of businesses that establish subsidiaries in foreign countries to serve markets in those countries. Much more is provided when manufacturing subsidiaries are created than straight transfers of capital. By contrast, there have been large international capital investments in the past in extractive industries which have taken out natural resources without putting anything into the domestic economies of the countries concerned, though this does not apply to the modern companies which are finding profits in processing and selling part of their output in the source-country. There have also been government-to-government loans which have served to finance balance-of-payments deficits resulting from consumption imports rather than to stimulate increases in local production.

While foreign aid may have overriding political and military purposes, the governments of advanced countries also expect major economic results from direct loans to the governments of less developed countries and from tax concessions and risk insurance to encourage private foreign investment. Other countries grant favors to attract international firms for the same economic reasons. The transfer of capital does indeed tend to create immediate purchasing power as it is dispersed among contractors and their employees but this purchasing power may be used largely for imported clothing, motor cars, and Scotch whisky, which provide an ephemeral well-being. Under favorable conditions, it may, however, stimulate ancillary industries and even provide a catalyst for domestic capital formation.

Government capital investment, as well as large initial private investment, in facilities for extracting raw materials may, however, fail to stimulate further growth because the capital goods represent only one-time expenditures. The installation at Kitimat in British Columbia, which comprises hydro-electric power generators, an aluminum extraction plant, housing, and roads, is one example, because it has not led to the establishment of secondary industries. The large American expenditures on foreign military bases in the 1950's had the same effects. While they were being built, money and jobs were plentiful, men and machines were fully employed, and the local monetary authorities were hard put to control inflation. When these capital programs were completed, however, there was often a reaction. Such investments provide facilities that can be operated by few people compared with the numbers required to build them, and they do not engender other industries. The construction men and machines cannot readily be moved to other work, even when such work is available. Even when public investments are specifically planned to earn profits by contributing to increases in the production of other industries or reductions in their costs, there is often a long delay before such results are achieved.

Neither capital investment in preference to other expenditures nor sheer quantity of investment is enough to explain economic changes. The quality of investment must also be understood and taken into account. One problem is that large capital investments have not, as demonstrated, led uniformly to permanent gains in investment activity or in employment. The successes of companies with foreign subsidiaries have, however, extended to national suppliers, customers, and staff and have thus acquired interest and importance as material for new empirical studies in international economics—and as a possible medium for more effective international assistance.

Investment in fixed capital assets has a prototype in British railway-building of the nineteenth century. That investment produced a great deal of international economic development. It is astonishing how much scope still remains for improvements in transportation. Many of these improvements employ capital profitably by connecting products with markets. A new harbor is built, and the Orinoco is dredged to help release the wealth of iron ore in Venezuela. A new railroad was necessary to bring out the ore from Canada's iron mines in remote Labrador. The new St. Lawrence Seaway moves this ore to the smelters in Ohio. Oil and gas pipelines complement the discovery of wells in Alberta or the Algerian Sahara. The Volta dam in West Africa will require immense expenditures on transmission lines and transformers to distribute its electricity.

Even Britain, where such investment has continued since the Romans made stone roads and the Normans built stone castles, can still absorb large amounts of new capital for new oil refineries on the Isle of Dogs, steel mills at Margram in Wales, superhighways like the M-1, and such improved distribution facilities as supermarkets. Britain also illustrates capital attrition. The coal mines, railways, and harbor facilities, for example, can continue to absorb vast sums of money that they can no longer transform into profits. The old investments yield diminishing returns. Pouring in more capital does not reverse this trend.

What Capital Does

A distinction is often made between capital and current expenditures. While this distinction serves useful purposes, it should be recognized as an accounting convenience that is often applied arbitrarily. An expenditure is classed as a capital investment when it is expected to yield economic benefits over a considerable period of time. Public accounts, however, are notorious for the way entries are shifted between capital and current expenditures to suit political convenience. The fiction that there is a difference in kind between capital investment and current expenditure serves its purpose in the accounting of a firm, where it is recognized as subordinate to and, in fact, a function of profit-earning capacity. It can be misleading, however, if more merit is attributed to so-called capital investments than to expenditures charged to current operations.

There is a grey area between capital and current expenditures. Intelligent maintenance of buildings and machines, for example, can include replacement of parts with improved types that increase or prolong earning power while being charged to current expenses rather than capital. The same is true of most costs of developing new and improved products, from research to expensive introductory advertising. In public expenditures a parallel to this example can be found in the practice of American highway departments, which continually make improvements in the course of their maintenance work on existing roads. Making provisions for improvements an integral part of the costs of operation and therefore deductible before profits taxes is encouraged by the profit motive guiding private companies. Many international firms grow not merely through enlarged markets but through better processes and improved products as well. This growth requires continuous expenditures that are quasi-capital in character because they yield future income yet offer corresponding benefits to the economies in which these companies operate. These investments may be written off annually out of current revenue, but they may have more influence on growth and profits than capitalized plant extensions or public works.

For national economies, one most important quality of capital investment is the assistance the industries receiving it provide to other industries. Thus the development of oil in Venezuela and Canada transformed the financial position of those economies. Yet the large influx of investment in oil in Venezuela has not, as yet, induced further and continuing development in that country—partly, of course, because of an oversupply of oil in international trade. These expenditures might have been more profitable if they had stimulated more demand for oil within Venezuela by the development of integrated petrochemicals industries. The quality of investment is related to the persistence and continuity with which diversification is pursued. These conditions may be provided through the concerted action of international firms.

Ten years ago, India was considered a poor economic risk because of the pressure of its population on its resources. There also seemed to be considerable risk to private ownership because of the socialistic policies of the Indian government. This opinion appeared stronger among American investors and in American financial columns than among the British who knew that a democratic socialist government like their own and India's need not preclude private enterprise. Socialism is not to be confused with communism. There are degrees of socialism in all western economies, including the United States. In the case of India, a newly independent government imposed some restrictions on international enterprise. Britain had taken the lion's share of the profits in the Indian market since the days of Clive and Warren Hastings. Intervention by the new Indian government was obviously necessary to create industries based on the needs of India rather than the profit or military advantage of Britain. That policy, however, did not preclude private enterprise, Indian or international. India became an example of the advantages a mixed system of state and private industry can offer an underdeveloped country. It was fortunate that humanitarian and strategic considerations outweighed early economic assessments and brought large amounts of foreign capital to India. This influx occurred primarily on a government-to-government basis, through the Colombo Plan, for example. Later, international firms discovered that India's vast population could provide a tremendous market. Today India ranks high in the number of branch plants of foreign companies that have been established there.

Preliminaries to Investment

Private investors approach a new economic territory armed with market surveys and with dynamic forces for market development—product demonstrations, advertising, and publicity.

A really dramatic innovation generates out of profits a large part of the capital that finances its production and market expansion. This has often happened in the recent history of international firms. Although it may seem paradoxical, capital can be called forth by bold enough demands for it, the explanation being that hidden resources are mobilized. When Kaiser undertook to manufacture motor-cars in Argentina, people were found to subscribe to the stock as well as to buy the product. In the public sector, by contrast, there may be a problem to find sufficiently imaginative improvements and some of the so-called development loans may have failed because their purposes were not sufficiently specific and dramatic. Every private business organization recognizes that accountants are invaluable for looking after the money and controlling it after it has started to flow in, but they cannot generate that flow. An inventor, a salesman, or usually a combination of the two, is required at first. Government loans have sometimes amounted to blind money, unable to see where it is going.

The expenditures of private international firms, especially in manufacturing, have the great advantage that they can be and usually are planned on a gradual and continuing basis. Plant is designed so that it can be extended. Investment often carries losses in early years while building up stocks and trade inventories and financing introductory advertising. International firms have a record of pursuing a policy of expanding sales volume even when they must take initial losses or narrow profit margins in order to obtain optimum use of plant and an influential share of the market.

When a number of international firms are active in a country, the continuing nature of their investments is intensified. When Procter & Gamble enlarged their Canadian plant in 1947 to make synthetic detergents, Colgate and Lever followed suit within two years. Chemical suppliers like Dow and Monsanto also enlarged or built plants. Package manufacturers expanded to provide for the greater bulk and faster consumption of the new type of product. The requirement for extra retail shelf-space contributed to the enlargement of supermarkets. A similar chain reaction was strikingly evident during the establishment of the frozen-foods industry, again involving suppliers of packaging and distributors, as well as manufacturers. A new industry was created in Canada by Hussmans of the United States and others, providing refrigerated retail-store display cabinets.

Diversified development is also sustained by efforts of international firms to keep growing. Some of them have actively sought local suppliers and encouraged them to reduce costs and assure continuity of supplies of raw materials and components, thereby eliminating the risks and delays associated with importing. A brewer and a cosmetics manufacturer can both be interested in a local bottle factory, and in fact such a combination was responsible for the start of one in Indonesia. An early beneficiary of an international consumer-goods manufacturer is the local printer of labels, packages, and store-display material. The versatile silk-screen printing process has made many such local industries practicable. Shipping containers are another immediate necessity when a new industry is established. Geiger has reported that "in the early 1920's, when GE [General Electric] first began to manufacture lamps, it required containers. . . . At that time there was no producer of paperboard containers in Brazil. Accordingly, the company found a small paper-products manufacturer who was willing to venture into a new field. GE lent him the funds to purchase the necessary machines and received reimbursement in the form of containers. Today, this Brazilian-owned firm of Costa Ribiero is one of the largest manufacturers of paper products and paperboard containers in Brazil." (Geiger, 1961, p. 71.) International firms are also avid users of advertising media. This demand has had large social consequences in the spread of mass media and in the improvement of their technical quality. The prosperity that has come to communications media from commercial advertisers has also reduced their dependence on the support of governments or political parties.

The easiest way for the international company to ensure local supplies and services is usually to invite firms with which it is already dealing to join it abroad. This practice multiplies foreign control of national industry. Continental Can and its associate, Metal Box, have the same customers in many countries. The

J. Walter Thompson advertising agency set up a number of its foreign branches at the invitation of its international clients to provide superior American skill in this important specialty. Lever's Lux Toilet Soap advertising, long associated with Hollywood film stars, is prepared for all countries by branches of J. Walter Thompson. Advertising agency services are exclusive and thus give their international clients advantages over local competitors. In either case—through local suppliers or through the attraction of foreign branch suppliers—expenditures, production, and income within a country are multiplied when an international firm enters with new products or new processes.

The initial deployment of capital in a country by a foreign firm may be modest, inconspicuous, indeed furtive, to avoid alerting competitors. It may consist of an option on a parcel of land and lawyers' fees to incorporate a company and obtain a building license. Even before these moves, an international firm will probably have sent a Joshua to spy out the land and turn in a report, with colored maps and graphs for easy assimilation by the board of directors. After the decision to expand has been made, the publicity begins. Bafut is to have a new industry, aiding economic independence and standards of living, which puts pressure on any government officials who may have been slow to cooperate with permits and even on bankers about the line of credit the company wants. No country wants to lose a new industry.

International Business and Modernization

Investments in market studies, legal advice, and public relations correspond in the private sector to the expensive feasibility surveys that precede public investments. International firms have found that the best local lawyers can be their most valuable allies. Beside keeping their clients within the complicated foreign law, good corporation lawyers can handle delicate and confidential negotiations for property, permits, and staff. They can also make disbursements for fees and special services

that may conform to local customs but may be interpreted as
clumsy attempts at bribery if undertaken by foreigners. This
function includes contributions to political party funds, which
many companies continue to make in advanced countries, but
which must be made with great skill and discretion, best provided by people of high personal and professional probity.
Good lawyers are expensive, but no auditor or tax collector
relishes challenging a lawyer's bill for professional services.
International firms have become strong supporters of a prosperous independent legal profession, which is now the backbone
of an upper middle class in a great many foreign countries.
Lawyers are the first local directors of foreign subsidiaries.
They become investors themselves and sometimes even active
managers. Education, travel, income, independence, and some
leisure enable and encourage them to foster cultural activities.
These uses of the increased opportunities and rewards afforded
to lawyers by participation in the local subsidiary operations
of international firms contribute, directly and by example, to
the diffusion of middle-class values and vocations.

Professional accountants, as well as lawyers, are permanent
beneficiaries of international business because additional employment is provided in preparing the more elaborate financial
reports required by a branch for its home office—and there is no
quibbling about fees for work that provides an adequate basis
for control over distant branches.

Independent local warehouse and delivery truck operators
and selling organizations also prosper. The international firm
may eventually form its own services in these fields. Even so,
the rates of remuneration will likely be above those prevailing
previously. Companies with good cost accounting are willing
to pay for efficient service, and particularly commissions and
bonuses to salesmen who help to increase business.

The most common policy on the payment of labor adopted
by the leading international firms allows no less than the going
rate for each particular area as the basis of their wage scales.
Many have also introduced job-rating, which enables them to
pay higher rates on a productivity scale.

The expenditures of international firms for raw materials show

characteristics that might seem mutually exclusive. Discounts
are demanded for quantity and continuity of purchase. At the
same time, price premiums are offered for quality. The international firm is more confident than local competitors of being
able to pass on to customers the relatively small additions to
cost incurred by buying premium quality materials. Superior
cost accounting may reveal to the international firm that the
apparently higher cost can be offset by avoiding waste. The net
effect is to strengthen the market for quality materials. Modern
firms expect their suppliers to earn profits. Robert Woodruff of
Coca-Cola has said, "We want everybody who has anything
to do with this product to make money." (Quoted in Kahn,
1960, p. 82.) There are many instances in which firms have
provided technical know-how to their suppliers. International
food-processing companies, for example, brought in field men
to advise their farmer suppliers.

International firms have gone much further than local competitors in finishing their products by packaging for consumers
and even for industrial buyers—and in such industrial design
features as the use of color on machinery. Such expenditures
encourage a wide variety of ancillary industries particularly
noticeable in relatively primitive markets. The value of modern packaging is conspicuous there, providing as it does, sealed
packages of food and medicine. The use of advertising by
international firms is so significant that it requires a separate
chapter (see Chapter 13).

The Importance of Marketing

Marketing is one of the most important areas of expenditure
for international firms. The new foreign branch is designed not
only to produce but also to sell its products. In the public sector,
it is not unusual for a new facility, like the road from the
Venezuelan harbor and airport of La Guaira on the coast to
Caracas the mountain capital, to have large spare and idle
capacity. The stimulus of investment is temporary, and the lag
in utilization of the new facility is wasteful. In contrast, the

international firm includes in its expenditures provisions for directly stimulating the consumption that will keep its capital equipment working at full capacity. Often there need only be distribution of the product to convenient outlets, in the case of scarce and obviously necessary items. There was, for example, immediate demand for penicillin in Belém on the Amazon in Brazil. A factory in Saõ Paulo solved the foreign-exchange problem. The product, however, had to be delivered to Belém quickly and regularly and, with it, a refrigerator was required to store it in a Belém pharmacy. Foreign drug companies in Brazil have since built a network of depots to provide services, including fast delivery and credit for supplies and equipment, that were lacking because of the lack of any substantial wholesale trade.

In other cases, arousing demand involves displays of new products, demonstrations, testimonials, subtle appeals to hidden motives, emphasis on particular values shared by people in the market (sometimes at the expense of other values—for example, "buy and enjoy now" versus "save for the future"). These efforts comprise the field of modern marketing. Companies that make marketing an integral part of their operations increase the returns on their investment.

In order to adjust production to consumption, an attempt is made, as part of the marketing function, to predict responses to economic changes, including new and improved products, advertising, and pricing. Marketing experts are now aware of the influence of attitudes, motivation, and values on buying habits, and they are also becoming acutely conscious of the changes that occasionally take place in people's values and the far-reaching effects these changes can have on buying patterns. Statistical projections on the impact of lower prices on the sale of Buicks, for example, become pointless when people suddenly and apparently spontaneously decide that they do not need, want, or even like the traditional big Buicks. Those big Buicks were extremely successful in the early 1950's, but Detroit is still trying to find out what happened at the end of the decade. The consumption of steel and gasoline, as well as of automobiles, is also affected by such changes, which cast doubts on the validity of production indices of these goods as economic indicators. The weakness of projections based on production statistics is that they do not yet give any reliable indication of when and why sales volume will fluctuate, causing wide repercussions in the rates of business activity, profits, and employment.

Marketing research offers to economists a few slightly encouraging successes in trying to discover inductively how people react to price and product changes and how their behavior in the market is affected by changes in their social and personal values. Previous methods of forecasting were deductive from abstract ideas of the elasticity of demand, projected from old and unreliable statistical tables. The shaky condition of the structure still in use for economic forecasting is revealed in a speech by Dr. Walter Heller, Chairman of the President's Council of Economic Advisers, at The American University Conference on Business-Government Relations in Washington, D.C., on March 30, 1962, in which he said—less than three months before the worst stock market crash since 1929—that all the economic indicators were favorable. With reference to consumer incomes, Dr. Heller did remark, however, that for some mysterious reason people seemed reluctant to part with their money. An interesting new indicator, which gets closer to the human factors in the market than graphs of bank-rates, car-loadings, or wholesale prices, is periodically compiled from questionnaires to a sample of the public on intentions regarding purchases of consumer durable goods. This survey on consumer buying intentions is made for the United States Treasury by the Bureau of the Census. For an interval, it was made at the Survey Research Center at the University of Michigan, which has continued to work and publish on this subject after the official survey was resumed by the government. Important extensions have been made by the McGraw-Hill Publishing Company and by the Federation of British Industries, which send out questionnaires to companies on their intentions with regard to capital investments.

The causes of change in intentions to purchase and invest,

which this writer considers to have significant influence on the business cycle and on the rate of growth, are still a mystery. However, some methods of influencing intentions have been evolved by trial and error by people engaged in marketing consumer goods throughout the world. Their accomplishments have been specific and practical—making the daily brushing of teeth a general practice, for instance—but there is broad economic importance in their purpose, which is to link consumption to production and avoid the waste of idle resources. Expenditure in this field holds promise of yielding methods that will improve economic science and ultimately the returns from all investment.

Criticisms of International Business Expenditures

There are, however, several complaints about the spending policies of international firms that must be noted. One complaint is that when an international firm obtains control of a subsidiary without having supplied all the equity capital, the dividend policy may be unfair to the minority shareholders. The international firm draws the profits needed to pay its shareholders from France one year, for example, and from Mexico the next. It does not have to recognize one national minority's interest in receiving regular income. The international corporation may prefer to plow profits back into expansion. Such criticism of dividend policy may simply reflect ignorance of the importance given by international firms not merely to adequate depreciation but to investment in growth. Experience has taught them that in order to keep up with modern competition and technological change it is not enough to stand still. It is necessary to be always trying to move forward. As Professor Hirschman has put it, "foreign capital is needed not so much *qua* capital as because it brings with it certain abilities and skills that are in particularly short supply. . . . An example is what has become known as growth mentality, which, among other things, stands for the plowing back of profits in substantial quantities, rather than for the 'milking' so often practiced by local capitalists." (Hirschman, 1958, p. 39.)

There is, however, more than a mere possibility that the power of the international firm will steam-roller minority shareholders. Indeed, a policy of reinvesting profits has often been used to mask pressure on minority groups to sell out to the international corporation. Furthermore, the international organization can take profits from a foreign subsidiary without sharing them with the minority through dividends—by calling them royalties, fees, and service charges. A dominating management may also pay itself high salaries and bonuses at the expense of dividends. This practice is not peculiar to international firms. There is, however, less publicity about the operations of foreign subsidiaries.

Foreign firms have been accused in some countries of spending part of their money to obtain political influence in order to increase or maintain concessions from governments. Political influence may come, not only from bribing politicians but also from frightening voters by advertising and publicity threatening loss of jobs. Political influence is of course sought by companies in advanced countries as well as in developing countries—and not only by international firms. Recent examples are the Billy Sol Estes business in government grain-storage contracts and some companies supplying the United States stockpile of strategic materials. These examples also show the risks. Exposure under the glare of modern journalism can cause political activity to boomerang. Reaction against business influence in the politics of foreign countries is particularly dangerous because it involves nationalism.

Some companies try to avoid every kind of publicity not limited to their products. Secretiveness, however, even when inspired solely by a desire to avoid involvement in political controversy, can also cause criticism. This possibility is increasing as economic literacy spreads and people find that they lack the information by which to judge the advantages and disadvantages of international business. Company managements are chary about giving out any news except what is strongly favorable because news often leads to discussion that may get out of hand. They then find themselves involved in explanations that may become arguments. Disclosure of the favorable quantities and terms on the provision of local capital to the subsidiaries of international firms, for example, would probably arouse further criticism. A basic theme of this book, however, is that the only possible way to resolve conflicts that loom before international companies is to take the initiative in providing information and explanations to the public in all the countries where they operate.

Another complaint may seem minor, but it has exerted an insidious influence on the public relations of many international companies. This complaint is that they do not contribute to local charities in the same proportion as their local competitors or as their home offices contribute to home-country causes. The excuse given may be that donations are made from net remitted profits only by the head office, but this excuse is not accepted, particularly in developing countries where the obligation of charity has not been lightened by public social services.

A comparatively new criticism is that international concerns make their contributions to higher education almost exclusively from the head office and to the country of origin. This procedure encourages centralization and monopolization of research and scientific technology (see Chapter 12). Contributions to higher education, moreover, are seldom entirely disinterested. There are publicity and influence with government, shareholders, and the general public to be gained by the home company. When this policy is not internationalized, it will eventually boomerang. In 1960, General Foods made a spectacular donation of over $1 million for a nutrition laboratory at Harvard University. The publicity was widespread. General Foods must anticipate that there will now be questions about their contributions in Australia, Britain, Canada, Germany, and the other countries where they operate.

Limited objectives and shortsighted attitudes toward social responsibilities do not destroy the practical advantages of international business expenditures. Expenditures are made on the basis of assessments of market potentials, including both psychological and physical factors. They tend to be continuous and progressive. They mesh with local industries and services, helping to form the complex of structures and activities, classes and occupations that lead to a modern developed economy. There are, of course, economic requirements that are beyond the scope or interest of private industry, especially public utilities. The accounting in the latter is now required to allow for social benefits that are not included in the selling price. There is all the more need for penetrating calculations of those benefits and what they cost although such calculations are not easy to make, and feasibility studies, especially on large government investments have too often been characterized by sweeping and unexamined assumptions about people, their economic responses, and their political reactions. Some progress has been made, however, in digging better foundations for investment policy in the study of the behavior of consumers and of industrial purchasers, including their intentions. International firms are forerunners in the interpretation and use of this material.

9

THE PROFITS OF
INTERNATIONAL FIRMS

ACCORDING to Sir Roy Harrod, Maynard Keynes, his great mentor and friend, never spared much time or thought for international investment because he considered that the losses it involved were excessive. (Harrod, 1951, p. 349.). Lord Keynes, with his many other preoccupations and his financial rather than industrial associations, did not see the possibilities of the new kind of foreign investment that was being developed in his time by his compatriot Lord Leverhulme. Keynes evidently drew his conclusions from the bankers' kind of investment, which appeared well protected but was so on paper only. Bonds, mortgages, and other formal written contracts are unfortunately unreliable without people to see that they are fulfilled. Human factors make attempts to reduce investments to figures on paper as premature as simple linear projections of economic growth.

International lending has indeed always been fraught with losses. Many of the world's railways were built by local companies financed by bonds, sold frequently in England. Neither the British issuing houses nor the British purchasers either could or wanted to exercise any continuing participation in the management of such foreign operations. When companies defaulted on the interest due on their bonds, the bondholders received legal authority over the management, but they had no organization to exercise it. Also, by the time that a company defaulted on its bonds, it was often too late for salvage work. Protection from these foreign dangers was sought through the alternative of making loans directly to foreign governments, which then issued bonds that were sold to the public in Britain, the United States, and other advanced countries. A variation of this technique was the issue of government-guaranteed bonds. Both of these types of security, Russian and German bonds, as well as those of many South American republics, often ended in default. When that happened, the individual investor was, if anything, worse off. A bondholders' protective committee of lawyers may be able to hire managers and move into a private corporation, but intervention with foreign governments becomes a matter of international relations, and political considerations enter into the situation.

Rich profits have often been garnered, however, by international firms that have invested in the management of foreign businesses, as well as in their fixed assets. This profitable kind of investment has included control and the provision of appropriate knowledge, as well as money. These principles were adopted by import-export firms from the East India Company and the Hudson's Bay Company onward. They put their own managers in their own trading stations all over the world. The great development, in depth as well as in scope, has come, however, since the Second World War, and the main stream of investment has been from the United States.

The volume of profits earned by international enterprise has been shown for a number of firms in Chapter 4. Information for American companies in aggregate is given in *U.S. Business Investments in Foreign Countries,* issued in 1960 by the United States Department of Commerce. The book value of American direct private investments in 1957 is given as $25 billion. The over-all net earnings of these enterprises in 1957 are given as $4 billion. $400 million is deducted from the $4 billion for the share of profits accruing to foreign equity participations. The neat 10 per cent figure looks like an estimate. It nevertheless leaves the over-all net profit to Americans from operations at all stages of development at a healthy 14.4 per cent and lends support to estimates that American direct private investment had risen to $30 billion in total book value by the end of 1959 and to $32.5 billion in 1960.

More information on profits seems certain to become available in the near future. The unwritten convention accepted by many countries that wholly-owned subsidiaries are private companies because they have so few shareholders—usually the one or two individuals who represent the parent company and vote its stock plus the local lawyers—is giving way to recognition of their economic and social importance. This recognition makes knowledge of the activities of foreign companies even more important than the information previously required, mainly for the protection of local shareholders, from domestic companies financed by public stock issues. More and more countries are passing laws like those of Brazil, which require foreign subsidiaries and branches to publish the same information as domestically-owned companies. The United States Department of Commerce also requires, since 1062, reports on the figures of all foreign businesses in which American interest is more than 10 per cent.

The profitability of an international operation can be considered in relation to the total profits of the firm, as a percentage of foreign sales, or as a percentage of capital invested. Firms that obtain half or more of their declared profits from foreign subsidiaries are still comparatively few, judging by the examples given in Chapter 4. The highest percentages are naturally those of companies that originate in countries that provide only small home markets (like the Netherlands and Switzerland) but have successful subsidiaries in the United States.

More striking are the rates of profit, and particularly the growth-rates of profits, in the few cases where the figures are already available. The foreign profits of Colgate tripled in the decade 1951-1960. In 1951, remitted and retained profits of Colgate overseas operations were $5.6 million, and in 1960 they were $16.1 million. In the case of Ford, J. S. Bugas reported to the stockholders at the annual meeting on May 18, 1961, that "earnings after foreign income taxes from operations of

affiliates and branches have grown from $19 million in 1951 to
$72 million in 1960." Heinz net income from foreign subsidiaries
grew from $2.4 million in 1953 to $8.7 million in 1959. Kodak
dividends received from abroad were $4.9 million in 1953 and
$10 million in 1959. Although these figures are only isolated
examples it is common knowledge, as Professor Fayerweather
has noted, that "the profit margins in most countries are substantially higher than in the United States." (Fayerweather,
1960, p. 501.)

Profit margins, that is, rates of profit on sales, are not a
perfect measure of the profitability of foreign investment. Higher
volume in a large home market, even at declining margins, may
contribute a greater amount of profit than better rates in smaller
markets abroad. There are indications, however, that yields on
increments of capital for established companies have been greater
in new markets, and that these markets are most readily found
abroad because the products of these companies are still new
to the people in many foreign countries.

Published capitalization of foreign subsidiaries is a measure
that may actually obscure the profitability of direct foreign
investment. The capitalization may properly reflect access to
patents and trademarks, retention of profits, revaluation of land
and buildings, but the amount of investment by transfers of
cash also needs to be known. High rates of profit on net cash
foreign investment will very likely prove to be the true incentive for the great surge of international enterprise in the 1950 s.
On declared assets, the profits of Sterling Products in 1960 were
16 per cent abroad compared with 5 per cent in the United
States; General Motors made 14 per cent of its profits abroad
on 5 per cent of its assets; Gillette earned 45 per cent of its
profits on 23 per cent of its assets. The president of the Lever
Canadian subsidiary complained that the 1959 profits were
only 1.5 per cent on the investment. The return on actually
transferred capital could be considerably better. This case raises
the question of when and why foreign profit rates are high.
Lever in Canada, along with Procter & Gamble and Colgate,
have swamped all local competition. The international firms are

left to compete with one another. When this happens, do their profit rates revert to their home market levels or lower? Is the foreign profit rate a reflection of the faster economic growth that now appears to have taken place in the Fifties in many countries other than the United States and Britain, the leaders in foreign investment? Which came first, the fleshy foreign chicken or the golden eggs? Was the rate of growth attributable to the influx of foreign enterprise? Oddly enough, American companies in Britain appear to have grown faster than domestic companies (compare Procter & Gamble's Hedley subsidiary with Lever, Esso with Shell, Monsanto with Imperial Chemicals), and so have foreign companies in the United States (Beecham, Carling Breweries, Ciba drugs).

Reasons and explanations for high foreign earnings are important, but the investor is even more interested in learning whether the apparent income can be realized or is only paper profit in blocked currencies or a paper capital gain. Foreign-exchange control was widely practiced in the first ten years after the war. Its purposes, however, were control of imports and prevention of flights of capital. Countries with sufficient skill in exchange control exempted profit remittances. Some countries, notably Brazil, ingeniously deflated high profits flowing from internal monetary policy by permitting purchase of exchange for payment of foreign dividends on the free market only. Even under these conditions, international firms that remitted profits as soon as earned, received attractive remuneration in dollars, pounds, and francs.

Currency devaluations are another and perturbing complication. They cause a write-down of working capital and sometimes of total assets of the subsidiary affected. Devaluation, however, usually follows a period of difficulty and leads to conditions in which higher profits are earned. That happened in Mexico, and in Brazil expansion has kept pace with continuous inflation for many companies.

The international investor who has taken the recent but obvious precaution of having his own men—the directors and lawyers of a foreign branch or subsidiary—look after his interests has in fact received preferred treatment in most countries. He has earned higher profits than he could earn at home and also higher profits than domestic companies could earn, partly because of protection for his foreign patents and trademarks. He could use these profits freely to buy up more foreign assets by expanding his branch or absorbing other businesses. He could take profits home at a very generous rate on the money he had put in, even from countries that at times desperately needed foreign exchange for machinery and raw materials.

The long-term outlook for international profits may not be so favorable. Much depends on the willingness of the investor to take payment in kind, that is, to permit his subsidiaries to export, or his willingness and that of his compatriots to consume its products as tourists. There has been large foreign investment in Canada, a substantial amount in manufacturing. But how can this investment lead to exports of manufactures to the United States, when Canadians make only American-style cars, toothpaste, and cake-mix? Furthermore, what American wants to tour Canada to eat Kraft cheese, drink Four Roses whisky, and look at Esso billboards? Mexico is comparatively fortunate to have its distinctive Indian-Spanish culture and its handicraft industries.

The disposition of earnings by international firms has been unexceptionable but often unimaginative. Venezuela is unusually fortunate because international capital and enterprise, as organized in the Rockefellers' International Basic Economy Corporation, are using oil profits to promote a diversity of other local industries, even though the reality does not yet approach the ideal. The Rockefellers have a long view and a long purse, but many international firms are now able, thanks to their foreign earnings, to follow the Rockefeller example and become increasingly imaginative and creative in their investment policies. When they adopt this orientation deliberately, international firms may be able to contribute more to diversified growth than local firms alone can do with operations developed by accident or in response to local circumstances. Among the advantages of international firms are the facilities they can provide for the encouragement of product development, particularly their broad knowledge of markets in many countries.

If international enterprise is to continue to remit profits, it may also have to diversify into more active partnership with local enterprise as another means of obtaining more diversified products. In 1962, *Time* took the pioneering step of contributing its publishing techniques to an Italian magazine with Italian staff, content, and financial backing—an advance over the so-called Canadian editions, which brought down on *Time* and *Reader's Digest* a government investigation featuring charges that they were smothering Canadian journalism. It should not have been difficult for the *Digest* principle to be adapted to a 60 per cent Canadian content, as required by law in Canadian television, and to be adapted to similar interest and support for national writers in other countries.

The higher profits of international firms abroad have been attributed to better know-how than that of local competitors. Fayerweather has claimed that "where competition comes from local businesses, U.S. companies often find that their advanced operating techniques or size give them advantages which still further increase their profit margins." (P. 501.) In some cases, the international enterprise has a monopoly of specialized know-how. This kind of competition is often regarded as unfair, even in the United States, when it comes from abroad. There is still, however, a general willingness in foreign countries, including Belgium and Japan, which have been accused of unfair competition in their exports to the United States, to consider foreign subsidiaries favorably. They reason that if the international firm increases local productivity, it more than earns its profits by the benefits it spreads.

The "Invisible" Investment of Know-How

Additions to the capital of a country made by an international firm comprise the quantity of capital transferred, the quality of the capital investment, and the even less measurable value

of know-how. Quantitatively, foreign capital from private investment can be very valuable to an underdeveloped country.
It can provide a high proportion of the net addition, particularly
in the early stages of the change from stagnation to growth.
Procter & Gamble contributed to a major change in the economy
of the Philippines by investing in plant to manufacture hydro-
genated fats as substitutes for crude coconut oil in the deep-fat
frying that is the main method of food preparation in that
country. The plant was expensive, and the machinery had to be
imported. There was, however, a large saving of labor for the
economy as a whole in the preparation and handling of edible
oils and a reduction in waste from rancidity in the crude oil.
The change made edible fat a commercial instead of a domestic
product, providing cash income for distributors and encouraging
ancillary packaging and transport industries. Labor was freed
for industrial and commercial employment. There were incidental benefits in the convenience and cleanliness of the commercial product. By-products like soap were provided. Efficient
mechanized extraction of the oil from copra provided a surplus
for export or to supply a larger population.

The quality of the capital investment of international firms
during the last fifteen years has probably been higher on the
average than that of domestic capital, partly because of their
wider knowledge and connections and their head offices' emphasis on research. The recent spread of companies abroad
has brought to underdeveloped countries the latest models of
machines and plant layout. In many cases, this superior technical efficiency is associated with patents taken out by the
parent companies and extended abroad through the International
Patent Convention. The scope of patentable knowledge in industry appears to be increasing with the rapid extension of the
applications of science to production. Important new industries
develop within the lifetime of the original patents, rather than
during the several generations it once took for the gradual
spread of such knowledge. Examples are plastics, synthetic
fibers, computers, frozen foods, dehydrated foods, synthetic detergents, and medicines—the antibiotics, the anticoagulants, the
antispasmodics. A country that does not create modern capital

in the form of new inventions, accompanied by the legal rights and the machinery and the know-how required to carry new ideas into actual production, can enjoy the modern type of scientific industry only through foreign investment.

There is wide recognition of the economic importance of know-how. Historical examples are numerous and familiar. Refugee Huguenot immigrants to Britain in the seventeenth century imported highly productive capital in the form of their knowledge and skill in the manufacture of cloth. The British colonists in America invested a small capital of superior tools—their axes, plows, and guns—but they also brought a large fund of know-how in agriculture and manufacturing. Nowadays, governments, opinion-makers, and the general public view with new respect and pride their Institutes of Technology and Hochschulen. These institutions will largely determine the rate of growth of the domestic economies of the advanced countries—provided, of course, that they do actually stimulate imagination and innovation. Scholasticism can fill business and government with organization men, as it did the medieval church.

The practical applications of the know-how of international firms have immediate effects in production and also in the general management of branches or subsidiaries. In production, the international firm uses the latest machines, and tends to use more of them. It shifts technical directors from country to country. This practice increases know-how in production management but incidentally decreases any feelings of loyalty or responsibility, except those to the firm, and reduces compunction about displacement of local labor. Thus the utilization of labor by the international firm is likely to be determined solely by efficiency, subject to any restraint imposed by local unions, which are often weak. Compulsory retirement at sixty-five, or even sixty, and no hiring over forty are practices introduced into many countries by international businesses. These practices are related to the requirements of insurance plans. These undeniable benefits have the effect, however, of reducing tolerance for the marginal services of the old or the dull and increasing the need for unemployment and other welfare services.

In general management, the know-how profitably introduced

by the international firm includes its accounting and marketing methods. The analysis and constructive use of both production and distribution costs is a highly sophisticated exercise, in which the international firm far excels the average national company. The average managerial ability in the foreign subsidiary and the indigenous and independent company may be much the same. The same men may run the local factory after it is taken over by an international firm, but the management tools will be different, and managerial judgment will be based on more facts, better arranged. An obvious example is the technique of budgeting, which is still not as well understood among indigenous firms as among companies originating from the advanced countries.

Practically all international firms operate today on careful estimates of sales, selling expenses, and the costs of producing estimated quantities. Independent competitors are still apt to be working with historical costs. They do not have any precise measure of the economies obtainable by increasing sales through investment in promotion or through price changes. The foremost international companies supplement their official annual budgets with five-year plans, revised every year. These plans take into account the delayed and cumulative effects of product improvements, price changes, and advertising, which are now known to extend forward beyond the normal accounting period of the fiscal year. It is no wonder that competitors still fail to understand the forces that cause their position in their home markets to deteriorate.

There is one important development, however, which may gradually balance at least part of the present advantage of the international firm on the accounting level. For indigenous companies in an increasing number of countries, there is recourse to improved accounting methods made available by the recent international expansion of consulting services by firms like Urwick of Britain; Arthur D. Little, McKinsey, and Booz, Allen & Hamilton of the United States; and Clarkson, Gordon of Canada. Management consulting is offered also by the pioneers of international professional accounting, Price Waterhouse. This development may be an indication that the international spread of know-how in management will be accomplished in the future without the ownership of regional operations having to be transferred outright to international concerns.

But the know-how of producing profits goes beyond production and business systems into sales or, more comprehensively, marketing, which harnesses the activities of market research, advertising, and selling. Marketing is a business activity pioneered by large concerns, most of which operate internationally —partly because of their superiority in marketing—and it is an activity still practiced in most countries almost exclusively by the international firms.

Market surveys, which require specialized know-how in de sign and use, are now carried on in a number of countries. There is also a strong international firm in this field, A. C. Nielsen, which has an exclusive technique for projecting inventories and sales from a sample number of stores in areas where there is a stable pattern of retail distribution. Incidentally, this technique is not applicable in countries where development involves rapid changes in the retail pattern—countries like Brazil, Mexico, and Venezuela. Difficulties have also arisen from the growth of house-to-house selling in the United States, which distributes goods outside the usual channels measured by Nielsen. Even where statistically reliable trade and consumer surveys are available, the productive use of this material calls for special skills in formulating hypotheses and interpreting results. The international firms have almost a monopoly of this knowhow because it requires years of investment in the training and deployment of people with special aptitudes. Here again, ordinary management in international firms can overcome indigenous competitors with the superior information available through facilities supplied by the parent organizations.

Even before the advent of such techniques as distribution surveys and motivational research, the international concern could invest in a foreign market its copyrighted trademarks and its tested advertising themes and methods of presentation and dissemination, and could derive great profit advantages. Market research has strengthened this form of capital investment by putting the results of experience on a measurable and comparable basis and reducing the time involved in applying them in different countries. Dramatic examples abound. The Beecham Group, formerly a minor Britsh patent-medicines company, has grown in ten years to one of the commercial giants of the world. Beecham experimented with television advertising in the Californian and West Central regional markets of the United States when this medium was in its infancy. Nielsen supplied detailed bimonthly results. Beecham acquired important early experience and, by using intelligence and enterprise, the company turned this experience into a know-how capital. This capital was invested in Canada in 1954. It yielded profits and additional know-how. Further experience—and profits—were obtained in Argentina, Brazil, Cuba, Mexico, and Venezuela. By the time that commercial television became available in the British home market, the Beecham management had the knowledge and the confidence to use it fully, even transferring advertising money from other media like newspapers. The company became one of the three largest television advertisers in Britain. It was able to buy other companies to acquire products on which to use its know-how still further. It also expanded, through television advertising, in other countries where this medium became available, notably Australia and Italy.

It is a relief, after the serious problems and dire warnings of much economic discussion, to look at international business. Here profits are made. Furthermore, they are clearly rewards for enterprise, far exceeding interest on capital. Favorable odds awaited companies with patented inventions and modern marketing and accounting methods, but they did not know it in advance. They had to go abroad, and that seemed a big risk to many company directors. For a generation brought up on the missionaries' tales of straw huts and shell money, it seemed hardly plausible that, in less than a generation, vast numbers of Africans would seriously be seeking industrialization. In many cases, adventurous executives traveled and set up foreign operations, obtaining the directors' concurrence afterward—because the amount of cash needed was comparatively small. Other true adventurers were the managers who went to live abroad with the problems of foreign branches and foreign social conditions. The companies profited from grub-staking them.

That the people in developing countries have generally welcomed new industries from abroad is another refreshing affirmation of the enterprise system. They have paid the prices for the new products that have yielded such high profits. Only monopoly conditions can continue to maintain abnormally high rates of return for foreign investors, however. Such profits cannot be expected to continue, except where and when they are a form of forced saving that is used for reinvestment through continuous successful innovation. Otherwise, publics and governments will object. In all cases, established industries will be required to bear their share of social costs, including welfare and, particularly, education.

10

ORGANIZATION AND CONTROL

ALEXANDER the Great, Tamerlane, and other historic leaders formed vast empires, which seldom long survived the personal loyalty or fear those individual leaders inspired. "You know, Hannibal, how to gain a victory, but not how to use it," said the Roman general Flavius, according to Plutarch. The Romans, on the other hand, made great conquests and kept them, century after century. They introduced superior forms of organization. Their armies were organized on a structure that was simple but ensured strong group solidarity, intense group loyalty —so that one hundred men could be maneuvered as a single unit simply by an order given to the centurion. This system worked for mediocre as well as for inspired generals, in the mountains and on the deserts, with recruits from Britain and Gaul, as well as native Romans.

The organizational efficiency that distinguished the Romans is the aim, model, and prototype for modern business. The system requires that action be taken in accordance with orders passed down from the top, where the power to enforce them rests. Medieval guilds and modern democracy, to name two organizational alternatives, have been found inadequate as patterns for business, although the guild pattern is used in professions like law, medicine, and accounting. Democracy is professed by the labor unions, which, however, often rig their elections with slates, making the executive co-optive and creating absolute power similar to the power in business organizations. The Roman Catholic Church has of course adhered steadfastly to the original Roman system of organization, providing a surviving parallel and example for business. For "emperor" read "pope," or "company president" or "chairman." For "senate" read "board of directors" or "college of cardinals." Foreign subsidiaries are managed by governors, archbishops, or executive vice-presidents.

Another form of organization is that of the Soviets. Russian military organization attracted some notice during World War II because it included political commissars, who were staff officers at various levels. International firms now have personnel officers to watch over the morale of senior management, as well as of the rank and file. A soviet is a council or committee. The development of this organizational device appears to be the distinctive feature of the higher levels of communist management. The difference between a committee or soviet and a board or cabinet lies in the greater executive authority of the committee secretary, compared to the board chairman, prime minister, or president. Stalin was Secretary of the Supreme Soviet of the U.S.S.R., and Khrushchev also held that position. In theory, although apparently only in theory, a secretary's powers are limited to carrying out the joint decisions of the committee.

A company president, like an army commander, receives information from his directors and staff, but he makes his own decisions and gives directions for their execution. He may formally seek the concurrence of his directors, or he may assume that if they disagree on fundamentals, they should resign. There are frequently situations in business when the secretary of a committee exerts great influence by controlling agenda, information papers, and minutes, but no cases have been reported in which business has deliberately employed the secretariat for executive purposes. It might be useful to consider borrowing this organizational device to help spread the executive load in the higher levels of the large and complex modern international firm. Secretarial staff members, who now concentrate on recording decisions, could follow them up to see that actions are taken and thus could exert considerable executive influence.

"Management by objectives," in which the demands of the job stimulate action without supervision is another organizational possibility. This alternative is discussed by F. Harbison and C. A. Myers. They recognize, however, that it is not a common practice. (Harbison and Myers, 1959, p. 43.) It is an attractive utopian ideal like philosophical anarchism, in which laws and governments are superfluous because people know what they ought to do and do it.

The Organizational Structure of International Business

The international firm is autocratic and hierarchical in its organization, although no more so than local or national firms. The head of any western company is in an extraordinarily secure and strong position, despite the publicized occasions when presidents are ousted—usually following a substantial change in the ownership of the company's stock. While subject on paper to annual re-election by his board of directors, the president frequently selects who is co-opted to the board. Unlike his subordinates, who are often moved or removed without consideration for seniority, the emperor abdicates only because of age or illness. The hold of the president on his office was illustrated in 1961 by the re-election of L. L. Colbert of Chrysler, despite the severe drop in sales and profits and the scandals about conflict of interest among senior executives that the firm had suffered. His subsequent resignation appears attributable to the outside influence of public opinion. This peculiar power of the head of the firm in modern industrial organization extends to the presidents of foreign subsidiaries.

The secure tenure of presidents contrasts with, and their power is strengthened by, the weakness of vice-presidents and all other executives down to the level where employees are protected by unions. Civil servants, both high and low, in advanced countries (except the United States) enjoy secure tenure of office. University presidents do not have the power to remove professors from permanent appointments. The only amelioration for business executives has been the recent tendency to compensate them financially for loss of office. In Britain, there are legal precedents for compensation based on the number of years of enjoyment of income that could reasonably be expected. This occasional price paid for the maintenance of absolute authority has not yet had any noticeable effect on the typical organization of the firm, either national or international.

The organization charts of international firms are deceptively similar to those of one-country companies. They all follow a remarkably standardized pattern of line and staff organization. In this pattern, the orders and the power are, of course, transmitted through the line officers, while staff officers may advise at various levels. Operational authority descends directly from the president to the sales organization and the plant management or, in the international firm, to executives in Australia or Venezuela. In between, but still in the direct line of descent, there is usually a vice-president for foreign operations in the international firm. He is on the same level as the vice-presidents for production, sales, and finance in the home company. His appointment is a recent concession to the importance of foreign operations. The old structure put such operations under an export manager responsible to the home sales manager. Companies as successful abroad as Coca-Cola and I.B.M. have formed separate organizations, Coca-Cola Export and I.B.M. World Trade, with their own presidents and staff and operational autonomy. These arrangements offer functional, as well as tax, advantages. They are connected with their parent companies through the financial control and licensing of patents and trademarks, accompanied by control over products.

Companies with large and widespread foreign interests, like Colgate, I.B.M., and Unilever, have problems owing to too many lines of operational authority. Colgate formed regional groups with assistant vice-presidents for Australasia, Europe, and Latin America. Procter & Gamble followed this example in 1962. Unilever uses its twin company in the Netherlands as a decentralized management for Continental Europe, and its United Africa subsidiary for central Africa and the Near East. For the remainder of its foreign operations it uses an overseas committee composed of several members with operational authority, supplemented by staff services that provide advice to subsidiary company managers on production, finance, marketing, and legal matters. Standard Oil of New Jersey has a new top management structure that includes an executive committee like Unilever's special committee and directors with area responsibilities like Unilever's contact directors. Standard Oil of New Jersey is also forming submanagements for regional groupings of national companies, with their own staffs of special advisers. The Beecham Group took an early step toward this type of international organization by placing a management nerve center—embracing line authority, as well as accounting, technical, and marketing staff—within the western hemisphere geographical area for which it was responsible, close to the North and South American operating companies rather than to the head office in London. This innovation was abandoned by this company after five profitable years, however, to re-establish the direct and complete authority of an overseas director.

The similarity of international organization charts to those of one-country companies conceals similar confusions and conflicts. The most common of the conflicts is between line and staff. An old army game is played in business. The operational commanders seek complete local autonomy and heed direct orders only. They see overlapping and contradictions in the advice of the staff services. The staff officers are also apt to be power-hungry, especially if staff work is only an interval in their administrative careers. They try to have their advice converted into orders. Oddly, the pressure to translate advice into action seems greater from outside consultants than from internal advisory staff, perhaps because fee-paid consultants feel a greater need to show quick results.

Relations between the Head Office
and Foreign Subsidiaries

In the international company, the tactical advantages in the quest for power lie with the field commanders. Distance decrees decentralization, even though communications have improved considerably since the Rothschilds' carrier pigeons—which reportedly flew from Brussels to London with the politically and commercially important news of Wellington's victory over Napoleon at Waterloo. The problem now is such volume and velocity of information that judgment is often overwhelmed. In the late 1940's a wily manager of a foreign branch appointed and encouraged a staff officer of his own to invent a system of comprehensive reports that anticipated and forestalled inquiries from head office, thereby substantially increasing the manager's freedom of action. In any case, local conditions are so various that long-established international firms have made it their practice to give maximum scope to their provincial governors, the heads of their foreign operating companies. British companies tend to go farther than American or European companies in this direction. American companies have often started their foreign expansion in Canada, where proximity has permitted close control by the head office. British companies, on the other hand, have found that in places like distant Australia, for example, they need a man who will run the business as if it were his own. All the bigger international companies are now tending to raise the status of managers of foreign operations. Former managers and vice-presidents are being made presidents of foreign companies.

This pattern of organization for overseas operations has been evolved rather than planned. In many cases, these operations began with unsolicited imports by an indigenous distributing firm. The growth of such trade led to formal recognition of the distributing firm as an exclusive agent. Subsequent stages provided local labeling to meet language requirements and government regulations, then local assembly, then local manufacturing. At this last point, a share of the ownership of the local agency was taken by the parent company in return for financial support of moves toward local production or for vesting of patents and trademarks in the indigenous company. Eventually the local proprietor was bought out. This sequence was often a single-generation cycle, and the transfer of ownership came naturally when the man who started the trade approached retirement age. He might have been retained, however, as local president. With forethought and determination, he could often obtain the succession to this position for his heir. There are several foreign sales agencies, now wholly owned subsidiaries of American firms, in which the sons of former agents are currently presidents. Throughout the early part of this evolution, the chief local representative of the international firm was usually independent and in business for himself, not a salaried employee. That situation may have something to do with establishing the unique status in modern business of the head of a foreign subsidiary.

The autonomous power of the president of a foreign subsidiary is becoming a significant social phenomenon. The influence of large corporations in modern society is growing. They control the livelihood of an increasing proportion of the population, as industrialization and concentration of large concerns proceed in more and more countries. Their social influence is widening, as companies become more and more involved in community affairs, education, relations with government, the projections of "images" of themselves and business in general, consumer attitudes and scales of values, and even the arts.

In the home country, at least in theory, management is responsible to the shareholders and must win an annual vote of confidence. Annual reports are published. Even in the home country, however, the influence of shareholders is notoriously vague and weak, in direct proportion to the degree of "democracy" in ownership. Even this slight check on the expanding power of company managers does not extend overseas. The home shareholders and public receive no information about operations in specific foreign countries. This secrecy is an indirect and unintended result of the financial reporting technique of consolidated accounts that was pioneered by Price Waterhouse with U.S. Steel in 1902, as an improvement in the information and protection given to shareholders at that time. Such accounts can conceal mistakes in foreign operations—the cost of strikes or local government intervention provoked by irresponsible foreign managers who have turned into petty dictators.

Power without responsibility is a historic menace to human rights. It has usually destroyed institutions in which it has become embedded. The American public is mystified about why the United States is associated with imperialism even in neighboring countries with politically sympathetic governments. An explanation may be found in the number of despots in charge of foreign subsidiary operations. International firms have unwittingly and unintentionally contributed to adverse political reactions by using a system of delegation of power that contains fewer safeguards against abuse abroad than at home. The depths of feeling that can be stirred by imperialism in international firms have been demonstrated in Cuba, and previously in the part resentment against exclusive control of business by Anglo-Argentines played in the rise of Perónism.

The strong position of the presidents of foreign subsidiaries results from a combination of influences. The historic background has already been described. The kind of man chosen for these positions is shrewd, determined, self-reliant, and enterprising. It is natural that he should exploit distance from the head office, private responsibility to only one man—the overseas director or his equivalent—and knowledge of local language and law, officials, and customers to increase his importance in the organization. International firms have deliberately encouraged overseas managers to act as Roman governors of conquered, if unpacified, provinces. The theory has been that they need almost complete freedom to make the best use of their knowledge of local conditions and to take prompt actions. There has also been an unacknowledged readiness to shift some of the heavy weight of responsibility that burdens the top management of a large concern. Why should the parent company look for trouble? Let Jones, who is on the spot, follow his own way, which he says is the African or Australian way, so long as he makes profits.

As a result of this system of organization, when something goes wrong at the foreign branch-manager level, the trouble is serious. The organization does not provide automatic remedies for mistaken appointments or for the deterioration from climate, age, family troubles, or too long enjoyment of absolute power that occasionally occurs among foreign representatives. This problem has arisen in important subsidiaries of several large and successful international firms within the last decade. The problem cannot be solved simply by dismissing the manager. It is a major operation to remove the head of a foreign subsidiary. Much power has been delegated to him—and his power, prestige, and perquisites are not willingly abandoned. The minimum cost is early retirement on full pension.

Autocratic and hierarchical principles of organization are adopted by all firms, whether local, national, or international, for their obvious efficiency. This single criterion is warranted when the purposes of the organization are specific and limited. The checks and balances and other historically necessary features of government are assumed to be provided at a higher, political level. Business is subordinate to government in the United States and Britain. There is a question, however, whether the political regime in Venezuela, for example, is more powerful than the oil companies. In such situations, a government may be completely dependent on one foreign-controlled industry, while the foreign companies have other large resources elsewhere. Some of the new international business organizations are larger and also more efficient than many of the national governments to which their subsidiaries are nominally subject.

The Role of Staff Specialists

One explanation for the rapid extension of the international firm is that it seems to have better organization, especially staff organization, than indigenous firms. Staff experts, specialists, and technologists develop and maintain higher standards in the operations of international subsidiaries than independent indigenous firms can achieve. Staff contributions may not always be recognized or welcomed within a company, but they are nevertheless pervasive and profitable.

Advisory services are substantial in all successful international firms, whether or not they are formalized on organization charts. They may be provided in several ways. The branch manager may be sent out from the home company with the latest knowledge in his head—operational knowledge may be kept up to date by rotation between home and foreign service. Another way of disseminating knowledge is through annual conferences of foreign managers like those held by I.B.M. Home leave is used by Unilever as an occasion for informal refresher courses. When the head of a foreign branch is a native citizen, he may be assigned an assistant from the head office, who must ingratiate himself with the boss but carries head office authority with the rest of the branch organization. There are frequent visits from head office top management. Small wonder that Unilever finds it worthwhile to own and operate its own travel agency, which buys tickets and books hotel rooms.

The largest and most experienced international firms now have permanent advisory departments. Some serve both home and foreign operations, while others are for foreign operations only. The British and Europeans incline toward the former, the Americans toward the latter. William O. Beers, Vice-President of the International Division of the National Dairy Products Corporation has nevertheless stated that "What we're aiming at is a truly international company, one in which our engineering people in Chicago are equally interested in and directly concerned with new buildings and machinery being built both in Louisville and Liverpool." (Quoted in Dowd, 1960, p. 45.) In American companies, however, there is generally a problem of scale between home operations and the separate units abroad, no matter how important the latter may be in aggregate.

The function of the advisory services is seldom to strengthen the decisiveness of the local manager, and advisers quickly learn to avoid getting in the way. Rather, their contribution is to make wiser decisions possible—mainly by providing better information, although their own experience and judgment can be tactfully introduced.

The primary area in which the international staff shows its influence is production. Uniformity of product is increased and costs go down; appearance of the product is usually improved. Real inherent quality is more debatable because the international technical advisers have all the latest news about synthetics, substitutes, and production short-cuts—which have not always provided improvements. It is a strict rule among the long-established international firms to manufacture the same products or to deliver the same services on which their home success was founded in as many countries as possible. If one of these products will not sell in a country for peculiar national reasons (soap with a carbolic smell was associated with brothels in France), the international concern prefers to withdraw rather than to modify the product. Accepting variations would leave the company without consistent standards, which could disturb its accounting and its marketing, as well as its production, arrangements.

A peculiar variation occurs in the international motor-car industry. British Ford and Taunus of Germany (owned by Ford) and General Motors' British Vauxhall, German Opel, and Australian Holden have developed independent designs. On the other hand, there has been no Canadian-designed car since the old McLaughlin, which was made by a company later bought by General Motors. The main reason for this difference in subsidiary operations is that the so-called manufacturing of automobiles is in fact largely an assembly job. The necessary parts have always been freely and readily imported into Canada from the United States, whereas distance, duties, and foreign exchange restrictions forced the use of available parts in Britain, Germany, and Australia, thus forcing the development of designs incorporating them. Other reasons for special designs of cars for Britain and Europe included license fees proportionate to engine horsepower and high prices for gasoline. These factors restricted the size of cars that could be sold in quantities that would permit mass production based on standardized parts, which was the real American competitive advantage in motor-car manufacture. International technology had to apply its standards on basically different designs, for example four- and six-cylinder engines in Europe, compared with eights in America. Only the American companies succeeded in organizing to handle such variations profitably and only in the motor-car industry. The nearest British parallel is Unilever's American companies. They originated Lux Toilet Soap, Lux liquid detergent and the Lipton line of dry soup mixes. These were quickly taken into the parent product line and manufactured in many countries on uniform quality standards applied internationally. A possibility of greater flexibility, however, is indicated by a new plan at Massey-Ferguson to meet different market needs in farm implements with particular designs, drawing on all the parts manufactured among all the different subsidiaries. This plan is highly dependent on easy international trade in components.

The technical or manufacturing organization of international firms comes close to contradicting what was said earlier about the separation of line and staff. Exclusive scientific knowledge makes the university-graduate engineers who now handle production a fraternal order or secret society within business. They have their own codes and passwords and mutual assistance policies. The technical man from the head office advises the branch factory manager, and the branch president often does not know what they are talking about. The organization chart shows the branch production man as a subordinate member of the branch management, like the sales and accounts managers. In some subsidiaries, the general manager is a glorified production man. Even then, he is apt to have lost touch with modern technical progress. The actual production manager or technical director will be discreetly deferential at management meetings. He must, however, have head-office technical support. His advancement is most likely to come by transfer to a bigger company in a larger country, on the nomination of the home-office technical staff. This situation welds the loyalty of the technical man to the firm and detaches it from the country where he is temporarily stationed, with more force than applies to other staff. This relationship among the production men and the technical advisers of international firms does not show on charts, but it is one of the most important factors in their competitive strength. If the production manager and his head-office technical adviser agree that a new machine is needed, the branch president has to accept the expense. If they agree that the president's favorite supplier and golfing companion is not meeting specifications, a change must be made.

The closed circle of technologists may contribute to the centralization of research and development in international firms. As noted, the senior technical adviser can subtly exert executive authority. He also usually has direct line control over research. Decentralized laboratories attached to foreign subsidiaries are likely to be restricted to quality control without any budget or authorization for research. If a subsidiary happens on a promising development in its own factory or laboratory or from an independent competitor or a university, this new idea will be picked up and transferred to headquarters. The increasing superiority of the larger countries in scientific development derives in part from the fact that international firms provide the most advanced countries with agents to watch for and report new ideas from anywhere in the world in their early stages.

Another area of management in which the staff of international firms makes a distinctive contribution is accounting. The place of accounting in the organization of the international firm is vital because, obviously, a widespread business cannot be operated without prompt, accurate, and manageable figures. One of the earliest international firms was the auditing partnership of Price Waterhouse, which originated in London. This firm placed its first foreign resident partner in New York in 1890, on behalf of British investors in American breweries and railroads. It subsequently acted for prominent international firms like Coats thread and Lipton foods. The New York position was taken in 1901 by Arthur Lowes Dickinson who was a Master of Arts from Cambridge University as well as a chartered accountant and a brother of the famous classical scholar G. Lowes Dickinson. Incidentally, Dickinson's advanced internationalism was demonstrated when he became an American citizen in 1906, while pressing Price Waterhouse to adopt a policy of encouraging national citizenship for its overseas management.

Firms of professional accountants raised the standards of accounting and greatly facilitated international expansion by improving communications and the basis for control. Price Waterhouse work for Standard Oil of New Jersey has been described in terms directly related to international organization. "One of the purposes of the new [accounting] manual was to assure uniformity in the financial statements of all the companies in the Jersey organization. . . . The magnitude of the problem was apparent from the fact that the holding company owned and operated a great many subsidiary companies, of which 80 per cent in number and 47 per cent in assets were foreign companies or companies operating in foreign countries." (DeMond, 1951, p. 203.) The accounts of companies in the United States, Canada, Mexico, the West Indies, Central and South America, Continental Europe, and North Africa were covered in the first consolidated balance sheet of Standard Oil of New Jersey, produced in 1934. It involved work by thirty Price Waterhouse offices.

Uniform accounts make better accounts for the purposes of subsidiary managers, in many ways. They provide foreign managers with more complete and accurate information, more clearly presented. They provide familiar and well-understood tools of management for anyone who has worked in any part of an international firm. The development of uniform accounts was the key that enabled a firm to become international, in the sense that it provided intelligible communications between the foreign branches and the parent company. Uniform accounts enabled the central management to understand the positions of the foreign branches—a prerequisite for central control. Uniform systems of accounting show what has happened and supply the basis for budgeting and planned development. International firms are even more meticulous about the reports that branches provide on employment of capital, raw material and production costs, inventories, cash position, and trading results than about patents and trademarks and production formulas and standards. On organization charts, this concern shows in the elevation of branch accountants to branch boards or management committees. These men are closely advised by head office accounting experts. They do not form the kind of inner circle identified with the production scientists, however, perhaps because no one can succeed as the president or general manager of a branch without also remaining thoroughly conversant with his figures and completely the master of his accounting department.

The Importance of Communication

Other communications beside bare financial figures are important in complex modern business. A service resembling that of certified public accountants has come to occupy, in the postwar period, an integral relationship in the organizations of international companies that distribute through grocery- and drug-store channels—the Nielsen audit of shares of market. Nielsen has led the way in putting sales statistics, not merely for a company but for an industry, on a current and exact basis. The importance of these figures in organizations to which they are available is a striking example of how specific information, like the early figures on national currency in the history of economics, can help create a framework of policy. Nielsen reports from foreign branches are second only to financial statements as a source of head-office information and a basis for control and policy. They focus attention on share of market, fostering intensive competition, particularly against the vulnerable indigenous companies and sometimes at the expense of current profits on the theory of increasing long-term returns.

The provision of market share figures by Nielsen—and now by other organizations like Attwood's in Britain and on the Continent—has stimulated interest in other kinds of statistical returns obtainable by other methods of market research, including psychological investigations of consumer preferences, attitudes, and intentions. International organizations provide departments in their subsidiaries to collect those kinds of data and departments at home to compare and evaluate them. International firms are generally better informed about their overseas markets and the positions and progress of their subsidiaries than indigenous companies are about their positions.

The figures from the accounting department and the market research department are not always self-explanatory. The parent company wants to know what caused them and what is being done about them. Visits to and from the foreign subsidiaries are one way of communicating this information. For the purposes of an organization, as distinct from management individuals, written reports about such visits are essential. The resistance against this systematic necessity among the average senior businessmen is astonishing. One elementary advantage enjoyed by the international firm is that it employs—and must employ—senior managers who can read and write or at least recognize the value of these skills to the extent of using assistants to brief them and keep notes for them.

Another channel of information that is used in international organizations involves written reports from the subsidiaries themselves, growing out of the explanatory notes required by the accounting statements. Still another communicative procedure employed by international firms is the circulation of minutes of monthly management meetings held by all the operating companies at home and abroad. These minutes keep the head office informed and also ensure that managements of subsidiaries discuss and systematically record their problems, decisions, and actions. This system constitutes a higher level of organization and communications than the often cryptic and perfunctory minutes of the legally-required type of directors' meeting.

The part-time external director whose only required appearance was at the monthly directors' meeting is losing his place in the international firm. He cannot contribute to management of such a complex organization or represent the interests of shareholders unless he is on the job full time with no outside business interests and little time or surplus energy for private interests. Standard Oil of New Jersey and a number of British companies have changed to the working director who is also a salaried employee.

A few international firms like General Motors and Procter & Gamble have elected foreigners to their parent company boards. This move appears to owe more to public relations than to any intention of making the managements responsible either to the considerable number of foreign shareholders in such companies or to the foreign countries that contribute to the profits.

The working boards of directors of some of the most progressive international firms are currently evolving into a new organ of management. They are being used as pools of talent from which men are drawn to head departments or to handle special assignments. They are not required to include specialists in these fields but men with knowledge and judgment on the broad policies and purposes of their firms and with skill as chairmen of specialist staff groups. The successful head of the cosmetics division of one British concern is now directing its food companies. The advertising director in another firm is now in charge of personnel, with special reference to foreign subsidiaries. His predecessor in personnel is directing this same firm's food companies, while one of his immediate assistants, the head of a food operation, is a certified public accountant and was formerly the firm's chief financial official. This rotation system provides a supply of fresh minds of tested high caliber without going outside the firm and continuously stimulates its top men to exert their abilities by throwing them into new situations. This system is similar to the one that has evolved through many years of government experience in the assignment of offices in the British Cabinet, which moves men like Sir Winston Churchill from Home Office to Admiralty to Exchequer.

Generating Fresh Ideas

The progress of international firms in methods of organization, and particularly in communications, has been rapid in recent years. Even so, there are problems that progressive firms recognize. An upward flow of information from the men in factories and on sales territories to the executives and an inward flow from foreign subsidiaries to the head office are required to provide the facts for current and well-timed business judgment. Reporting systems like those mentioned above are intended to provide facts on products and methods of production, costs, margins and profits, and shares of market.

To get an upward flow of creative ideas, however, especially in marketing and public relations, is difficult. Head office has trouble in encouraging this important kind of commercial intelligence because the facts have to be combined with a "feel" for local conditions that is difficult to demonstrate or evaluate. Intelligence services are notoriously weak in anticipating public opinion. The essential that they so often lack, whether they are working for governments or businesses, is a real sympathy for the needs and hopes of the people with whom they are supposed to be concerned, especially the rising generations rather than the established, conservative, middle-aged groups. Some outstanding successes in international enterprise can be traced to an inspired or accidental appeal to the emotions of the masses of young people in developing countries—for motor transport (Vespa, Volkswagen), for good health (penicillin, vitamins), for personal appearance (nylons, cosmetics). In the United States, the enthusiasm of young people for sports cars caught American industry napping and made large contributions to the dollar earnings of Britain and Italy.

Viewed historically, the systems of organization and control developed by international firms, comparatively recently and quickly, are a remarkable achievement. They stand comparison with the Roman and British Empires and the Roman Catholic Church. Their strength arises from their power to create wealth; their power over the livelihood of their employees, suppliers, and distributors; and the support they can give governments by providing tax revenue and employment. Such power has not always been handled responsibly, among other reasons because of distance and lack of an informed public. But parent-company requirements for information and control are creating some checks and balances within international firms, related mainly to "the interest of I.B.M. World Trade Corp. as a whole," for example. Broader concepts of the interests of firms may develop out of more enlightenment, particularly about demands by foreign countries for assurances that their interests will be served. Services through which companies now obtain market information are capable of exploring the relationships of the firms with the social needs and purposes of the countries where the firms operate.

11

PERSONNEL IN INTERNATIONAL BUSINESS ORGANIZATIONS

PEOPLE buy the land for factories and stores, design the machines and hire the people that run them, design the packages and hire the people that sell them. People pay and receive the wages earned. Economic institutions are means toward ends that are always ultimately to serve human wants and needs for products and activities. John Maynard Keynes gave the basis of his studies an illuminating insight when he said at a professional meeting that "economists are the trustees not of civilization but of the possibility of civilization." (Quoted in Harrod, 1951, p. 194.) He thus acknowledged that an economy must do more than maintain itself.

Values expressed in money have lent themselves to study because of the ease with which they could be measured and compared. The great economists were not inhuman calculating machines, however, as is revealed in the lives and original writings of Adam Smith, Alfred Marshall, and even Thomas Robert Malthus, traditionally the prototype of the "dismal scientist." Sir Roy Harrod has counterbalanced his own highly abstract theories with his warmly-written biography of a great exponent and champion of the enjoyment of living, John Maynard Keynes.

While measurement has been developed for some of the human factors in the production and distribution of wealth, the
productivity of labor, for example, is known to be more than a
function of the capital supplied and to involve more than cal-
culation of man-hours. Output has been shown to be affected
by the working atmosphere, specifically by air-conditioning and
the use of color on machines and surroundings and more generally by attitudes and motivations that are influenced by social
relations, rather than by money incentives alone.

The greatest variations in productivity of labor after those
related to the tools supplied, arise from skills and talents. Skills
are acquired and can be increased by education. Natural talents
are inherited, but they must be discovered and encouraged.

In international economic comparisons, differences in skills
and talents are considered as important as variations in applied
capital in accounting for differences in productivity. M. F. Millikan and W. W. Rostow have declared that "one of the most
serious bottlenecks inhibiting the development of absorptive
capacity [for capital] in the underdeveloped countries is a
shortage of managerial and administrative skills." (Millikan and
Rostow, 1957, p. 61.) A similar opinion led D. K. David to go
still further in saying that "the central issues of foreign economic
policy cannot be dealt with effectively . . . by the mere export
of capital. The answers will be found, I am convinced, in the
massive export of the managerial and entreprenurial talents as
well as the productive skills that reside in the American business
community." (David, 1958, p. 7.) These ideas are valid, however, only if they are acknowledged to be temporary. They
resemble dominant British opinion in the Kipling period that
law and order could be provided in many parts of the world
only by sending out British judges and administrators.

It is notable that the skills and talents now reckoned as scarce
no longer include mechanical aptitude, the ability to operate
machines, or even the ability to maintain and repair machines.
Africans and Chinese have proved capable of performing these
operations, given a chance to learn. For a long time, it was
presumed from the concentration of mechanized industries in

Western Europe and North America that the people inhabiting other areas were like happy children, lacking in dexterity and powers of concentration. It took the wartime manpower shortage to break the white monopoly on the handling of powered equipment within the United States. The remaining claim for superiority in management skills can derive *post factum* from the preponderance of American control of large concerns which owes much to the large home market and the recognition of American patents by smaller countries.

The level of managerial ability on the scale of human achievements is easily exaggerated in societies whose main accomplishments to date have been industrial. The difficulty in acquiring managerial skills owes as much to lack of opportunity as to lack of ability. Where conditions are favorable, more people have climbed from the bottom to the top in industrial management than in such other occupations as law, which imposes formal educational and informal social requirements. There is much evidence of business success among immigrants and ethnic minorities, the Syrians in Brazil for example. Managerial talent is not necessarily scarce, but opportunities to exercise and develop it in modern industry have been rare and limited mainly to advanced countries.

Favorable conditions for encouraging managerial talent are necessary. They include financial rewards and social recognition provided by such marks of respect as the titles given in Britain and Australia and the appointments to foundation and university boards in America. There are also taboos and punishments for violating the rules of the game in industrial management, which some people in advanced societies find confusing. Some go too far in padding their expense and entertainment allowances; some accept excessive gifts; some take investment opportunities that create conflicts of interest. At lower levels, the acquisitive impulse is often so undisciplined that bonding of staff members who handle cash and policing of retail stock against pilferage by employees are necessary on a large scale in the United States. Professor Hirschman has argued that "the pattern of values and attitudes with which underdeveloped countries set out today on the path of modernization and industrialization is probably less suited to the successful accomplishment of these tasks than the pattern which prevailed in Western Europe at the beginning of the Industrial Revolution." (Hirschman, 1958, p. 137.) Close acquaintance shows that the values and attitudes in so-called advanced societies are not uniform and are not what they appear to be on the surface. There are, however, complex rules of business behavior, and they are thoroughly policed, all the way from the shop steward to the Securities and Exchange Commission.

The basic question concerning the adaptability of people to industrial organization is whether or not they have the necessary motivations. The answer to that is clear. For most people throughout the world, to recognize the benefits of industrialization is to want them. In the countries that have been industrialized for some time, there may be people who look back nostalgically to Thoreau's Walden Pond, but there simply is not enough room in the world anymore for the self-sufficient solitary life. Professor Myrdal points out that "the drive for economic development in underdeveloped countries is not the feeble brainchild of scheming economists; it is a living political force of immense and irresistible power in our contemporary world." (Myrdal, 1956, p. 173.) Knowledge of the people in the developing countries reveals also that factory and office working conditions are as important benefits of the industrialization they seek as the products manufactured.

The problem is getting to know the rules for succeeding in business. Many of these rules are not written; many, like those governing fair competition, vary according to the time and place and kind of business. From the outside, management may seem a Masonic mystery, and, until very recently, there has been a taboo on discussing publicly the roles of wives and secretaries, expense accounts, club memberships, and the like. Defiance of this taboo is one reason for popular interest in Vance Packard's *The Pyramid Climbers* and a Broadway play entitled *How to Succeed in Business without Really Trying*. The rules are "sensed" by members of industrially successful communities, particularly by the middle classes who do the work of managing industry. People with social awareness but not too much *noblesse oblige*, people good at figures and literate but not bookish, people with responsible ambition derived from having something to lose but more to gain, have naturally come from the middle class. This fact has led Professor Rostow to suggest that "the middle class, in a sense, was the most important of the economic innovations of modern times, and it is not susceptible of rapid diffusion throughout the underdeveloped regions of the contemporary world." (Rostow, 1953, p. 254.) It is arguable that economic development through industrialization with local participation automatically produces a sizable middle class. Modern industry, with its greatly increased proportions of skilled and supervisory staff, does provide a middle class susceptible of wide diffusion in a single generation. This last fact is most clearly seen, paradoxically, in the cradle of the modern middle class, Britain, where this class has grown vastly since World War II.

Staffing the International Business

The quality of personnel plays an important role in determining the success of international firms. It is clear that international firms enjoy important advantages here and that they have, in fact, successfully coped with shortages of managerial talent and skill. The staff that international companies can send out makes up for initial and temporary local deficiencies, but it is not their sole advantage. Their ability to find, develop, and pay native personnel is superior to that of indigenous competitors because of advanced methods of personnel selection and job rating. International companies also have the benefit of expert advice on how to use improved working conditions to increase productivity. Above all, international firms are skilled in practical business education. Nestlé of Switzerland, for example, is responsible for one of the leading institutions for education in higher mangement in Europe. International firms are likely to do more for the rapid and wide diffusion of a middle class than native industrialists, who tend to form capitalist clubs and keep mere skill and talent subservient.

The training and supervision of production staff is a primary concern of international firms. The first man to move into a foreign country for an international company is often the man with the formula book, a jealously guarded compilation of the firm's successful experience as to specifications and production processes. Companies with widespread operations are now employing native production managers under close supervision by international staff, which includes key control of secret processes. Companies with large home operations have a reservoir of trained and experienced technical personnel from which they can draw for foreign operations. Plant experience is important, and the international firm has an advantage in being able to provide it. Even when a country catches up in some branches of academic education, its graduates often still lack plant experience. Although Lever Brothers have had a factory in Canada since 1899, the Canadian technical director is an Englishman. Libby's Canadian plant, just across the border from the United States and engaged in the relatively simple food-canning industry, is run by an American. Beecham sent a man from its home production organization in England, with its own specific plant experience, to run its new factory in Clifton, New Jersey. When Beecham hired a graduate chemist in Argentina, it took him abroad for six months in-plant training.

Efforts have been made to foster production skills in underdeveloped countries independently of the activities of international companies. Government technical assistance programs have sometimes yielded disappointing results—wasting the home taxpayers' money and weakening foreign confidence—because the men they have been able to recruit were theorists from the schools or discards from industry. Also the training experts have been hampered, regardless of their ability, by not having the up-to-date formula book of the commercial organization. They have done better, however, in agriculture, where most research is public property because it is done in state-aided institutions. In food processing, Clarence Birdseye invented quick-freezing and gave a head start to the companies that bear his name. This head start, however, has created a monopolistic position only in food-importing countries like Britain where domination of the frozen foods industry is an outgrowth of enterprise in distribution. In producing countries, quick-freezing has raised many problems involving seed varieties, cultivation, harvesting, and handling that involve the public facilities for research on food and agriculture. These problems have given opportunities to indigenous enterprise in foreign countries. In contrast with agriculture, effective technical assistance in manufacturing and distribution has depended on the willingness and ability of international firms to supply the men with the know-how.

Incentives for Foreign Business Service

Men are available for foreign service with international companies from reservoirs of trained personnel at home. Foreign service with such firms need not involve a break in a man's career. The declared policy of international companies is to look after their people, although there are in fact gaps and difficulties, especially with other than production staff. However, men are recruited on this promise. A man will therefore go to Nigeria for an international firm, who would not accept employment by a Nigerian company or a government assistance scheme because he believes the international firm will bring him home after a reasonable time, with accrued seniority.

One inducement provided by foreign service with some companies is the chance to be a "nabob," as the earlier executives imported from Britain by the East India Company were called, and to build up a fortune early enough to retire and enjoy it at leisure. Men going to low income-tax countries on home pay scales plus living allowances, company cars, and company houses, can accumulate substantial savings. Americans working for American subsidiaries in the socialistically-taxed Britain of the postwar Labour government period enjoyed the fruits of a special agreement between the American and British internal revenue departments. They could be paid only enough salary to cover their expenses in Britain. This income was taxed by Britain at British rates but with the usual family and expense exemptions. They could at the same time receive additional income in dollars at home, which was taxed on the American scale. Under graduated and progressive taxation, the rates were thus lower in both countries. This arrangement did not apply to colonials or foreigners imported by British companies. It was a special concession designed to encourage the infusion of new blood into the war-ravaged British economy. It was a price Britain was prepared to pay to secure American personnel and their superior know-how.

Foreign staffs have in many cases been superior to those available locally, for either foreign or local companies. Some of the reasons have already been indicated. One is better education in the advanced countries, including the range, as well as standards. Law is taught as well in Mexico as anywhere, but the number of scientific courses, especially at postgraduate level, does not yet compare with those in Sweden or Switzerland and still less with Britain, Germany, or the United States. Business administration has been taught only at American universities until very recently.

Another reason for the superiority of staff drawn from the advanced countries is that companies often make experience and secret know-how available only to trusted employees. A Dutch firm, for example, will trust a Dutchman anywhere in the world more than an employee of another nationality. Other reasons are security of employment and family protection and better pay and conditions provided by international companies. Big firms do not begrudge salaries and allowances. With better accounting they are in a better position to assess the contributions of superior skill and talent. With profits taxes of 50 per cent or more, the government pays half the difference between the pay rates of ordinary and of superior staff.

International firms have led in the provision of staff benefits. Fifty years ago, employment at Lever's Port Sunlight in England provided practically everything a modern union leader can demand in the way of fringe benefits, except an annual wage for the factory staff, which was pioneered by Procter & Gamble. As these firms spread internationally, so did their enlightened policies. Were these policies adopted because profits permitted generosity? Or were the policies themselves profitable because they increased productivity? Did firms expand internationally because home profits provided the capital? Did enlightened labor policies offer competitive advantages abroad? Cause and effect are inextricably intertwined. Some international firms have been more enlightened and generous toward home staff than toward foreigners. The fact remains, however, that international concerns generally have been ahead of native practice in base rates of pay, recognition of unions, provision of pensions, insurance and health services (particularly important in underdeveloped countries), training programs, university recruiting, community services, and company social life.

Base pay by international firms is generally at the top of the going rate in a particular locale. Wood and Keyser reported that "wages, hours of work and conditions of employment at Sears (Mexico) are apparently better than competition and consciously kept so." (Wood and Keyser, 1953, p. 34.) Lever in Canada negotiated on the basis of five cents an hour under the highest local hourly rate, that of the breweries. International companies are anxious to avoid spoiling the market by overpaying and arousing the resentment of other employers, but they are equally anxious to avoid labor troubles and to attract the best personnel and thereby achieve maximum productivity. "High pay has proved to be no extravagance on the part of Sears. The ratio of payroll to sales in Mexico is about the same as in Sears stores in the United States." (P. 34.)

The big bad foreign company used to fight unions, especially in the extractive industries, but it does so no longer. Large international firms have a greater fear now, which displaces their fear of unionization and taxation—fear of expropriation. A contented union can offer valuable political support to the international firm.

Health services also interest enlightened employers. International firms have simply been more enlightened than native employers in underdeveloped countries. It has paid them and also benefited their employees to set an example for others. Lever Brothers transformed the usual factory first-aid post into the first Canadian industrial health center, designed to serve their entire staff—office, factory, and management—with preventive medical consultation instead of merely treatment of injuries. Many companies, especially those employing women, have subsidized in-plant meals to counteract the effects of undernourishment or unbalanced diet on health and efficiency. The contribution of international firms, however, must be only that of pilot operations, since, even when they include the families of their employees as does Standard Oil of New Jersey in Venezuela, they can serve only a small part of the population. This difficulty also arises in connection with pensions. Why should people lucky enough to get jobs with foreign firms enjoy preferred treatment? This question is beginning to interest government tax experts, who realize that the national revenue loses at least half of the tax-free contributions of profitable firms to employee pension plans, while demands for social services for the whole population are increasing.

International firms have also led in staff training, which improves the quality of local labor. Wood and Keyser stated that "any young Mexican who lands a job with Sears is soon busily learning the way merchandising is done in the United States. This has included a number of innovations that are having an effect on other merchants in Mexico." (P. 37.) This training has often been the only way in which citizens in some countries could acquire many of the important new skills. I.B.M. trains programers for its computers and offers comprehensive courses for managers in the use of the new figures. International Harvester teaches its salesmen to teach farmers how to make the best use of its tractors and attachments. Selling is like teaching in many respects, and international companies are experts in salesmanship.

The training activities of many companies have recently been expanded to provide accelerated orientation programs for university graduates. These programs provide a source of management personnel that is an alternative and a supplement to promotion from office, factory, and sales forces. Recruitment from universities, offering early advancement into business management, raises interesting possibilities, not the least being the formation of a class society in ostensibly democratic countries

like the United States. The only question we are concerned
with here, however, is the international effects. Most management training schemes are still operated exclusively by the
parent company. The graduate managers go anywhere and
everywhere, but they are drawn from home universities only
and are limited to American, British, Dutch, or Swiss nationals,
according to the location of the home company. The penetration of university graduates into management via training
schemes is actually increasing the national complexion of the
management of some international firms, as these men take over
the direction of more and more foreign subsidiaries. An attempt
to counteract this tendency was made by Unilever immediately
after World War II, when the trainee scheme was opened to the
larger subsidiaries. Men from universities on the economic frontiers were given postgraduate training in their home countries
and abroad, but they were to return to the subsidiaries in their
own countries rather than enter upon international careers.

New Developments in Staff Policies

Noel Coward has written a song that goes, "Uncle Harry's not
a missionary now." The array of benefits that international
firms have offered to backward countries has been a sufficient
substitute for missionary enthusiasm, especially among the university graduates offered opportunities to see the world without
any anxieties about their expenses. There has been an outlet for
Harry's zeal in international business—an opportunity to raise
living standards, if he could handle money and men, similar
to that of the scientist going out to fight the anopheles mosquito
or the tsetse fly.

It is a rare missionary who acknowledges that even his
favorite convert can be his Elisha. The mantle of employment
has been spread, however, by some companies, up to the level
of local management. Coca-Cola Export Corporation had 5,500
employees in 1958, of whom only sixty were Americans. (Kahn,
1960, p. 33.) National Cash Register had only six Americans
in a total of 22,000 overseas employees in 1958. (Fayerweather,

1960, p. 372.) National Dairy (Kraft foods) had two Americans working abroad. (W. O. Beers, quoted in Dowd, 1960, p. 372.) The United States Committee for Economic Development found that "of the 1,000,000 employees of U.S. companies in Latin America in 1957, about 2 per cent were sent from the United States. . . . The U.S. employees are relatively much more numerous in the higher positions, accounting for 20 per cent of those in management, professional and technical categories. It is natural that most of the people sent from the U.S. should be specialists of some kind." (Cabot, et al., 1961, p. 43.) Of the managerial, supervisory, and technical personnel of General Electric in Brazil, "nearly 90 per cent are Brazilians," but "of the 51 highest managerial positions in the company, 35 are held by Brazilian nationals," that is only 70 per cent. (Geiger, 1961, p. 58.) The staff of Unilever's subsidiary, United Africa Company, was 4 per cent African in 1939 but 30 per cent in 1960.

The converts want to take part in the service. As long ago as 1931, Mexico passed a law decreeing that 90 per cent of the employees of foreign firms must be citizens of Mexico. This requirement, however, could be met at the lower levels without opening the few top management positions to Mexicans. Questions are now being asked about the authority held by foreigners in local subsidiary companies and the salaries they receive compared with citizens of the host countries. In some countries, nationalist sensitivity has developed even against business missionaries sent out only temporarily to train native staff. Delegates to the Conference on Latin America, held at Lake Couchiching in Canada in 1960, warned that there is a new attitude in Latin America, a determination to develop their own methods of industrialization without foreign bosses and foreign advisers. Instead countries are seeking to train their own technicians, sending their own people abroad, when necessary, to acquire foreign know-how. This attitude is important to all concerned with the distribution of advice, whether gratuitously through foreign aid and technical assistance or charged by companies to operating expenses of the subsidiaries receiving the advice. People in countries that consider themselves underprivileged or even ill-treated, rather than underdeveloped or backward, prefer to go to the United States, Europe, or Japan for education and training. Here is an interesting alternative to economic warfare. Although this approach does not ensure direct economic control, it may provide more abiding influence for western methods and values if these visitors convert themselves.

There are, in any case, limits to the profitability of staffing foreign branches with managers and expert advisers sent from home. The direct cost of the higher pay they command compared with native staff has usually been earned by their superior knowledge and productivity. But indirect and delayed costs have been substantial. It has become customary to allow home leave. This custom began when men were sent without their wives to feverish tropical posts, and their health and morale required frequent trips home. Modern health provisions plus air-conditioning, however, have made life in the Philippines, for example, as safe and comfortable as life in Florida. For the women, modern appliances and convenience foods along with plentiful domestic help make life easier abroad than at home. They still want to see their relatives and friends at regular intervals, however. Such home leaves have become established at three-year intervals for some companies and even two-year intervals in the case of American banks. Foreign service people also want their children to receive secondary school and university educations at home, where family connections can help their careers and they can meet and marry people of similar backgrounds and attitudes. The privileges granted foreign personnel create difficulties when native personnel rise to equivalent ranks. Some companies have given home leave trips to the United States or Britain to Latin American managers and their families —particularly Anglo-Argentines, who are of Anglo-Saxon ancestry but were born in South America and have often never been abroad before.

The most awkward problem arises when a man claims to be repatriated on the grounds that he has given his share of loyal foreign service. This service does not necessarily equip him to fit into the larger, more complex home company structure at an equivalent level. The wasteful and expensive answer often adopted is to pay off such people, frequently in their prime of life but at an age when they would find it difficult to re-establish themselves in other businesses.

Apart from political reactions to the prevailing use of personnel from the home country and the problems that affect both firm and the individual, there may be economic disadvantages for the less developed nations. Jahangir Amuzegar has gone so far as to write that "the popularly believed shortage of technicians in the underdeveloped countries is purely operational. That is to say, underdeveloped countries cannot at present afford to pay for the skill, knowledge and wisdom that they wish to employ in order to have higher standards of living," and he adds explicitly that "Americans are the most expensive technicians in the world, and their productivity happens to be highest at home." (Amuzegar, 1959, pp. 256, 260.) His criticism applies, however, to intergovernmental technical assistance programs more than to international businesses, which have their profit figures acting as governors on their use of staff from home.

The fact is that foreign experts and managers may continue to yield profits for the firm after they have become undesirable socially and from the point of view of an integrated economy. A foreign ruling class arouses deep resentment and sometimes actual resistance to reasonable and helpful suggestions. Objections to the foreign representatives of international firms can also be well-founded. Some of these people have contributed to the establishment or perpetuation of economic colonialism because their view is exclusively that of their company, and it is not easy for them to take a full view of the needs of the local economy. Their job is to cultivate the local market and their method is to provide that market only with the goods and services on which the firm has been built. They are not favorably disposed toward exports, which are often of critical importance to a developing economy, because exports of standard products might compete with other subsidiaries in their business family. They also fail to encourage exports because they do not approve of local differentiation in products that could provide the basis for export demand.

When international companies, all pursuing this policy of uniformity, become predominant in an economy, they stultify economic growth. This risk has already been examined in Chapter 7, and it will reappear in Chapter 15. What is significant here is that this problem represents a conscious and deliberate policy on the part of the university-trained managerial class in international firms. But how is a developing country to gain exports from its secondary industries and reduce its dependence on commodity marketing, when standardized international products and standardized international men and minds are in control? The replacement of foreigners by nationals may be speeded by economic as well as social forces and may represent much greater local autonomy than even the most progressive international firms yet realize.

Although the future staff of international firms will consist mainly of nationals, such firms still offer inherent advantages in the training and operating experience they can give production managers, for example. This ability gives them competitive strength and profit potential. Talent is discovered and skills are taught in countries where there once seemed to be shortages of people with the qualifications needed for industrial progress. Attention to education and advancement, exemplified in the supplementary courses and conferences and counseling services that are associated with American business leadership, represents investment in the progressive middle classes, and these classes have strong interests in progressive government.

The problem of conflicting loyalties is a possible basis for constructive development. In the era of colonies, divergent interests were not recognized. Now, nationalism exaggerates such differences. Working for international business is giving people of many nationalities experience in practical cooperation. This experience leads to international understanding and a feeling of participation in international service—parallel to the spirit that has been kindled among the permanent staff of the United Nations.

12

RESEARCH AND DEVELOPMENT

THE WORDS "research" and "development" are frequently used as if they were magic incantations, and the spell has even more power when the terms are combined in the phrase "research and development" or "R & D." Laboratories are built today instead of the temples of previous ages, for the wish, hope, and belief is that research will cause development. Companies devote ever increasing expenditures to R & D, and shareholders enthusiastically approve. When enough companies are active in research, the public expects that the whole economy will prosper. Lest these private burnt offerings prove insufficient, governments provide tax concessions and subsidies for research. They even build public laboratories. Few people appreciate or understand research itself—a laborious, frustrating, unsocial occupation. It is the development they want.

The significance of research and development can perhaps be most readily grasped by comparing them. The word "development" has two distinct applications: one to products, the other to national economies. Business R & D involves product development, that is, work in the factory and in the market to evolve new or improved products. This process has become elaborate and expensive—an important and profitable factor in the operations of successful companies. It is also important to the overall functioning of highly-developed economies. This development work is applied, however, to inventions or ideas for new products that were conceived earlier, sometimes in a laboratory, sometimes during a lonely walk in the woods, as a sudden inspiration. Occasionally the development process does produce a fundamentally new idea, but its main purpose is to modify and adapt. However, Albert Einstein did some of his important thinking while strolling in the college gardens of Christ Church, Oxford.

Product development is important. It is derivative certainly, but it is not secondary. Original inventions usually require a great deal of development before they will work. The notebooks of Leonardo da Vinci are full of ideas for which the market and production facilities did not appear until the twentieth century. One of the most striking recent inventions, Sir Frank Whittle's jet engine for airplanes, required the development of new alloys to withstand the intense heat. The development stage is more attractive for company investment than is the search for original ideas, partly because profits can be realized only when new products are ready for the market, but partly also because the use of capital in product development is better understood. A man alone in a bare room can conceive the idea of a hydraulic transmission to displace gears in an automobile, provided that his mind is steeped in motor mechanics and the theories of physics. It is possible that such ideas are more likely to come, like the artist's and writer's inspiration, in a garret. A small company like British Daimler can build the first few units and find a market at a high price among connoisseurs and enthusiasts. The financial and technical resources of General Motors come into play in producing thousands of variations until a version is found that can be mass produced and also mass consumed. The latter requirement includes reliability and low maintenance, compensated brakes and engine power. The company must also teach the public how to use the new convenience and dispel their doubts and fears. Large investments in demonstrations and advertising are often required.

A parallel situation occurs in the development work required with a new medical discovery. After the discovery is made it must be tested on thousands of cases, over a long period, to determine the risk of abnormal or delayed reactions. If all goes well, there remains the job of spreading the news among thousands of busy doctors and informing the public. The investment that can be absorbed in testing new products and then making them known is staggering. This cost is one cause of the heavy demand for capital for product development. A discovery that has taken a great deal of time and money to test and publicize is the value of fluoridized water supplies for reducing tooth decay.

One kind of development can occur in companies without new or improved products—increase in output of existing products. The market for established products may grow because of increased population or, at least for a time, because of rising purchasing power, although the latter ultimately leads to demand for more variety. An aggregation of companies with increasing production, even without more product variety, enriches the total economy. Nevertheless, like a forest in which the existing trees are growing but no new seeds are germinating, a healthy economy requires continual new sources of growth. There is doubt that straight volume increases in existing industry can continue indefinitely. Broad economic development implies increases in variety, as well as in quantity. Furthermore, such variety furthers the integration of an economy by encouraging interdependence for materials and markets. In discussing the development of backward areas, people often forget that production increases concentrated in a few export commodities do not provide true economic development unless they are extended to industrial diversification.

There is a close relationship between economic development and product development. The formation of new and diversified industries depends on the practical work of finding, making, and selling new and improved products. This growth is the essential living substance of economic development. There are, of course, many and complex conditions that determine the environment for development, but they cannot substitute for the creative process itself.

Public interest in the processes of development is now acute. They are less interested in the direct results; there is seldom any overt demand for new products until it has been stimulated. But the public has become aware that there is some mysterious connection between "development" and more and better jobs. Development provides the opportunities to move from the farm to the factory and from the factory to the office or the control room. Americans have already taken advantage of the first opportunity, and now they are looking for more of the second. Other countries still have great numbers of casual laborers who would be glad of any steady job. The widespread yearning for development could not exist but for the hope that it is attainable. That hope is offered by research.

The development of new industries requires new products, which, in advanced countries at any rate, must be invented. And much more is involved in original invention than product development or applied research as now practiced by industry. Applied research finds mass production and quality control methods for penicillin, but only after the principle of penicillin has been established by a Fleming and a Florey. That original flash of inspiration, however, seems to come as a stroke of lightning. Can inspiration be produced at will? For industrial development, useful inspiration is required in a steady flow. There are profits in development, and much money is being spent for this purpose. Is it being spent well?

Money, Research, and Invention: Theory and Experience

The factors of production are defined in classical economics as capital, labor, and land. Is research a form of capital, or is it labor? Or is the human ability to produce useful inventions a fixed and scarce factor like land? Perhaps ability is most comparable to minerals like nickel, which is very irregularly distributed and very expensive to extract.

In the classical theory of Adam Smith, the industrial arts were viewed as an outcome of the division of labor and therefore as a function of capital. More capital applied to industry, by producing more specialization, would lead to more inventions. Adam Smith, however, gave no assurances that invention would follow in any definite ratio or according to any specific timetable. Capital had to be applied on the broadest scale. For American investment to obtain Burbank, Edison, Ford, and Kettering, the country had to produce thousands of intelligent and unconventional young men and women and had to provide spare time and incentives—the prospect of riches or honors.

One of the most original of contemporary economists, Professor J. Kenneth Galbraith, has expressed views on development that are basically the same as Adam Smith's. Galbraith has stated that "economic growth—the expansion of economic output —requires an increase in the quantity of the productive plant and equipment of the country or in its quality or, as in the usual case, of both. . . . The increase in quantity is called capital formation. The increase in quality is what we call technological advance. . . . Modern economic activity now requires a great number of trained and qualified people. Investment in human beings is, *prima facie*, as important as investment in capital. . . . The improvement in capital—technological advance—is now almost wholly dependent on investment in education, training and scientific opportunity for individuals." (Galbraith, 1958, p. 271.) This reasoning could be applicable, however, to straight-line and potentially limited growth, without providing for original new inventions, a rate of invention, or the ultimate requirement for an increasing rate of new inventions. Professor Galbraith goes on, however, to assert that "innovation has become a highly organized enterprise. The extent of the result is predictably related to the quality and quantity of the resources being applied to it." (P. 272.) Here then is specific assurance from economic theory that progressive development can be achieved by progressive investment. The condition is that it be applied to "education, training, and scientific opportunity for individuals." (P. 272.)

The theory that development can be increased by increased investment of capital is receiving a thorough test right now in the American economy. Professor Daniel Hamberg has estimated that the total R & D investment by American companies, universities and government agencies in 1959, after adjustment for changes in the value of money and in the definition of such investments, shows an increase of 2,000 per cent over 1929. (Ham berg, 1961, p. 17.) The biggest increase followed the war, but the new rate has been maintained. The rate of growth in the American economy as a whole, however, has apparently been unaffected by this increase, falling behind that of such other areas as Western Europe and becoming almost indiscernible in the late Fifties and early Sixties.

The ways in which R & D investments are directed and controlled are brought into question by Professor Hamberg in view of the failure of such vast increases to yield, as yet, the returns that might be expected. The complexity of modern science entails specialization in practical use among industrial firms and leaves most of the critical and speculative review of fundamentals—the basic research that opens up new fields for industrial development—to those who teach science in the universities. Professor Hamberg points out that, on this basis, the proportion of total industrial R & D investment in *basic* research has fallen from about 20 per cent in 1929 to only 8 per cent in 1959. (P. 18.) There has nevertheless been an absolute increase in the total amount spent which is large by any previous standard. Government investment, which has led the increase and become the largest segment of the total is not all spent on applied research or development. Three large government programs—atomic energy, space, and national health—include important basic research programs.

Perhaps there has not yet been time for postwar basic research to stimulate fermentation throughout industry. There is, however, a much more serious possibility that disturbs Professor Hamberg and others, including members of a special committee appointed by the Engineers' Joint Council of the United States (*The New York Times*, May 26, 1962, p. 27.), the possibility that fermentation has been inhibited. Professor Hamberg touches a vital point when he criticizes the tendency of government and business to try to focus basic research on specific short-term objectives, and in the case of government, military objectives. In addition, there are the obviously sterilizing effects of government "classification" of research. Such classification prevents diffusion of new knowledge among the large number of people and companies that could develop commercial applications. For the best economic results, the Atomic Energy Commission, for example, would have to throw open its laboratories to tours and meetings of groups, not only of physicists but also of biologists, chemists, and engineers.

There seems to be great waste in research, where the normal standards of efficiency—working toward a purpose, relating costs to results, or even working steadily in regular hours—paradoxically do not apply. Harm is done by too much direction and control. Adam Smith's example of an inventor was a boy who preferred play to work and who, left unsupervised, achieved early "automation" with a piece of string tied from one machine to another, which he was supposed to operate. (Smith, 1910, p. 9.) The machine that puts vitamins into gelatine capsules, justifying its cost by providing exact dosage and glamorizing the appearance of medicine, was invented by a man who quit a regular job because he did not like to get up in the morning.

One limitation of present efforts to increase intellectual ferment is too close correlation with industry and particularly with budgeting. Research and development funds are purposefully allocated. This system is appropriate for development, but an alternative for basic research is necessary. Such an alternative might be to adopt the approach of wealthy patrons, individuals, companies and foundations, toward supporting the arts. They do not invest, they donate. Significantly, also, individual donations are only large enough to keep the artist painting or the musician composing. The number of recipients is more important, and the continuity of support. In richly creative Britain, individual and government donations in the form of annuities or sinecure appointments have benefited a surprising number of contributors to the arts and sciences. When in doubt about how to select worthy individual recipients, a benefactor endowed fellowships at a university. These endowments were quite different from typical modern research grants, which demand reports and results. Some universities, however, are now becoming as systematic and organized as companies or government departments, and they are beginning to be staffed with executives. Business and government in the United States could scarcely be more generous toward research, but they could be more liberal. Allocation of funds to more individuals as pure donations, even as modest life annuities—and a wider distribution of grants among smaller institutions—to replace investment in directed and budgeted research projects in large institutions would be more conducive to creativity. Company accounts provide for donations, which are deducted before profits tax if made to officially recognized charities and educational institutions. Since creative ability is not easy to recognize, it is important for business and government to adopt a more liberal attitude.

However they originate, ideas serve companies—and nations —as a kind of capital from which new products and new industries can be developed. The American economy has been stimulated by a series of new industries providing products that have drawn forth surges of consumer demand—for automobiles, electric stoves and refrigerators, radios, automatic central heating and air-conditioning, air travel, and television. The efforts people have made to acquire these new goods and services—the number of women working to help the family carry the time-payments, for example—have helped to finance the growth of these industries. These new products have fired the imagination of potential buyers. The same is true of industrial goods. The warehouseman gains status, as well as efficiency, when he adopts dramatic new mechanical fork-lift trucks for materials handling. Far more concerns have installed mechanized accounting equipment than can show savings from it. Even hard-headed accountants have been swept along by fashion and the sales promotion of I.B.M. and others.

The modern drug industry provides a remarkable example of research and development. It pours investment funds into development, and it is increasing its contributions to pure research. Some of the capitalized reserves that are now being invested in R & D can be traced back to profits made in the vitamin business. Discoveries were made in pure research, for example by Lord Boyd-Orr and the Mellanbies, husband and wife. There was widespread publicity and popular interest, factors that certainly influence development more than is commonly realized. They may even prove to influence the original creative process by increasing and spreading interest in a specific field of research. In the case of vitamins, genuine inventiveness in packaging machinery made precise dosage possible and simultaneously reduced waste of expensive ingredients. The new package was the attractively colored, translucent capsule, which was also convenient and easy to take. The business financed its own growth and provided profit surpluses for reinvestment in the search for other gold-mines in the drug field.

The International Diffusion of Innovations

Vitamins were discovered in Britain. So was penicillin. Yet today the strongest companies in the drug business are American and Swiss. For many years, American genius has focused on the commercial development of ideas—for example, the telephone invented by a Scot, Alexander Bell; radio invented by an Italian, Marconi; locomotive and truck engines invented by a German, Diesel; the tranquilizing drugs, discovered centuries ago in India; and the protein concentrates, traditionally recognized by the Chinese in soybean sauce. Many advances in atomic research were borrowed from Denmark and Italy by way of Britain during World War II, and in space-rocket research from Germany later when the men with the ideas were physically transported to the United States.

Development in Western Europe, especially in the period since 1955, has outstripped that of any other comparable area. A capital of innovations was available after the war from the United States, ready for use in many cases with little or no development expense, not even the cost of providing information to the public. Europeans knew about, desired, and felt they could afford cars, appliances, prepared foods, television, and paid vacations. Aroused demand created a great variety of new jobs and incomes in the production, installation, and service of these innovations.

Subsidiaries of American companies and European companies with American connections have been in the van of European development. They had an accumulation of products that were still new in Europe, along with know-how that embraces the complexities of modern physical distribution and the subtleties of advertising, pricing, and time-payments, as well as the techniques of production. The profits of innovation have financed a great deal of this development. The same thing has been happening, of course, although more gradually, in other parts of the world, from Australia to Venezuela.

Firms with foreign subsidiaries gained profits from the new products they introduced, and from participation in the rapid economic development that occurs in countries where the activity of a variety of industries creates a compound effect on employment and purchasing power. These gains also interact on development—and possibly on research—by providing finance and motivation for pushing the search for more new products.

It is not suggested that there is any necessary connection between R & D and international enterprise. General Electric,
until recently a company mainly concerned with American
domestic business, has as its motto, "Progress is our most important product." General Foods was involved in a program of
systematic innovation before it embarked on a wide international development program. On the other hand, Corn Products'
largest foreign venture was the purchase of a Swiss company
that gave it the Knorr line of new products. Chrysler bought
Simca of France for quick access to the booming small car
market. The search for innovations *can* be aided by international
connections.

The activity of international firms in research and development is stimulated by foreign profits. Some firms charge the
whole cost of research and development to the budget of the
parent company. A more sophisticated arrangement is to make
a levy on all member companies of the group. This system has
tax advantages wherever the local authorities can be persuaded
to accept research, even though carried on elsewhere, as a cost
to be deducted before profits. Consolidation of these contributions from subsidiary companies yields funds for research that
are beyond the capabilities of most one-country companies, except those with very large markets in the United States or West
Germany.

The number of companies that have policies directed toward
growth beyond the next ten years or so cannot yet be high.
There is of course the difficulty, not to mention the unpleasant-
ness, of peering into the foggy, unionized, and government-reg-
ulated future. There is also the inexorable fact that the active
span of top-management executives has temporal limits. But
the frequent and expensive shuffling of control among corporations where the management has not risen to successful planning
demonstrates competitive weakness.

Long-term corporate development requires a flow of new and
improved products, which in turn requires facilities and skills
in product development—plus early access to basic research
discoveries, which is best obtained by participation. In product

development, however, needs are easier described than filled. The search for profitable ideas, whether in company laboratories or among independent scientists, requires faith, luck, and pertinacity, the familiar ingredients of personal success in any activity.

Acquaintance with developing companies suggests that for success, the head of the firm must engage personally in the search for improvements. The chairman or president can buy a big research laboratory and hire brilliant assistants, but he must himself use and help to test possible new products. If he is strictly a politician of business or a banker, he must have the ability to choose as his right-hand man a Lord Cherwell, as did Sir Winston Churchill during World War II, or a Charles F. Kettering, as did Alfred P. Sloan of General Motors during one of its great periods of growth, and the willingness to clothe this man with his power. Responsibility for development cannot be delegated, though the work can be decentralized. It is still a top-management responsibility to provide functional independence and strong support. One of the organizational advantages of large firms is that they can afford to delegate all the normal operations, leaving time and energy at the top for working with problems for which no policy has been established. Here is another reason why the international firm can drive its smaller national competitors into obsolescence.

Professor Hirschman has observed that "one of the real difficulties of development is lack of knowledge of and uncertainty about the market." (Hirschman, 1958, p. 120.) Successful development links product and market, scientist and consumer. Arthur C. Nielsen and his firm have built up dramatic documentation on gains and losses in the process of innovation, much of which is, of course, unpublished. The rate of failure of new products is shocking, despite obvious improvements in the preparation of new items and their introduction to the market. One of the highest costs of innovation is evidently at the stage of launching new products. The leading companies embark on introductory marketing calculating the risks and planning for strategic retreat if necessary. Formerly, and among independent companies in smaller countries still, a failure in development could lead to bankruptcy.

The technique of test marketing is an important part of the process of innovation. The facilities are superior in the advanced countries. American government statistics are steadily improving compared with those of other countries, and the United States is far ahead of the rest of the world in the theory and practice of market surveys. In this field, government and industry obviously gain from collaboration. The Census Bureau provides the statistical foundation, notably the censuses of population, production, and distribution. Gallup, Nielsen, Schwerin, and others have built up sampling procedures that provide quick answers to specific questions at economical costs. The homogenous, compact British market has proved suitable for similar methods, and market testing is well developed there. This part of the innovation process is largely confined, as yet, to these two countries. Elsewhere, studies are made primarily on possible variations that might be accommodated by minor adaptations. This situation has adverse long-run effects by limiting the amount of market research on original products in other countries.

It must be acknowledged, however, that the practice of innovation, even among the leading firms, is not confined to the procedures that have been outlined. Procter & Gamble, long and strongly associated with the baking industry through its cooking fats and equipped with laboratories that must have mastered every detail of cake-making, bought the Duncan Hines home cake-mix business. Unilever, a world authority on the technology of producing and distributing oils and fats of all kinds, bought the small but growing Success Wax business in Quebec, Canada. These purchases of products that were already on the market can be understood as reflections of the very high cost of the market development phase of the process of innovation. They also suggest that the obstacles facing any smaller country anxious to safeguard its independence by self-sustained innovation are indeed mountainous—although they may be passable in intervals of propitious weather. Chance and time still appear nearly as important to establishing a new product as do money and laboratories. Small countries may be able to provide both as long as they protect local industries from being swamped by international mass-production and as long as they are not drained of all their resources of inventive talent.

The requirements for the adaptation that is part of product development are facilities and talent. The facilities of large international companies are generally superior thanks to financial contributions from many branches. Talent, moreover, is distributed throughout the world, and international operations have better chances of finding the people gifted with the originality required for successful product adaptation as well as for original invention.

In the generation of original ideas, which is the object of basic research, the search for talent is aided by wide operations. International firms can spot creative work at long range. Stacks of scientific books and periodicals from all over the world are a familiar feature of every research laboratory. An international firm obtains reports in advance of publication. European margarine companies with international connections were following closely the first investigations into the possible relation of cholesterol to heart disease being done in California before 1950. International scientific congresses also make a recognized contribution to research. Within international companies this kind of stimulating discussion, among executives and experts who have been exposed to a variety of conditions and countries, is going on continuously and is becoming an established part of the technique of innovation. The interchange of ideas, which American industry has used so profitably in the past can proceed still more systematically through the channels provided by international enterprise.

The Centralization of Research and Development

Research investment and most product development tend to be concentrated in the home countries of international firms for both technical and policy reasons. Ideas are drawn from wide areas, but the people who originate them can be brought to the center. The stated reason is efficiency, but security and nationalism are undoubtedly considerations. Knowledge is power, and never more so than today. Boards of directors and national governments are becoming increasingly aware of this fact and are jealously watching that the sources of power do not get too far away from them. There is also a practical problem: Research and development can absorb a great deal of money and, particularly in development, the money must often be spent at one time and place and cannot be spread out. A pilot plant cannot be divided up among different countries.

Most companies centralize their research and development. Unilever, larger and more international than most, established primary research facilities shortly after the Second World War in three different locations. The original research department in Port Sunlight, England was duplicated in the Netherlands and in the United States. There was internal political pressure for this step. The Dutch part of the peculiar Unilever corporate Siamese twins had to be allowed a brain, as well as arms and legs. The American company was in the largest market, exposed to the fiercest competition, in a geographical region that was being deluged with new products at that time. The chairman of Unilever at the time yielded to these pressures, despite his misgivings about the cost of duplication on the grounds that all research involved great risk and apparent waste. He could, however, afford to duplicate in the hope that the odds in favor of profitable discoveries might be improved while keeping expenses to a small percentage of his large concern's profits. Other companies like Ciba of Switzerland have also duplicated their home research departments with facilities in the United States in order to assure participating in the American flow of new developments.

Centralization of research has a number of disadvantages, some economic and some political. Talent, especially for pure research, is widely scattered, and some people may not function as well if transplanted. Furthermore, the costs and uncertainties of research have already led some progressive organizations to another technique of innovation. Instead of relying exclusively on their own research departments, they are collaborating with universities and with government and commercial laboratories. Initial grants and subsequent royalties to these organizations may be more economical than the long-run costs of maintaining a strong enough internal research program to ensure parity in the competitive race for new and improved products.

This approach is manifest in Cambridge, Massachusetts where Harvard University, Massachusetts Institute of Technology, and organizations like Arthur D. Little, Inc., carry on industrial research. A similar development is appearing in the "research triangle" formed by Chapel Hill, Durham, and Raleigh, where Duke University, North Carolina State College, and the University of North Carolina, and various commercial research facilities are located. Another concentration is growing around Washington, D.C., under the impetus of rising government spending on research.

If it is practical and worthwhile for companies to farm out research and development to Cambridge, Massachusetts, it should be equally so in Cambridge, England, or Ottawa, or Mexico City. The only obstacles are distance, which air travel has reduced; language, which is slight among scientists; and nationalism, which requires serious, frank discussion. The facilities are becoming available. In the neighborhood of Ottawa, the government has created a National Research Council with its own facilities and associated with an atomic energy research laboratory. There are, as well, scientists and facilities in other departments of the Canadian government, an experimental farm and agricultural research laboratories, for example. Informally but closely associated with them are the science departments of two universities, one French and one English. Now the newest large private research establishment in Canada has been added in this area by the Northern Electric Company, a subsidiary of the Canadian Bell Telephone system, to supply communications research that used to be obtained from the United States. Government and university research are available to Canadian companies, including American subsidiaries, at bargain rates, since the installation and overheads of these establishments are largely covered by government grants.

The cumulative effect of the concentration of research and development in the advanced countries, to which the centralizing practice of many international firms contributes, is potentially very dangerous. Simply as a matter of research technique, centralization is a short-run and short-sighted economy because it fails to give the widest possible encouragement to intellectual ferment and activity. In the long run, it clearly has adverse effects on the economic development of other countries. It is politically dangerous to international companies and their home governments because it can seem like a new kind of colonial exploitation.

Financially, the research of international companies is costly to most countries, a debit in their foreign exchange. In some cases, research expenditures receive exemption from taxation and priority for foreign currency. Charges made to support centralized research are transfers from the less developed to the more advanced countries. As the pace of R & D investment has increased, the charges against the less developed countries and the income of the more advanced countries have increased.

Even in Canada, a country that is not backward in the education of potential research staff or the use of up-to-date equipment, the rate of expenditure by private industry of all kinds on research is only one-fourth the rate in the United States and the practically identical rate of Britain. (Coyne, 1960, p. 20.) The Canadian drug industry spends only 1.21 per cent of sales on research, while it devotes 24.9 per cent to advertising and promotion. (Howard, 1961, p. 5486.) By contrast, little Switzerland, because it is an important parent country for the pharmaceutical industry, spends the equivalent of $20 million on R & D, compared with the United States figure of roundly $110 million. (Keele, 1960, p. 27.)

The adverse influence of some current product-development policies on the economic development of the less advanced countries can be illustrated by the example of instant coffee, which has been so widely and rapidly accepted. The processing involved in this product, which simultaneously economizes on the raw material, coffee beans, and commands a higher price from consumers in return for convenience, is carried on in the highly developed consuming countries. They gain the employment and profits of the new industry, dominated by the American and Swiss firms that developed the process, while more efficient extraction has actually depressed the raw coffee market and worsened Brazil's terms of trade and relative economic position vis-à-vis the United States.

The Brazilians find themselves powerless to cope with this situation. It might be argued that they could establish instant-coffee manufacturing in Brazil, ignoring the foreign patents, in order to compete in the United States and Europe through savings from shipping concentrated soluble coffee extract instead of bulk beans. The foreign processors could, however, make patent claims in their home countries against the Brazilian manufactured product, and they are also strongly entrenched in distribution by heavy investment in sales promotion and advertising. Indeed, a still more serious threat impends—the synthesis of the essences that give coffee its flavor and aroma.

Increasing the Flow of Innovations to Developing Countries

The less developed economies and some advancing countries like Australia need research facilities and activities, not merely the results of research. It is not sufficient for Mexico to have an industry that consists largely of satellite plants making American products with Spanish labels. Initially these plants serve development by displacing imports and increasing Mexican employment. Eventually, however, Mexico and the other countries in the same position will try to build up their own research and innovation because they need manufactures with export potential.

Increased manufactured exports are essential for continuing development among the former economic colonies, and they are important also to the advanced countries—for instance, as substitutes for the coal Britain used to export and the cotton and other farm products the United States still disposes of abroad. Industrialization offers emancipation from reliance on commodity production and marketing, which reinforce the economic pattern based on peasants, landlords, and speculators and which yield uncertain foreign earnings. Industrialization however, even when highly integrated, requires an inflow of specialized equipment and components and therefore an outflow in payment, best provided by complementary specialized products, which are readily exportable to other countries. The United Nations *World Economic Survey* for 1961 is entirely devoted to developing and documenting this argument. Trade between Europe and the United States has reached this form and level and it is a high and mutually beneficial level that could not have been achieved by free trade. It has become possible because research and development are strong and independent in both areas.

Furthermore, there are indications that different lines of industrial development may be needed in other parts of the world from those prevailing in the United States. In Canada, the automation that is increasing American productivity is of very questionable benefit. It has not produced substantial cost reduction in industries serving the small Canadian market but it has produced mass unemployment and consequently adverse effects on the apparent productivity of industries that are working part time. In small markets with rapidly increasing populations, where the effects of mechanization are most sharply felt, research is particularly needed to find labor-intensive innovations. In a number of countries, distinctive handicrafts, organized like the cottage industries of eighteenth-century Britain, have provided exports and given people a way out of subsistence farming or fishing or unemployment. A recent example is the cultivation of artistic talent among the Eskimos and the development of an international market for their distinctive sculpture.

Governments and the informed public throughout the world have come to recognize and respect research almost to the absurd point of worship. They will not tolerate the continuation of the monopoly at present maintained by Britain, France, Germany, the Netherlands, the United States, and Switzerland.

This domination by the advanced countries may not be intentional, although the desire for power, especially military power, is a factor in the allocation of investment and in restrictions on publication of results. The trend could have resulted from the momentum acquired in their earlier industrialization, augmented by the policy of centralization adopted by most international companies.

To the outsiders, the smaller and newer countries, it looks as if they are only receiving crumbs of knowledge from the rich men's tables. They think their growth is being stunted. If they come to believe that foreign subsidiaries are a significant factor —a continuation of colonialism in a new, subtle form in which profits, power, and even knowledge are siphoned out by foreigners—nationalistic reactions can be expected. Governments may intervene for political reasons, ignoring the poor record of government efforts in industrial research and development. Governments may increase their grants for research in their own countries by national companies, financing them by increased taxes on foreign firms. Protection for foreign patents may be withdrawn. If reprisals are attempted by the foreign companies or the governments of the advanced countries, foreign subsidiaries may be nationalized by the less developed countries. The hunger for a share in economic progress will not be denied, and before it leads to negative reactions such as these, it must be recognized. The smaller countries must be allowed to share in knowledge and the pursuit of knowledge.

Myrdal has expressed the pessimistic opinion that "nations like social classes, almost never give up existing privileges except under pressure." (Myrdal, 1956, p. 267.) The interests of international companies and their parent governments now include the economic development of the many countries where they operate, and there is no obstacle, in principle, to a wider spread of research and development investment and more independence in its use. For most companies, however, it means a revolutionary change in policy, beset by immense practical difficulties.

Undue risk and expense still attend the comparatively straightforward operation of developing new products in large, advanced countries. Some large companies still prefer to buy from small, independent innovators who have been lucky. Applied research, seeking commercial applications of new basic discoveries, may take such long periods of time that it is hard to accommodate it in the financial planning of any except the most farsighted companies. Most basic research carried on within companies or through grants must in practice be written off the books, whether or not the necessity is recognized at the time of allocation. If this situation exists in the advanced countries, what reasonable basis is there for multiplying the number of places in which such expenditures are made—and probably also multiplying their amount?

The dubious record of American R & D might be adduced as an argument that private investment should be reduced and more of the field should be handed over to governments as a social responsibility like general education. But innovations continue to appear and to earn profits for companies that, by one means or another, gain access to them. Risk and enterprise are essential for western progress. Internationalization can be a means of spreading the risk and extending the enterprise. In practice, more companies will have to organize their operations to clear more time for top management to foster development— including more travel to lend their advice and encouragement in more countries. There are functions, on which top management now spends time, that can be delegated, notably finance. Even obtaining money becomes easier when a company is growing, and the surest influence for growth is development within the company itself and in the countries where it operates.

In an opinion handed down on a Sherman Act case, United States v. United Shoe Machinery, 1953, Judge Wyzanski of the District Court of Massachusetts made a comment that sums up the possibilities offered by the international expansion of research and development. He said, "industrial advance may indeed be in inverse proportion to economic power; for creativity in business, as in other areas, is best nourished by multiple centers of activity." (Quoted in Neale, 1960, p. 122.)

13

THE INFLUENCE OF ADVERTISING IN INTERNATIONAL BUSINESS

FIRMS THAT are very successful internationally have been among the leaders in the development and use of advertising. In many countries, foreign subsidiaries are the largest and shrewdest users of advertising. This business activity is associated with rapid economic development. While advertising is not necessarily a cause, economic changes do reflect alterations in human behavior—and advertising is an attempt, at least, to influence human behavior.

There is strong disagreement on how advertising works in the advanced countries and on what, if anything, it contributes to human well-being. Controversy is sharp between economic theorists and advertising practitioners and is coming to involve the public and governments. Professor Alvin Hansen of Harvard University has said that "an educated citizenry would laugh out of court a high percentage of our current advertising—a form of 'inverted education.' We are expending an immense effort to make people believe things that are not so." (Hansen, 1960, p. ix.) Businessmen who allocate most of the money spent on advertising claim profit advantage or competitive necessity, but they are not in firm agreement that the over-all effects are beneficial to the community or even to business.

Government regulation grows steadily more strict and detailed, yet public expenditures on advertising are also increasing —to attract tourists, to influence the location of new industries, to obtain public cooperation with health and safety measures. As to the magnitude of advertising expenditures, Prof. A. W. Frey has calculated that advertising has hovered closely around 2¼ per cent of the gross national product over the long period of growth in the American economy from the 1920's to the 1950's, except of course during the war years. (Frey, 1960, pp. 460-461.)

Advertising has proved to be commercially effective, as soon as the level of supply of goods or services rises above obvious shortage. The first stage of advertising is the bare announcement of the existence and availability of the product. A prototype would be an announcement by a merchant in colonial Williamsburg, Virginia, of the arrival of a shipment of manufactures from London. A surprising amount of modern advertising is still of this kind—for example, "classified" advertising and a good deal of retail store and new product advertising. Professor Hansen does not say what percentage he regards as high, but Professor Frey shows that retail and classified ads alone still absorb more than 40 per cent of current advertising expenditure in the United States. (Pp. 460-461.)

It is sometimes assumed, for the purposes of economic analysis, that the market is composed of reasonably knowledgeable people, but modern advertising is based on the realization that it is not so and furthermore that it pays to tell and retell the simplest messages. The great expansion of advertising occurred, however, when cash income was first achieved by great numbers of people with no more than primary schooling, which accounts for some of the characteristics of past advertising. Practical advertisers are currently in danger of underestimating the knowledge of the people in the market. In a number of countries, the new generations have nearly all been through secondary school, and, in the United States, the number going on to college is approaching 30 per cent. These people are obtaining much more economic information from general news services, from publications like *Consumer Reports,* through increased mobility and foreign travel, and not least by word of mouth. Television is a tremendous influence, and it appears to be educating the consumer at a pace faster than the commercial sponsors are learning.

The response to informational advertising can be a dynamic influence, particularly when there is a new product or a new market, as is frequently the case in foreign countries. Astonishing reserves of purchasing power have been tapped for quick-frozen foods in Britain, to give a recent example, and for "sneakers" among the traditionally barefoot country people of Brazil and Mexico.

How Product Information Fosters Economic Growth

Advertising is a factor in economic growth analogous to the recently discovered influence of hormones in biological growth. Just as increased income in an economy is capable of increasing employment, demand for goods and services can so powerfully affect people's behavior that it creates new purchasing power. British coal miners had an extraordinary record of absenteeism to attend funerals or dog races until their wives began to aspire to electric washing machines and, even more important in the soggy British climate, gas clothes-dryers. In British colonial days in Africa, labor resources were mobilized by the primitive method of imposing a head tax on the tribes. Unilever's United Africa Company replaced such methods by establishing the Kingsway department stores, which flaunt before the copra harvesters and cocoa planters fascinating arrays of brilliantly colored textiles, hats, shoes, bicycles, cosmetics, and patent medicines.

More recently, in a wide variety of economies, from the most advanced to the comparatively underdeveloped—and affecting an equally wide range of industries—there has been the phenomenon of television. Television has created demand for itself and for the products that support its programs. The experience in

Britain following the advent of TV advertising, and then in West Germany, reinforced the American experience, which provided from its beginning a case history in advertising and publicity. An early American TV personality, "Betty Crocker," has been associated with a transformation in American methods of food preparation, which has greatly profited her sponsor, General Mills, as well as its competitors and companies offering the same convenience principle in other types of food. Television has already hurdled the obstacle of illiteracy that restricted print advertising in areas of Latin America, and it holds the same promise for other areas. The British "telly" has been part of a social revolution in which the historic British "working classes" have engaged in a mass migration to the higher economic ground that they saw on their television screens.

One reason for the response to advertising, which has generally been complaisant or even cordial in the mass levels at which it has been aimed, is the emphasis on product standards. Although not necessarily high, they are at least uniform, and the public is certain to get the same product time after time, wherever they buy it. The pressure for standards in advertised products arises from the fact that the initial investment in creating a new customer, which is the largest cost of advertising, must also lead to repeat purchases to be economical, and repeat purchasing depends on uniformity of product. It is hard to remember in advanced economies the adulteration, substitution, and short-weighting that used to be commonplace in the market place. In the public markets in Hong Kong or Mexico City, however, the difference to the consumer between the wrapped and sealed, branded and advertised product compared with local commodities is still conspicuous.

Some advertising has also been welcomed for a reason that, while not narrowly economic, is nonetheless real. Much good advertising has been genuinely entertaining. The opposite is also true and, regardless of the importance of advertising to the economy, public rejection may result from advertising that is offensive or merely dull or too great in volume, dangers that are apparent in the United States today. Nevertheless, the original medicine show was a welcome interlude in the dull routine of pioneer life. In the years when radio advertising was pre-eminent, Jack Benny and Bob Hope made their commercials for Lucky Strike cigarettes and Pepsodent toothpaste part of the fun. Cadillac ads in the magazines brought dreamy escapist pleasure to millions. Earlier calendar pictures opened the world of art to a generation of corner-grocery shoppers. The mail order catalogue was the farm family's encyclopedia.

These considerations are still important in less developed markets—a drug company's almanac has the largest circulation of any publication in Brazil. If they are no longer as important in the advanced countries, it is because of the failure of advertising practitioners to keep up with rising standards of taste and more sophisticated demands in entertainment. Dreary similarity in advertising is commercially ineffective as well as esthetically offensive.

International Applicability
of Advertising Principles

Great results have been obtained from advertising in many otherwise dissimilar countries by following a few elementary principles. One of them is that advertising, though often considered to be a form of mass communication, conveys messages only to individuals. It may be designed for mass publication but its appeal is directed to the individual. Hence the ubiquitous use of the word "you" and its foreign equivalents. The most common human interest being self-interest, the message of most advertising emphasizes benefits known or assumed to be sought by individuals. During wars there has been considerable advertising for social purposes—campaigns to avoid waste, buy bonds, and the like—but even these campaigns have been linked to the security or survival of the individual. Commercial advertising offers benefits to prospective customers. With reference to international applications, it is particularly important to recognize that these consumer benefits are assessed by the customer, not by the supplier, the government, the church, or an independent testing laboratory. The benefits chosen often

look trivial. They are often superficial, literally the package
rather than its contents. But people consider appearances important. Advertised benefits must be recognizable and acceptable to the buyer.

Although the elements that make effective advertising have
often seemed slight or irrational or far-fetched, particularly to
the intellectual critic who is free from the problems of the
woman in the kitchen or the girl going on an important date,
new tastes can be cultivated by advertising. There is profit in
appealing to rising standards. Recordings of classical music have
become popular as have cheap editions of literary works in
Sir Allen Lane's fabulously successful Penguin editions and
their imitators. These sales trends began with elementary advertising in the form of displays and publicity, but they grew
through the use of more systematic advertising, which made
known the availability of these new benefits to masses of people
throughout wide markets.

The heart of the problem of producing an advertising message
is amorphousness of personal and social values, in both advanced
and underdeveloped , countries. How can they be measured?
What do people really want? There are so many influences—
age, sex, income, education, geographical location and environment, health, previous purchases, family responsibilities, aspirations and taboos, and of course the promises of an established
competitor. Furthermore, the time involved in planning advertising and the even longer time involved in providing the
capacity for producing increased quantities or new varieties of
goods require that people's wants should be successfully anticipated. The people themselves can offer little help because
they cannot know what they will think about a new product
that they have not seen or had an opportunity to evaluate. Even
their future intentions with respect to existing products are unreliable beyond a few months. The young man intends to buy a
car but finds himself with a baby carriage.

The successes in solving or surmounting these problems are
better known than the failures, and both are more obvious than
the reasons. A talent for anticipating the thoughts and feelings
that will prevail among people in the market appears to guide

some writers who create outstanding advertising messages. This talent may have its roots in sympathetic emotional responsiveness as demonstrated by Albert Lasker, the head of the very successful Lord & Thomas advertising agency, who demonstrated his humanitarianism by founding the Lasker Foundation for the advancement of medicine. Such an intuitive basis for successful advertising is obviously even more difficult to achieve with people of foreign cultures.

Progress is being made, however, in broadening and deepening objective knowledge of influences on people's market behavior by the use of hypotheses and methods drawn from psychology and anthropology. The director of research in the London office of the American McCann-Erickson advertising agency, Harry Henry, has described some of the results in international applications in *Motivational Research*. While this scientific alternative to the advertiser's intuition offers obvious advantages in foreign cultures, the importance of a sympathetic attitude remains high—because in advertising, as in other literary forms, the emotions of the writer toward his audience are frequently revealed involuntarily.

Selection of prospects and of means for reaching them are the most exact aspects of modern advertising. They can weed out those who are unlikely prospects because of income, age, or attitudes. They can measure the exposure provided for an advertising message on a billboard by a physical count of the passersby. A magazine page can be evaluated by the audited paid circulation, the average readership per copy, and the percentage who read any particular page. A. C. Nielsen has developed electrical recorders for radio listening and television viewing, and other services obtain ratings from telephone interviews. From figures like these, it has been possible to project some patterns of audience behavior that appear to repeat themselves. These patterns are similar in different countries, offering opportunities for advertising experts from advanced countries to apply their methods internationally.

There are hazards in the measurement of potential market coverage provided by advertising media, particularly abroad. One occurs in presuppositions as to who are prospects for buying the product. It has often happened that more people have wanted products, especially in the developing countries, than their economic superiors who plot advertising had expected. This sort of bonus has provided some of the big profits attributable to advertising in the same way that rising life expectancy has profited companies selling life insurance on old actuarial rates. The opposite is happening, however, in advanced countries, where higher income no longer provides automatic prospects for more conspicuous automobiles.

Another hazard in measuring the reach of advertising is revealed in research by E. Katz and Paul F. Lazarsfeld of Columbia University on opinion-makers. (Katz and Lazarsfeld, 1955, p. 33.) They suggest that any population is a honeycomb of small groups of as few as a half-dozen people, who recognize individual leaders for various types of behavior. The advertising that works reaches the appropriate leaders. For example, food advertising should be aimed at the best cook in the suburban women's morning coffee club, the woman who most likely tests and discusses new recipes and ingredients.

Early American television provided support for this hypothesis. The first set-owners were proved by their purchase of this strange new device to be people who ventured into new experiences. Their friends admired them and respected their reports on new TV-advertised products. Markets were tapped by pioneer TV advertisers that could not be accounted for by any statistics of possible viewers. Discovering and reaching the opinion-makers for various goods and services in some foreign cultures are formidable tasks. For example, in India where many women are in purdah, much household shopping is done for them by men.

Television automatically solves another fundamental advertising problem which is to catch attention. If the television set is being used, the commercial will be seen unless a special effort is made to avoid it, which is not the case with press advertising where the page can easily be turned. Radio commercials can be drowned in a burst of conversation or a clatter in the kitchen sink.

Advertising must break out of the hum of distractions that

people have learned to ignore while listening or reading, and it must also break into the reverie that occupies most people's minds much of the time. The arresting photograph or caption or radio sound-effect is designed for those purposes. The effects of different pictures, phrases, and sounds in gaining attention are subject to measurement and comparison, but the reasons behind the differences require deep research into individual and social psychology. The most common words in the advertising lexicon are undoubtedly "new" and "now." This fact must be a reflection of a changing society. There have been classes and communities in which the new was not synonymous with the desirable. Attention-value evidently depends ultimately on the audience rather than the medium, despite the physical advantages of television. This fact is important for advertising in foreign countries.

Symbols in International Advertising

Symbolism permeates advertising, starting with the trademark —a design or word drawn in a distinctive way that identifies most advertised products. Many commercial design-marks have been adapted from devices that already had symbolic meaning in the societies where they are used—the seal, the crown, the arrow, the cornucopia. The photograph is also a symbolic representation; even elementary showcards proved meaningless in parts of the Congo where people had not learned to recognize perspective as marking a third dimension. Most children learn this before starting school by going through picture books with their parents. Television has had the effect of revitalizing the power of visual symbols in communications (including advertising), in contrast with the spoken words required by radio.

Symbols catch attention, convey meanings, and arouse emotions. A symbol can be purely intellectual—plus, minus, and πr^2, for example—although even they may have emotional overtones for people who have difficulty with mathematics. Young children often have favorites among the letters of the alphabet. Many people have lucky numbers. Seven appears on cigarettes

and soft drinks, and the number three and triples of other
numbers are often used because of favorable associations derived from their traditional use in religious symbolism. Conventionalized palm trees appear on the packages of many products
sold in the tropics. Snow-capped mountain peaks are found on
white wine and beer labels and on talcum powder sold in India.
Conventionalized flowers have symbolic meaning and influence,
from Swiss edelweis to the lotus of India and Indonesia. The
abstractions of Moslem design have a counterpart in the en-
graving of banknotes, which is still sufficiently important sym-
bolically to appear on coupons and trading stamps in the United
States.

Pictures do most of the symbolic representation in modern
advertising, especially since the perfection of color photography
and color printing. There are sex pictures, prosperity pictures,
and social-situation pictures. The uniform of the professional
nurse, worn by a pretty model, is a common symbol in advertising pictures, although it has been officially ruled out as misleading in some countries. The white laboratory coat and the
microscope are new symbols of science and progress. Modern
functional architecture in houses and furnishings and spacious
and expensive landscaping are often used as settings for advertised products. They attract attention and convey suggestions
of the social standing a great many people desire. Automobile
advertisers have worked hard to capitalize the symbolic value
their products have acquired—Cadillac and Rolls-Royce in particular. The neatest example is Jaguar, whose name, emblem,
body-lines, and concept of performance are all integrated. Even
its muffler has been adapted so that instead of eliminating
sound it releases a growl that strengthens the brand image.

The influence of symbols on the emotions has long been
understood by priests and artists. New efforts to increase knowledge of symbolism are being made today in psychology, and
new efforts to use symbolism are being made in advertising. A
symbol may be merely a device to telegraph information, or it
may be intended to exert influence through the emotions. Are
advertisers morally justified, or politically wise, in trying to use
people's emotions to sway their judgment? This aspect of adver-

tising is highly controversial. It is a separate question and a more subtle one than that raised by the common use of false logic to persuade, toward which most current criticism is directed but which can be detected and prohibited. Criticism has continued to build up, despite the reforms that have eliminated the lies and deception of the patent medicine era, and it appears to come from suspicion that people's emotions are being manipulated without their knowledge for commercial advantage.

In advanced countries, the free expression of rational criticism serves as a check on emotional advertising. This expression is provided not by young, susceptible media like radio and television but by the newspapers, which have traditions of free criticism going back to John Wilkes. The position in emerging nations is not so well safeguarded. Excesses are committed, however, by local imitators more often than by foreign subsidiaries. There has been no Western patent medicine in recent years that has claimed the cure-all and rejuvenating powers of the famous "Tiger Balm" of Hong Kong.

The Economic Consequences of Advertising

There are many ways to lose money in advertising. The first Lord Leverhulme once observed that one-half of his advertising was wasted, but he did not know which half. A sure way to lose money in advertising is to stop too soon. The high proportion of new-product failures in recent years may be related to the new theory of a launching barrage of advertising that can be cut back after six months or a year. On the contrary, success requires the budgeting of advertising as a permanent and increasing cost, to be paid by savings from volume production. There are two reasons why. One is the time-lag in changing human habits. It is necessary to stir people over and over before they will act—and to remind them again and again before they will form new habits, even when they have the best intentions and the strongest desires.

The other obvious reason is that a market, like Heraclitus's stream, is never the same. People are leaving it, and new people

are entering it all the time. The message has to be repeated for
the newcomers. The largest continuing source of new entrants
into a market is, of course, young people growing up. They
create a special need for constant revision of the form and
language of the advertising message to ensure that it does not
become dated.

The way continuity affects the results of advertising is very
important in making a foreign subsidiary a better means of
supplying a foreign market than exports. Assured continuity
of product supply is required to reap the cumulative benefits
of continuity in advertising. Exports require larger stocks in
depots abroad and in transit to offset the uncertainties of
weather, seasons, shipping, and endemic dock strikes. Other
hazards include import and foreign exchange restrictions. It is
no accident that foreign manufacturing and advertising are
associated.

The economic effects of advertising are seldom analyzed
dispassionately. The commercial interests involved are substantial and vocal—it is their business to be. Any question about
the economic soundness of current vast expenditures on advertising is met with a harangue about freedom of choice and the
economic basis of a free press from the plush offices of the
advertising agencies. This attitude provokes a reaction, prevalent in the comparatively austere rooms where academic economists teach and write, that advertising is economic waste, an
extra cost passed on to the consumer, and, worse still, an
interference with the free action of price competition and therefore monopolistic in its tendencies. Behind these criticisms is a
genuine and growing fear that sinister psychological forces are
conditioning for private profit not only people's judgment but
also their sense of values and even their moral code.

Informative advertising makes the same kind of contribution
to economic value as do physical distribution services. This
contribution is most evident and significant in connection with
innovation. Economic growth receives impetus from the rapid
dissemination of information among consumers, as well as from
the increase and spread of production know-how. A large market
for a new product, if it can be quickly tapped, makes large-

scale production and blanket distribution possible. Very large savings can be made, which are usually shared between profits and the consumer, the latter receiving lower prices or better values.

At the same time, the effects of advertising can be strongly monopolistic. Advertising emphasizes the originality, distinctiveness, and exclusiveness of a product. The traditional copyline was "accept no substitutes." This message, if successful, interferes with pure price competition. Professor Hansen has said that "the competitive struggle runs not in terms of price . . . but in terms of dubious advertising techniques designed to attract customers to a brand-name." (Hansen, 1960, p. 77.)

Advertising has effects similar to those of exclusive patents. But the influence of exclusive patents was considered so economically restrictive by the United States Supreme Court that, by its ruling on the Ethyl gasoline additive case, it compelled patent owners who licensed anyone to use their rights to extend their licenses to all applicants willing to pay for their use. This decision has had an odd consequence: It has enabled one oil company to use as its advertising slogan the claim that nobody can make a better gasoline. A company that has gained the initiative in advertising and built up habitual buying habits in its market is almost impossible to overtake if it uses its rights to obtain all worthwhile new product improvements offered to its industry. American compulsory licensing of patents has actually strengthened the position of the leading advertisers by making all technical product improvements open to them if they are granted to any company beside that one which originated them.

In large, advanced countries, the monopolistic influence of advertising is checked to some extent by distributors' brands, which are products sold by department stores and more recently by drug chains and grocery supermarkets under their own names and guarantees, rather than those of the manufacturers. This restraint does not exist, however, in smaller markets.

Actually, the monopolistic effects of advertising can go even farther in practice than standard theory recognizes, particularly in the less advanced countries. A company that has become a leader in advertising has two advantages, its monopoly profits and its superior knowledge and skill in advertising. Such companies are now actively diversifying. That is a euphemism for buying up less efficient firms in other lines of business where the new methods can be applied. Within the United States this situation has come to the attention of the Federal Trade Commission. The advertising trade journal *Printer's Ink* has reported that "in the matter of Procter & Gamble being ordered by the FTC to divest itself of Clorox, P & G's marketing skills were emphasized as contributing heavily to FTC's decision to make its demand on the company." And among advertising men, "there is uneasiness over the possibility that aggressive marketing practices, successfully applied, eventually may invite antitrust difficulties." *(Printer's Ink,* January 6, 1961, p. 16.)

International Advertising

Advertising by international firms outside their home countries raises some ticklish questions. The facts are fairly clear. International firms are the largest advertisers in many countries, although figures on advertising expenditures are not published in other countries as they are in the United States. In 1960, the J. Walter Thompson agency had thirty-six foreign offices in twenty-two countries, serving its important list of international firms, as well as some native companies. Thompson is the largest agency in the world in volume of advertising placed. For several years it has had larger billings in Britain, for example, than any British agency. The president of J. Walter Thompson has disclosed that "the five largest American advertising agencies operating in the international field handled a total volume of more than $304,000,000 of advertising outside this country [the United States] in 1960." (Strouse, 1961, p. 87.)

In the list of network sponsors published for 1960-61 by the Canadian Broadcasting Corporation, fifty-four out of sixty-three —86 per cent were foreign-controlled. In Mexico, Colgate is such a large user of radio and television that competitors find it very difficult to buy nonadjacent time. The Procter & Gamble subsidiary in Britain is one of the three largest TV advertisers. The foreign editions of *Time, Life,* and *Reader's Digest* have been made viable by international advertisers. *Reader's Digest* has advertised itself by stating that "Standard Brands, one of America's most successful international marketers, has increased its business overseas every year since forming its international company in 1947. It markets in more than one hundred countries, uses *Reader's Digest* editions in Canada, Latin America, Europe and Africa." (Advertisement by *Reader's Digest* in *Printer's Ink,* May 26, 1961.) Linkage effects are manifest in the further statement by Norman Strouse of J Walter Thompson that "*Reader's Digest*, published in 27 separate editions, and 13 languages, now has a circulation of 9,000,000 outside the United States." (Strouse, p. 87.)

Unilever established its own advertising agency long before the Second World War, with branches in many countries although not in the United States. It obtains extra profits, or advertising at lower cost, from the commissions allowed by advertising media on its huge international volume. It also ensures quality in countries were local services are not first-class. These instances of international advertising are mere straws in a strong wind.

The subsidiaries of foreign companies are the leading advertisers in many countries, for a combination of reasons. They often introduce new products to compete with the traditional products of native firms, and they have therefore more information to spread in the market and more profit to gain. Their accounting figures are better, and they can therefore measure the results of advertising and can take controlled risks by budgeting for advertising to be paid for out of increased sales. They have more expert knowledge in the preparation and placing of advertising.

Last but not least, international firms enjoy the efficiency and economy of tested advertising themes and forms of presentation. Benefits to the family, for example, are obviously of wide interest, and a company that has a distinctive family appeal for its product can use it widely. Colgate toothpaste can be advertised anywhere with confidence that "bad breath" is common and offensive and that a picture of a pretty girl and a virile boy who are not attracted to each other will catch attention and dramatize the problem. Of course, not all such tested themes have this universal application; Pepsodent's promise of white teeth, for example, is inappropriate in the betel-chewing regions of Southeast Asia where black teeth carry prestige.

Some successful international firms have gone so far as to adopt explicitly a policy of trying their tested advertising formulas wherever the market and other conditions look attractive, but of withdrawing and going elsewhere if the advertising fails, rather than incurring the hazards and expense of attempting to develop special campaigns. Originally, advertising was even manufactured centrally. Display material was printed, and matrices of press advertisements were made up and shipped out with the same artwork but in a great variety of languages. This procedure is still followed for small markets like Cyprus and Malta, Haiti and Santo Domingo. American artwork continues to be used for many advertisements in foreign publications, and American filmed TV commercials are duplicated for use abroad, with "voice over" in native languages, despite high customs tariffs on the full production costs. This system pays because the research, market testing, and creativity that go into the making of an outstanding advertisement are not traceable by customs valuators. These influences on the quality of advertising are applicable even where, as in Venezuela, the law requires that commercials must be remade with TV actors who are local citizens.

There are other special advantages that firms derive from advertising in the less developed countries. The pulling power of modern advertising is greater for the international firm abroad than it is at home, provided that the technical problems of language and symbolism are solved. It is common knowledge that brand loyalty is higher at lower levels of income and education within countries, as well as among nations. Coca-Cola, Colgate, Gillette, Heinz, and other heavy advertisers enjoy larger shares of the market and higher margins of profit in the less developed than in the more advanced countries.

Some of these results may be attributable to consumers'

childlike credulity. The outstanding reasons are, however, that the international firms make worthwhile and dependable promises, as few of their national competitors do. Their products are uniform—providing full weight, size, and number—and often in factory-sealed packages. Goods with accidental defects are replaced without charge. Products are often sold at prices that are published and policed by the manufacturer—which can be a protection for consumers in countries where trading consists of primitive haggling. There is more efficiency and less waste than in the advertising of native firms, whose efforts are apt to be fruitless because they are haphazard. The amateurs scatter their money over too many media, trying to use a little of everything, from billboards to television, and they also advertise in fits and starts. Imitating the big international companies without understanding does indeed produce advertising that is economic waste.

A limitation on the competitive efficiency of the advertising methods of large international firms occurs, however, in their internal organization. This limitation can be viewed as one problem of the scale of operations in smaller markets. The home market organization, like a centralized international organization, can be too complicated and cumbersome. In smaller markets it is necessary to concentrate on the bare essentials. Specialized services, like advertising audience measurement, and other frills, are unobtainable or too expensive. One man has to handle several jobs, buying printing as well as radio and TV time, working on budgets in the morning and adapting a piece of copy in a foreign language in the afternoon. Training and advancement via highly specialized departments in large companies do not provide this versatility.

Superficially, trainee schemes that circulate bright young men through several departments answer this problem by providing men who have a broad familiarity with the higher management levels of large businesses. But in fact these men are often carried upward on the shoulders of experienced professionals in each of these specialties. They do not acquire the competence to do various jobs by themselves that is required in the smaller foreign markets. Here is another reason for using personnel from branch operations, rather than sending people out from home companies, provided, however, that there is training in principles by an expert advisory staff.

The dynamic influence of advertising extends beyond the direct interests of the companies using it to include the fostering of development in backward areas. It facilitates the establishment of full-scale new industries, especially secondary manufacturing of modern consumer products. The advertising industry itself supports skilled labor and the professions, even the arts. It emancipates newspapers and other media from financial dependence on political handouts. The financial dependence of the communications media on advertising may have other effects of course, for example on public taste. Further evolution in recognition of weaknesses and criticism must be expected. The present stage is, however, a clear advance over the politically subsidized and suborned journalism of prewar France and over Goebbels' Nazi propaganda machine. The forward trend may be the mixed system represented by BBC and ATV in Britain, the public and private networks in Australia, and the part commercial, part subsidized CBC in Canada.

Restraining the Monopolistic Impact of International Advertising

The power of advertising to augment profits is great, in underdeveloped as well as in advanced countries, but in the latter it is increasingly regulated. Maximization of profits is the cardinal principle in the economics of the firm in a free enterprise system, wherever it operates. This principle means that the firm can, should, and must use all means that are within the law to increase its profits.

American law has regulated business conduct with the intention of maintaining competition. Myrdal has noted that "legislation was important . . . and has become increasingly so, as a means of laying down conditions for the individual's competition and cooperation within society. In earlier times . . . legislation often served the purpose of abolishing restrictive mores or institutional structures and of enforcing competition . . . but legislation has increasingly become a means for organizing competition and cooperation in a special way, which was felt to be in the common interest." (Myrdal, 1956, p. 24.) The great example has, of course, been the Sherman Act.

Some other countries have antitrust legislation, but few of them have spelled out its application to advertising with American exactitude. Despite the vagueness of foreign law, companies must consider their profits in the long run, and that is where the monopolistic tendency of modern advertising may hurt them by stimulating action by the power of the national state. More countries may follow not only the principles of United States law but also its specific applications to advertising. It is not in the long-run interest of the international firm to press its advantages monopolistically. It would be more profitable to share patents and superior know-how in market research and advertising than to incur discriminatory taxation or, in the extreme case, nationalization.

Both national governments and international firms are becoming concerned, from opposite points of view, about possible controls over the power of advertising. What can governments do to regulate advertising constructively? How serious are the dangers to companies and what must they do to avoid them?

Governments can stiffen antimonopoly legislation. They can find all the examples they need in the United States. Without, however, going to the American extreme of government interference, which few other countries are even considering as yet in the case of advertising, the danger of foreign domination can be greatly reduced by the simple and unexceptionable device of publicity. When public and government became alarmed over the prices of drugs in Canada, which were on the average 11 per cent higher than in the United States and which many people attributed to American, British, and Swiss control of the market through the use of patents and promotional skill, two official inquiries conducted public hearings on the subject. Prices came down. In Britain the Pilkington Royal Commission has held public hearings on the quality of commercial television and issued an adverse report that has stalled the establishment of more commercial networks. An example to the world in the use of public information to prevent abuses of economic processes and institutions is, of course, the system of hearings by committees of the United States Senate.

Profits do not have to be made by stealth in any part of the world. The glare of publicity in which the American automobile industry profitably operates reveals consumer preferences, consumer buying intentions, brand shares of market, and detailed advertising expenditures, as well as sales, investments, and profits. Similar disclosures in many other industries and other countries are both feasible and desirable.

14

STATE TRADING

INTERNATIONAL economic relations have not been left entirely to private enterprise at any time in history by any country of consequence. Long after internal trade has been liberated, foreign trade has often remained in the hands of government-designated monopolies or under close government supervision. Nineteenth-century Britain was an exception. Tariffs, subsidies, and quotas are now used by all governments in free-enterprise countries to control and direct imports and exports. They also sharply influence international finance. This appeared to be beyond the control of national governments while it was governed by the international gold standard and therefore by the Bank of England. Subsequent deliberate currency management by national banks—including the fixing and supporting of interest and exchange rates—has helped to restore and increase control by national governments.

The production of munitions has engaged European governments for centuries. From the Royal Arsenals in England, for example, friends and allies have been supplied with arms, in war and in peace, at prices based on considerations other than cost. A large part of Soviet export trade is obviously of this political character although figures are naturally not available. Recipients include Syria, Egypt, and India, as well as Cuba and the older satellites. This type of trade does not lead to the construction of branch plants that could leak military secrets.

Governments have also invested in a wide variety of industries for strategic purposes. Prime Minister Disraeli put the government of nineteenth-century, free-enterprise Britain into foreign business by buying a controlling interest in the Suez Canal Company. His purpose was to protect the short sea route from Britain to India for trade and defense. Later British governments bought into oil lands to ensure supplies for the British navy. The American government operated a mixed economic system in wartime, subsequently returning most of the munitions plants to private ownership but retaining the Atomic Energy Commission and its plants and properties.

Government participation has been extended to include natural resources, utilities, and foreign trade. The electric power industry of the United States is under mixed control, the Tennessee Valley Authority, for example, being a government enterprise. Many countries, from Argentina to Switzerland, run their railways as state enterprises. The United States subsidizes its merchant marine. The French government is involved in international business through ownership and operation of its merchant marine, and the British government through British European Airways and British Overseas Airways Corporation. During the war and the ensuing reign of the Labour government, official British purchasing missions arranged contracts for the importation of such foods as Argentine beef. The quantity and quality of Australian food exports to Britain are supervised by an Australian government body. German Volkswagen grew into the largest enterprise in that country with a very large foreign business under state ownership. (*Fortune*, August, 1962, p. 116.) Shares were not sold to private investors until 1961.

Most western governments now insure their exporters against political and currency risks. The United States buys agricultural surpluses and sells them abroad. The government appointed and financed British Broadcasting Corporation sells films and tapes for TV, cinema, and radio in foreign markets. It is hard to find any line of business in which private enterprise is entirely free of competition from one government or another.

In the large part of the world incorporated into the modern

Communist bloc, all trade and investment, at home and abroad, are entirely state controlled, directed and operated. This complete nationalization is an essential difference between the communist system and western mixed systems. While the physical foreign trade of the Soviets is marginal, the percentage increases in the 1950's were large, and the Russians have also made some substantial foreign investments—in India, Egypt, Tunisia, and Cuba, for example. Does this rise portend an important new factor in international business?

To view the foreign trade of Russia and other Communist countries in proportion, it is also necessary to examine the degrees to which free or private and state enterprises are intermixed in western economic organization. Some private corporations like the foundations are nonprofit organizations. Some state corporations use business accounting and endeavor to charge prices that will cover their costs, including interest and capital, and to earn profits.

On the other side, the Communists also now use "business accounting," which involves pricing to include planned profits and even allows extra profits as incentives to be shared among managers and staff. These Russian profits are still too restricted, however, to be comparable to capitalist profits, although Soviet Prof. Y. G. Lieberman made proposals in the fall of 1962, which, if adopted, would give more authority to plant managers, including more freedom in pricing and thus more opportunity to make profits. (Olsen, *The New York Times*, October 20, 1962, p. 4.) Meanwhile, the planned profit margins of communist production and distribution organizations are set by the state and may be altered to suit economic or political purposes, including sales abroad.

Exceptions are also increasing, however, in western economies. Railways and international shipping lines, like roads and schools, are increasingly recognized as social and strategic services that a country can better pay for from charges against the general income of the country—by tax-financed subsidies—than from charges against the immediate users. This principle applies also to other subsidized activities, notably agriculture, in the United States and Europe.

There was an extreme application of state participation in

international business by the postwar government of Britain, which was socialistic but decidedly not communistic. In the interests of employment and wages, the large-scale purchase of food and raw materials was controlled to favor British industry, at the expense of the suppliers. In the case of Iranian oil, increased profits on the final product were held in the wholly British refining and distributing companies, not passed down to the producing company, which was owned jointly with Iran. In the case of African cocoa, a British appointed marketing board reserved part of the profits instead of distributing them immediately to the producers. The argument was that postwar prices were unusually high and that the board's reserves could be used to stabilize producers' incomes in later years. The reserves were held, however, in sterling, which—under Socialist policies of full employment, with increasing wages and welfare for the people of Britain—was rapidly depreciating in purchasing power. The real price obtained by the Africans was thus reduced. These examples provide illustrations of direct use of power by the state in international business.

Legal and Political Complications

The direct participation of governments in international business—as buyers, sellers, and investors—has known domestic effects and at least two important international ones. At home, there is a familiar complaint that government in business is inefficient or, when it is efficient, that it constitutes unfair competition. The basis of this two-edged complaint is that the state trades on a different basis from that of a business firm. It may conceal or exclude some costs, particularly the enterprise-inducing cost of providing profits. The state's size is an advantage in successful operations but it becomes a disadvantage when it is weighted by bureaucracy. The state also has certain legal advantages—it makes the law.

In the international field, a common complaint about trading with Russia is that commercial disputes are disputes with government departments and must be taken for arbitration and adjudication to the government with which one is disputing. This illustrates one of the additional complications that arise when state trading extends internationally. Each state is sovereign in its own territory. It cannot operate as a state within another country, unless the sovereignty of that country is compromised. But the branch of a Soviet government department that builds a steel mill in India is subject to the Indian government while in India. Any permanent operation by a government within the territory of other governments must be organized in the form of a private corporation like the British Overseas Airways Corporation and Amtorg, the Soviet trading agency in the United States.

The other complication that cannot be avoided when states endeavor to carry on economic activities across the frontiers of other countries is that of involvement in political activity. Although organized as a nonpolitical business firm, the state trading entity must serve over all national policy—which includes political activities, as well as procuring materials, disposing of surpluses, and pursuing other economic advantages. When a government enters foreign trade, its guiding policy is that of the state rather than a commercial firm. Control by any country's government of a significant proportion of the business now carried on by foreign subsidiaries of its own companies would challenge the independent sovereignty of the other countries.

This problem is a major one for socialist governments in countries like Britain, which has become dependent on invisible exports, which are the profit remittances from foreign subsidiaries of companies like Dunlop, Imperial Chemicals, Shell Oil, and Unilever. The problem was recognized but not necessarily solved by the British Labour Party's eventual change of policy, to allow for the acquisition of a majority stock in a company as an alternative to outright nationalization. Extension of government control of the parent companies in Britain, in any form, however, would seem likely to cause other governments to insure their sovereignty by using nationalization to increase their control over foreign subsidiaries.

The distinction drawn here between international companies whose shares are held by private individuals, who may be citizens of various countries, and those that are government-controlled, may seem a fine distinction, since private companies cannot anyway carry on operations that conflict with policies of the government of the parent country—trade with Cuba, for instance. Governments can also press parent companies to use their foreign subsidiaries as instruments of national policy, by disseminating, for instance, American, British, or Dutch propaganda. Privately-owned companies are in a better position than government-controlled corporations to confine themselves to commercial activities. Furthermore, private companies appear to offer a comparatively easy means of achieving more truly international ownership and policies than organizations controlled by single states.

Soviet Barter

State trading is most commonly associated with the communist countries because government bodies handle all their imports and exports and foreign investment. There is the question, however, of whether or not communist foreign economic activity adds up to any more in money value than the international trade conducted directly by western governments and their agencies—including transport, insurance, and marketing of commodities like wheat and wool. If government-to-government grants and loans are added, as a form of foreign investment, the direct international business of western governments far exceeds that of the communist countries.

Differences in form attract attention to the trade of communist countries. These differences are also severe limitations on the possibilities for growth of communist participation in international business. Physical trade by the Communist Bloc with the rest of the world has been discouraged by several circumstances. They include the fact that territorial Russia was originally self-sufficient in a great variety of commodities; the nature of economic planning, which requires assured long-term supply and demand; the Russian desire for maximum self-sufficiency; and western restrictions on sale to Russia of strategic products. The satellites have been largely absorbed into the Russian trading system. They have been encouraged and assisted to build industries of their own on the base provided by their own material resources, supplemented only by materials from other communist countries. The apparently temporary Yugoslavian deviation seems related to difficulties arising from a western-oriented trading pattern. Russian foreign commerce has been chiefly directed toward obtaining products like natural rubber and industrial diamonds, which have been scarce or unobtainable internally, and to the products of the engineering industry. This latter demand has dwindled to the point of interest mainly in prototype products that can be copied to help advance the quality of their own industry.

Barter has served these communist purposes adequately in most situations. Barter has, however, disturbed international markets and created a fear that the communist group could upset the whole international business system. Barter is, however, an indication of the restricted interest of the communists in purely economic international activities, and it is severely limited in its potential. A specific deal with the supplier of the particular items needed—for example Russian timber in exchange for British engineering products—is much simpler to arrange than complicated agreements for multilateral trade and convertible currency. Much communist trade continues to involve barter, a recent example being the exchange of Cuban sugar for Russian and Czechoslovakian machinery and munitions. Russian exports were at first mainly commodities—timber, furs, gold, and even wheat, despite scarcities—since they were the only Russian products available for which there were open markets. There have also been substantial oil exports, even though prices were already soft when they began. Russian engineering has reached the point of providing heavy industrial plant and contracting for construction, notably the Bhilai steel complex in India, but trade is still bilateral.

Barter looks attractive to some countries that are outside the Communist Bloc, especially when they have surpluses of commodities. Barter appears to avoid both the profits of middlemen and their frequent inability to bring supply and demand together, especially in relation to the commodities and the manpower of the underdeveloped countries. The Soviet supply of goods has proved to be a problem. J. S. Berliner has reported that Burma "was unable to find a sufficient volume of Soviet goods of acceptable quality at reasonable prices to equal the value of the rice already shipped. As a result, Burma became an unwilling creditor to the Bloc by an amount estimated at $11 million toward the end of 1956." (Berliner, 1958, p. 82.) As long as the communist countries continue to plan only on the basis of internal resources, there will be no great scope for increased sales of any variety of their products abroad, or even for absorption of the commodity surpluses of other countries.

The offers of oil, tin, aluminum, and timber made by Russia and other communist countries in foreign trade have been priced to sell. State trading organizations handling the business have not been required to recover their costs plus profits if high prices stood in the way of obtaining the western products or currencies specifically required in communist economic or political plans. Russia and other members of the bloc have entered international business in another way, with purposes that are not so obvious. They have begun to make what looks like a form of foreign investment. This investment consists of long-term credits made mostly on a government-to-government basis at low interest rates and payable in the borrower's currency or products. It is not unlike equity financing. Such credits are mainly for construction of heavy industrial plant like cement works, steel mills, truck factories, and electric power stations.

Russian credits can look attractive to some noncommunist countries, as can the barter deals already mentioned. The means of industrialization are as desirable to the Indonesians, for example, when they come from Russia as when they come from private enterprise in Europe or the United States. In one respect, they look more desirable. Berliner remarks that "industrial establishments constructed under the Soviet aid program become the property of the recipient country. This contrasts sharply with foreign private direct investment, in which foreign companies construct plants and then continue to own and operate them for profit." (P. 164.) This political consideration for the recipients should not be underestimated. Coupled with the desire for industrialization is the fear that it is available only with hidden conditions that perpetuate economic colonialism. The readiness, indeed the eagerness, of the Russians to train in Russia the staffs for the plants they build abroad is looked upon as readiness to share know-how rather than as a means of political indoctrination.

The attractiveness of Russian credits to some countries is powerful because, as Professor Myrdal has pointed out, "this other type of economic organization—the Soviet type—presents itself as fundamentally a system for the development of underdeveloped nations." (Myrdal, 1956, p. 144.) The desire for independent development favors consideration of Soviet credits toward the purchase of industrial plant and equipment, and so do the apparently easy terms. The Russian example is the positive factor, suspicion of business imperialism the negative factor.

Russia has enjoyed rapid economic growth under a system of complete state enterprise. Professor Hansen states that "in the United States the trend rate of real income, that is, of Gross National Product at constant prices, compounded per annum, has been around three per cent during the last three decades. . . . The Russian GNP growth rate in real terms has been around seven per cent." (Hansen, 1960, p. 43.) The Russians achieved these results by themselves without foreign loans or foreign interference. It is easy to overlook the facts that in Russia the starting point was low, the resources were plentiful, and there was a backlog of innovations to maintain consumer demand similar to the one noted in connection with recent rapid growth in the European Common Market.

State Trading, International Enterprise, and Innovation

The growth that the underdeveloped countries seek and acceptance of Russian investment appears to offer is produced by a marriage of resources with technology. The centrally-controlled communist economies have been able to increase sharply their investment in the expansion of their productive capacity, by forcing up the proportion of their internal income devoted to capital formation. This policy increases gross national product, as long as there is unsatisfied demand for existing products and/or available technology for improved methods or improved products.

A stage can be reached, however, when more wheat production can be added to gross national product only by government purchase for storage, as in the United States, and when increased production of textiles makes diminishing contributions to the economy, as is happening in more and more countries.

The rate of growth was found to be affected as much by the innovational quality of investment as by its quantity in a recent study of Britain and several European countries made for the Organization for Economic Cooperation and Development. (Williams, 1962, p. X 2.) The significance of these several points mentioned for the developing countries is, first, that the communist method of obtaining growth involves more control over the disposition of income between saving and consumption than these other countries may be able or willing to enforce; and, second, that innovations provided by the importation of technology from Russia are still quite limited in their range. Specifically, cement and steel and locomotives represent industrialization, but they do not constitute a sufficient basis for the economic integration that many countries are seeking. Integration requires consumer goods, in which the Russians are still backward, and ultimately it requires continuous innovation, which no country can claim to have mastered but for which the Soviets are still dependent on the West. Rare exceptions, as in the field of rocketry, are achieved at great cost.

Soviet industry still lacks both adaptability and diversification, and, in the judgment of some experts, its organization has tended to inhibit innovation (Nove, 1961, p. 171). A great impression has been made by the contrast between the land of the muzhiks of fifty years ago and today's nation of the sputniks. The over-all Russian economic growth rate quoted by Professor Hansen is lower than that given by the United Nations for Japan, Israel, Venezuela, and West Germany.

The contribution to growth offered by communist investment in foreign countries may prove to be transitory. The innovation that communist countries have been able to generate up to now is not broad enough to afford a continuous flow to a wide variety of other countries. In the short run, the Soviet practice of building a plant, especially in heavy industry, training local workers and management in a framework of Russian economic planning, and then abandoning the project is even more limiting than colonialism. This Soviet type of investment is particularly weak in marketing, which is vital in any progressive economic integration. Even a cement plant profits from steady operation maintained by study of the needs and opportunities of its customers.

State export-import and investment activities have the same limitations, whether Russian, British, or American. They are more open to influence by national political considerations than is private investment and more likely to stir conflicts of sovereignty, already one of the most serious obstacles to the international spread of know-how for economic development. State investment, abroad or at home, has some advantages in industries where quantity and kinds of demand are known for a long time ahead. State operation is not conducive, however, judging from experience to date (including Russia's), to the originality and adaptability that are essential to integrated industrialization and development.

15

ECONOMIC DEVELOPMENT

AND NATIONAL INTEGRATION

PRACTICALLY everybody everywhere wants more economic development. People born in prospering families, communities, and countries recognize today that their islands of development are threatened by economic stagnation in the seas of population surrounding them. These seas are rising. Yet the only real development is that which increases output and consequently income *per capita*.

It is worth reiterating the principle that business and economics have to do with people and that figures derive their meanings entirely from ultimate benefits to individuals. This principle has a specific application that cannot be evaded. An adequate economic organization provides full employment. If private enterprise forms a large part of that organization, employment is the responsibility of business. Production of wealth without maintenance of full employment is socially and politically unacceptable. It is also bad business. Firms that trace the courses of their products to the ultimate consumers know it well. Customers are the aggregation of employees. Furthermore, the potential consumers are not limited to particular races or nationalities. The main limitation on potential consumption is the level of purchasing power, which can be raised.

214

Advanced countries require continuing development for their own citizens and to maintain seedbeds of ideas for the whole world. Backward areas cry for rescue from stagnation and from worsening living conditions caused by rising birth rates coupled with declining death rates. Some intermediate countries that were underdeveloped until recently now appear to have achieved a "take-off" that will enable them to continue developing on their own power—without the terrible sacrifices exacted by the communist system. This achievement has given rise to great expectations throughout the free world. Unfortunately, there have also been negative economic reactions, sometimes in countries that seemed most promising.

The concept of development includes an implied qualification that it must be continuing and practically continuous. Lurching, staggering progress imposes costs on business and individuals that nullify many of the benefits. It brings unemployment and interference with the smooth running of economic machinery to which so much effort is now directed. In practical business operations, continuous flow production has widely displaced batch production—with resulting great increases in output and reductions in costs. In other cases, the same effects have been obtained by use of computer technology to achieve sequential batch production. Channels of distribution have also been streamlined. Efforts have been made and some success has been achieved, within national economies, in adapting the flow of money to the need for continuity. Purchasing power is stabilized by welfare payments. A large amount of saving is automatic and some is compulsory, pension contributions, for example. Public investment is used to fill gaps between actual private investment and the level of investment necessary to maintain full employment of people and other productive resources.

Periodic maladjustments still occur. In advanced countries like the United States or in regional blocs like the European Economic Community, which are large enough to be relatively self-contained—and even in the sterling area—corrections are made quickly and effectively, and automatic stabilizers like unemployment benefits and agricultural support ensure that the adjustments necessary will be relatively minor. Unemployment, the

crucial indicator, has been kept well below 3 per cent in Britain
for most of the postwar period and similarly low in Europe
since the formation of the Common Market. The American rate
was also low until the late 1950's. Budgetary deficits incurred
in maintaining domestic levels of purchasing power in support
of employment have put the British pound under outside pressure at frequent intervals, and the American dollar weakened
in 1960, but the reasons in both cases included heavy defence
and foreign aid expenditures. Exports of the advanced countries remained strong, even those of Britain, which in addition
to other causes of exchange crises, faced a runaway tendency
of imports whenever restrictions were relaxed.

Business cycles continue to have severe repercussions on countries that depend on trade in commodities on world markets.
The economic disturbances in these countries are far deeper
than anything that has happened in the United States since the
early 1930's. The position of exporters of coffee, wheat, cotton,
wool, oil, metal ores, forest products, and so forth has already
been discussed.

The countries in recent difficulties include not only a number
of the underdeveloped countries but also others that previously seemed to be making substantial, self-sustaining progress.
Export prices have contributed to the difficulties into which certain of these once rapidly developing countries have been sliding
since about 1958. Countries like Argentina, Canada, South
Africa, and Venezuela were trying, however, to emancipate
themselves from economic colonialism and were widely considered to have passed the worst difficulties of the "take-off." This
failure of former economic colonies to grow, after promising
initial increases in size and variety of output, represents a challenge to theories of economic development. It is also very expensive to international business, which is deeply involved.

What was wrong with the industrialization of these countries
and with their built-in stabilizers? Did they simply use up their
international credit by climbing too fast, or were there struc-
tural faults in their growth plans? These questions are quite
different from the familiar questions about countries where
there has long been no growth or only slow growth. They in-

volve what might be described as "overdevelopment" in contrast to the problems associated with "underdevelopment."

For a dozen years after World War II two currencies were even stronger than the American dollar: the Venezuelan bolivar and the Canadian dollar. Recently, they not only have lost their premiums but also have been devalued. There has been political unrest in both Venezuela and Canada. In the former, there have been riots and attempted revolutions. Canadians have protested at the polls. In 1957, they turned out the moderate Liberals who had governed, except for five years, since 1921, in favor of the slightly more nationalistic but equally pro-business Conservatives. In 1962, Canadian voters protested against both the old parties, reversing traditional positions in both English Canada and French Quebec, in the latter giving a maverick group carrying the label "Social Credit" enough members of Parliament to hold the balance of power. The election of 1963 also failed to give any party a clear mandate.

Both devaluation and political instability are anathema to foreign investors. In both Venezuela and Canada, foreign control of industry is exceptionally high. Distrust between the people of these countries and international business firms has already caused great mutual losses.

Argentina and South Africa offer additional examples of relapses in apparently developing countries. Despite peculiar local conditions, these countries had given good indications of growth, although only briefly in the former—between the overthrow of Péron and the economic and political disturbances of 1960 and 1961.

Canada: a Test Case
for International Enterprise

Direct foreign investment has reached a peak, or an extreme, in Canada. More American foreign investments are located there than in any other single country or the whole of South America— one-third of the American total before the Canadian devaluation of 1962. There are also important British and European subsidiaries. American companies entered Canada sooner than they ventured into most other countries—du Pont, for example, has been there since 1876. Foreign firms control more than 50 per cent of oil, mining and smelting, and manufacturing industries of all kinds, thereby wielding power over the whole economy. The combination of natural resources and foreign development had produced in Canada a per capita income that, at its peak, was the highest in the world after that of the United States. It is unthinkable that Canada could react as Cuba did, following the cessation of economic growth there, and as other nations have threatened. Thus Canada offers an opportunity for dispassionate laboratory investigations on the effects of direct foreign investment, which may yield knowledge of great importance for future profits.

The economic development of Canada was continuous and rapid for twenty years, before 1958. The increase in gross national product was 5.16 per cent per annum from 1939 to 1955. (Royal Commission on Canada's Economic Prospects, 1957, p. 79.) Then it slowed, and in the first quarter of 1961, the gross national product, regularly calculated and reported by the Dominion Bureau of Statistics, actually showed a decrease. A recovery of 8 per cent in 1962 followed a devaluation of 7.5 per cent in the Canadian dollar. A large part of the development occurred in foreign subsidiaries. There are two features of this development that call for study, since they may have significance for other countries and for international business. One is the form that industrial development has taken; the other is its financing.

Venezuela has grown on exports of oil, subsequently supplemented by iron ore. Australia exports wool, meat, and metal ores. Countries are fortunate when they have surpluses of commodities for which foreign markets exist, for they are able to finance their development in the stages when they are still largely dependent on imports for the means of industrialization. How long do these stages take?

In Canada, from 1946 to 1955, a period of growth, primary manufacturing, a category that covers such processing of primary products as food canning, grain milling, and pulp and newsprint production, increased its contribution to gross national product only from 7.1 to 7.3 per cent. Secondary manufacturing, covering more extensive processing like metal fabrication, actually declined, its contribution falling from 22.2 to 21.6 per cent, despite the influx of more foreign branches. The greatest increase was in resource industries like mining and lumbering, which rose from 7.3 to 9.9 per cent. Agriculture fell sharply from 15.5 to 12.8 per cent. (Royal Commission on Canada's Economic Prospects, 1957, p. 83.)

Expectations were that the growth of processing and secondary manufacturing would reduce dependence on commodity and raw material exports. (P. 94.) These expectations have not been fulfilled. Principal Canadian exports are still commodities that are processed elsewhere, 63 per cent in 1959. (Senate Committee on Manpower and Employment, 1961, p. 33.) In the same year, 61 per cent of all Canadian exports went to the United States. (P. 34.) The earlier Royal Commission report on Canada's economic prospects included figures showing that secondary industry located in Canada exported 7.5 per cent of its output in 1929, less than 7 per cent in 1939, and less than 6 per cent in 1955. (P. 233.) After World War II, exports of farm products also declined. The lessons of this Canadian experience can affect the plans of other commodity-exporting countries who hope for improvement in the value and stability of their exports as a natural outgrowth of more domestic manufacturing, however obtained.

The directions of economic growth in Canada in the years following the war were influenced by the closing of the sterling area to Canadian exports of processed foods and the cars and appliances made in American branch plants that were established before the war to take advantage of Commonwealth preferences created by the Ottawa trade agreements of 1932. At the same time, American demand for imports of materials like nickel, iron, oil, aluminum, timber, newsprint, and electric power increased, as forecast in the President's Materials Policy Commission's *Resources for Freedom* Paley Report, presented to President Truman in 1952. The result, as already noted, was the flow of 61 per cent of Canadian exports to the United States in 1959.

The concentration of exports in unprocessed goods and raw

materials is natural and even advantageous in the early stages
of economic growth, since it earns the wherewithal for importing otherwise unobtainable manufactured goods for both consumption and additions to productive capacity. Indefinite reliance on commodity exports, however, leaves the producing
country exposed to fluctuations in demand which have generally
been greater for commodities than for manufactured products,
and to the increasing possibilities of advanced processing and
of substitution with synthetics, which can exert continuing down-
ward pressure on commodity prices. Furthermore, continued reliance on exports of raw materials fails to stimulate the profits
and the additional employment, particularly the higher grade
employment, afforded by manufacturing. Hugh Aitken has expressed the view that the only growth possible for Canada now
depends on raw material exports, mainly to the United States.
(Aitken, 1961, p. 184.) However, he does not consider either
the problem of employment or the possibilities of more advanced processing.

Manufacturing activity has increased in Canada, South Africa,
Venezuela, and Argentina, but the kinds of manufacturing that
have appeared have not been conducive to export and have not
been integrated to aid healthy growth. They have been accompanied by intensive efforts to stimulate domestic consumption.
Building plants and access facilities for exploitation of natural
resources provides only a temporary boom, especially in employment.

Construction increased from 4.6 to 6.5 per cent of Canadian
output between 1946 and 1955 (Royal Commission on Canada's Economic Prospects, 1957, p. 83), following closely the
expansion of resource industries. The government, however, was
subsequently forced into subsidized housing and public works
to maintain employment in the building trades. The owners of
raw-material deposits do not encourage processing at the source
because they have acquired the raw materials deliberately to
feed existing processing plants in the United States. Furthermore, higher processing would invoke much higher duties on
importation to the United States.

Building branch plants in Canada for local production of

industrial equipment and consumer goods has not improved the situation fundamentally. They have often been planned to do solely the minimum finishing required to satisfy the Canadian tariff requirements, while the ingredients are imported to Canada from the United States. These branch plants have not made any plans or efforts to become integrated in a self-sustaining development. They copy American products exactly. In Venezuela, there are at least Spanish labels, and some exports have been smuggled into Colombia.

As far as Canada is concerned, all smuggling has been from the United States since the end of Prohibition. The 44 per cent of Canadian manufacturing that is controlled from the United States (Dominion Bureau of Statistics, 1962, p. 59) provides no basis whatever, under present policies, for exports from Canada to the United States. The products are copies, production is not planned and costed in relation to exports, and the parent company's attitudes, the trademark laws, and American labor unions all stand in the way of profitable exports. American unions object even to exports from American subsidiaries abroad to third countries. The additional 13 per cent of Canadian manufacturing that is controlled from Britain and Europe (bringing the foreign-controlled total to 57 per cent) is not likely to contribute to exports to world markets because these companies also have other foreign subsidiaries and pressures to export from their home countries.

American automobile manufacturers in Canada provide an example of this complication in the development process by their persistence in simply assembling American parts, rather than developing local supplies—a policy that has been exposed and criticized in the report of the Royal Commission on the Automotive Industry. The president of the Ford Motor Company of Canada was quoted by the Toronto *Globe & Mail* on July 4, 1961, as replying that "no company in Canada is going to start out designing a new type of vehicle." (P. 19.) General Motors, however, has designed an Australian car, the Holden, which has achieved profitable export sales, particularly in South Africa. Sweden, another middle-sized country, has its own Volvo, although Sweden is near to an industrially more powerful neighbor,

Germany. These examples prove that countries with smaller home markets than Canada's can support a domestic automobile industry. The Australian example also shows that an international company can provide such an industry when necessary.

In addition to the currency debacle that has overtaken the bolivar and the Canadian dollar, there is evidence in Canada of a potentially more serious and less easily corrected maladjustment. This problem involves the failure of the kind of development that has occurred to keep the available human resources fully employed. Unemployment in Canada went up to 11 per cent in March, 1961, and in the large, politically sensitive French Quebec area, it reached 15 per cent. By comparison, the United States figure in March, 1961, was 7.7 per cent. The Canadian Senate Report, issued in June, 1961, warned that "there is a distinct danger that a considerable volume of unemployment will remain after the business cycle recovery now underway has reached its peak. . . . More is needed than an ordinary business revival; it is necessary above all to re-establish an adequate rate of economic growth." (P. 3.) The kind of growth is also important.

The explanation is often put forward that foreign subsidiaries entering countries like Venezuela and Canada have tended to be capital-intensive industries and that labor-intensive services come later. A gap or lag that allows unemployment of 10 per cent or more, however, stultifies the growth process. It destroys confidence among local consumers and foreign investors and forces governments into providing doles and public works financed by deficits that may jeopardize the foreign exchange rate and further deter foreign investments.

Improving the Structure
of Development in Foreign Countries

There are enough instances—General Motors in Australia, Ford in Germany, Hoover in Britain, Lever Brothers in India, General Electric in Brazil, Sears in Mexico, Procter & Gamble in the Philippines, the various Rockefeller activities in Venezuela—to demonstrate that international firms are flexible enough to aid integrated industrial development when the need is recognized. Firms are learning that profits are imperiled by lopsided development and ensuing unemployment. If that is not sufficient incentive for business to seek new policies, there is also the fact that government pressure is rising.

International companies may achieve increasing participation in diversified development of foreign economies by giving directors of their subsidiaries more authority over purchasing, product development, and export marketing. Specific efforts to provide employment are also possible, not only through more local buying of supplies and services but also through fuller evaluation of the total effects of the latest parent-factory labor-saving devices. On the local scale, these savings may be insignificant, while resulting unemployment and the use of scarce foreign exchange for importing the machines may be more significant. In any case, if these considerations are ignored in business planning, the initiative passes to governments.

Disinvestment by International Firms and Development

When a subsidiary is established in a foreign country, the implication is that it is there to stay. Investments in the costly papers required to obtain legal incorporation and registration of patents and trademarks, investments in the purchase of land, building factories, and even advertising, all seem permanent. The speeches about growing with the country are of course written by the public relations department, but the public and apparently the officials and even the economists of the under- and partly-developed countries have taken them literally.

In practice, the depreciation allowances granted liberally by most tax authorities give companies that make enough profits to take advantage of them a great deal of liquidity. This liquidity allows them the option of spending that money on the new equipment for which it is intended by the fiscal authorities or of transferring it to greener fields in other countries. If a large part of a country's industry is foreign-controlled and if a consensus develops that money can earn higher profits elsewhere, the aggregate result is disinvestment. If disinvestment is substantial or continued, it breaks the foreign exchange rate, causing devaluation as in Canada in 1962.

Devaluation is an obvious cause of profit reductions or losses for foreign subsidiaries. Before that stage is reached, however, failure to reinvest depreciation allowances and a portion of profits causes investment to fall seriously below savings. Less purchasing power is available, and plant and labor fall idle. When corporations control a large part of the investment in an economy, their combined opinions about the profitability of investments influence profits. In large, advanced, and relatively self-sufficient economies, governments can raise the rate of investment by public works and thus prevent drastic reductions in profits and employment. Also, the proportion of the depreciation allowances and profits of such countries that can be transferred elsewhere is relatively small. In smaller economies, with large proportions of foreign control, loss of confidence or simply outside attractions can result in a net outflow of investment and ultimately can depress profits. Government attempts to fill the gap can often only aggravate the difficulty.

No company would deliberately undermine the economy of a country where it has made investments, and not many are subject to panic. American investors, mainly corporations, remained remarkably steadfast in Latin America during the disturbance occasioned by the Cuban expropriations in 1960. Figures on United States direct net private investment in Latin America, reported in a new balance-of-payments statement produced in 1962 by the Department of Commerce, read as follows:

Year	New Investment	Reinvestment (in millions of dollars)	Total
1958	299	143	442
1959	218	202	420
1960	95	215	310
1961	203	200	403

It is understandable that new investment in Latin America dropped by more than half in 1960, as shown in the above table, but it is encouraging that new investment rose so far in 1961 and that reinvestment actually increased in the dark year 1960.

Private investment began to decline earlier in Canada, and the decline continued longer, with cumulative effects. Private investment dropped more than 15 per cent from 1957 to 1960. A further decline in 1961 was definitely traced by the Dominion Bureau of Statistics to increased foreign withdrawal of profits. (*Globe & Mail*, June 28, 1961, p. 19.) This withdrawal is in addition to movements of capital made possible through depreciation allowances. These liquid funds are often temporarily placed in the money market and could be the explanation of what have been described as sinister "hot money" movements.

The degree of control over savings and investments in Canada- and thus over the financial regulators of business activity— that have passed to the private business sector was revealed in the report of the Royal Commission on Canada's Economic Prospects. (P. 81.) In the years 1953-55, business savings through undistributed profits and depreciation allowances accounted for 53.7 per cent of the total investment in Canada. Considerably more than half of this sum would be under foreign control, since foreign subsidiaries predominate in the technologically most advanced industries and in resource industries (which obtain extra allowances for depletion of reserves as well as the regular allowances for depreciation of plant and equipment). Foreign financing accounted for 45 per cent of total net capital formation including the public sector in the 1959-60 period. (Dominion Bureau of Statistics, 1962, p. 49.)

There are no inherent disadvantages in the rising importance of corporate savings and investment. Indeed, it may improve the correlation of investment and savings by providing joint consideration of opportunities and financial resources at the corporate finance-committee level instead of at meetings in the money market between company promoters and individual investors. In countries like Canada and Venezuela the importance of corporate saving and investment is likely to be proportionately higher and concentrated in fewer firms than in the United States or Britain—and it is controlled from outside the country.

Back in 1958, when the tide of new investment in Canada

turned, there were no expropriations, no immediate threats to foreign trade from British entry into a protectionist Common Market, no slumps in either the stock market or employment. Yet it is clear that international firms were already at that time putting the brakes on expansion in Canada and also in Venezuela. A simple explanation is the increasing attractiveness of Europe—thanks to re-equipment and rising consumer expectations associated with the formation of the European Economic Community. Another factor may well have been that important men in New York, London, and Zurich began to fear that the twenty-year boom in Canada must be nearing its end. That kind of premonition among the men who control the rate of investment is often a cause of the anticipated effect. At any rate, the outcome was a general downgrading of the value of all foreign investments in Canada by the devaluation of the Canadian dollar. Furthermore, the Canadian government was forced into growth-restricting and profit-restricting measures like raising interest charges and tariffs on imports and reducing public expenditures to stabilize the foreign-exchange value of the Canadian dollar at the new reduced rate.

These severe reversals in Canada and in similarly situated, basically well-endowed countries, suggest that growth policies and recession remedies used by international firms and national governments may be based on some concepts that are not appropriate to or compatible with international economic development. The expectation that growth will be followed by rest or readjustment is itself an influence on economic activity, reducing the rate of investment. The assumption among international firms that maintaining continuity and aiding integration in any and every country where they operate is someone else's responsibility actually involves them in losses, as illustrated by the losses on Canadian operations that many American companies had to report to their shareholders in 1962. The freedom international firms demand to repatriate capital, which they use not to sell out to local investors and retire from a country but to transfer allowances intended for replacement of equipment from country to country, often offers apparent advantages to a particular firm, but it has contrary effects when exercised collectively.

In countries with high proportions of foreign-controlled industry, governments cannot maintain full employment independently. They can only succeed by restricting imports and directing investment and, if capital inflow dries up, by forcing savings from their own population. Thus they face a quandary. They must act, however, because democratic governments cannot survive mass unemployment.

The idea that a general reduction of tariffs overcomes these problems is unrealistic. Freer international trade holds no promise of higher exports from manufacturing subsidiaries of American companies in countries like Canada to the United States or to other countries where those companies have subsidiaries or where the market is dominated by exports from the United States. Tariff reductions threaten existing foreign manufacturing subsidiaries. Increased exports of raw materials do not offer compensating increases in employment.

Getting rid of obsolete theories and practices and finding constructive replacements for them are among the unfinished business of national governments and international companies. The former are strongly motivated by threats of unemployment, the latter by threats of losses. Both dangers are aggravated by the kind of development that leads to economic dependence on a narrow range of products and a small number of foreign markets and that therefore permits wide fluctuations in the rate of investment. International firms have direct control in these fields, governments only indirect, but there is a danger that governments may seek to acquire more control by nationalizing foreign subsidiaries. Companies, however, have the power to take direct, immediate corrective action. Basically, they can offer greater and steadier support for foreign subsidiaries.

16

BENEFITS OF INTERNATIONAL
BUSINESS ENTERPRISE

WHO GAINS from international enterprise? Who are
the beneficiaries? What do they gain? What are the benefits?
Answering these questions involves evaluation, not merely description. This chapter makes some suggestions, but the final
value judgments must be made by those who choose investments, careers, and governments.

Private investors are beneficiaries, but they do not invest their
money directly and exclusively in international enterprises, except for the few who buy stock in I.T.&T. and B. A. Tobacco.
The former operates largely and the latter entirely outside the
parent country. Decisions to invest abroad are made by the
investors' agents, the directors and executives of firms. The
tendency of corporation control to escape beyond the reach of
private shareholders—a tendency that Adolph Berle and Gardiner
Means originally discovered, documented, and explored—reaches
an extreme in the foreign subsidiary. Company officers vote the
stock in subsidiaries, and, by consolidating accounts, they avoid
reporting to the ultimate shareholders on separate foreign operations. Despite this lack of control or even information, companies with international interests have been popular investments. The outstanding "growth stock" recently has been International Business Machines.

Decisions that affect the market for securities, including the securities of international firms, are now made by professional investment managers. The significance of these groups and their opinions has been emphasized in Berle's recent book, *Power without Property.* Berle shows how control of investment through the selection of available stocks and new issues to be purchased, as well as the voting authority that represents power over management, have been relinquished by the primary savers to the trustees and executives of pension funds, insurance companies, and the like.

The number and variety of these intermediaries are great. A large block of Unilever stock was owned by the Church of England Commissioners. The Methodist Church of the United States for years held, by bequest, enough stock in the Scott & Bowne subsidiary of Beecham to elect one of their bishops a director. The Oxford and Cambridge colleges traditionally invested the accumulated wealth of their endowments in land. Between the two world wars, however, Lord Keynes's college, King's, Cambridge, and Sir Roy Harrod's Christ Church, Oxford, achieved profitable diversification with stocks. In the United States, a professional organization has been formed in this field, the Society of Security Analysts. The New York Security Analysts have made foreign tours, to Britain in April, 1961, for example, to view international business from the inside.

The common opinion of market experts about foreign operations is illustrated in *Market and Business Survey* issued in December, 1960, by E. F. Hutton & Company, members of the New York Stock Exchange. This survey noted that "over the past decade and a half a relatively few far-sighted managements have staked or reinforced their claims on the ground floor of what is now the most rapidly growing consumer market in the world—the European Economic Community. . . . Domestic firms have been transplanting techniques of mass production and distribution abroad, with a resulting high quality and low cost output. . . . The profits experience for well-managed companies has been little short of spectacular."

The most influential opinion in favor of investment in international enterprise has been, however, that of the finance com-

mittees of large concerns. They dispose vast investment funds
derived from depreciation allowances and undistributed profits.
Corporate managers also control patents, trademarks, and know-
how that can be turned into foreign investment. The reasons
why a company with distinctive products and exclusive processes should decide to open up new markets are obvious. The
money risked can be small, the rate of profit can be high, and
the aggregate volume can be great. Investors, especially the
professionals, encourage the step, partly to achieve windfall
profits, partly to hedge their investments.

Professor Galbraith has suggested that "the development of
the modern business enterprise can be understood only as a
comprehensive effort to reduce risk." (Galbraith, 1958, p. 101.)
The domestic risk in the advanced countries includes diminishing returns, declining profits, slackening growth. Every professional investor is now sharply aware of the need to supplement income stocks with growth stocks to provide capital gains
as an offset to inflation. Organizational investment takes foreign
risks, administrative and political, in order to escape the risk of
stagnation.

American, British, Dutch, and Swiss investments in other
countries since World War II have paid off handsomely. Temporary interruptions resulting from exchange difficulties in individual countries have not significantly affected the flow of
dividends. Beside higher income, there have been tremendous
capital gains. International enterprise has been highly beneficial
to the investor.

Managers as Beneficiaries

The directors and managers of companies that have undertaken international operations constitute a group with special
interests, generally in accordance with those of their shareholders
but going beyond them. These people have often been able to
show improvements in earnings ratios and large increases in
capital value, without going to the market for new money. This
success is ideal window-dressing. It earns them prestige at

home, while foreign activities add to their power. These gains are further reflected in the salaries they can justify to their shareholders, as well as to their home governments and the public. In some cases, international executives also receive from foreign subsidiaries fees and expenses that are lightly taxed. The capital gains from foreign operations can be particularly profitable to executives who have stock options. Thus international enterprise is attractive and beneficial to this group.

The younger men, the careerists in modern industry, are another group with special interests in international operations. They have before them examples like that of Hobart C. Ramsey, Chairman of the Worthington Corporation, who first joined his company in what was at that time the minor position of export manager. Foreign operations offer a variety of experiences and fruitful opportunities to acquire a profit-making reputation in growth situations. Foreign service offers glamour in business as well as in government. It also affords an outlet for the reforming zeal that inspires the best types of young men. The British Foreign Office has long enjoyed the pick of the graduates from British universities. International firms also attract the able and adventurous. In turn the men obtain broad knowledge and experience—and often real understanding of and sympathy for the people of other countries, especially when they marry foreign girls. This breadth can benefit them and their companies and can become increasingly important for international relations, especially for countries, like the United States, that maintain close liaisons among business, government, and the universities.

Voices of dissent have been raised, however, by labor-union officials in the United States. Some charge that international enterprise is a cover for the export of jobs to lower wage-areas. It is true that American workers are comparatively remote beneficiaries of foreign economic development. But the benefits of political stability from economic development throughout the world accrue to labor, as well as to other social groups in the advanced countries.

Foreign disturbances have stimulated investment, especially in defense, but they may also stir reactions on the domestic economic scene by frightening consumers and investors into short-term over-saving, which adversely affects business activity and employment. Foreign industrialization increases demand for machinery and specialized components, which have to be imported from the advanced countries. These needs stimulate increased employment, except when their influence is offset by the installation of labor-saving machinery. In the long run, physical exports and invisible exports like tourism gain in value from the spread of industrialization—as is demonstrated in the trade relations between the United States and Japan on the one side and Western Europe on the other. British laborers, however, who must rely on imports for bread and margarine, have had to accept adaptation of their exports from cloth to spinning and weaving machinery, from coal to electricity generators. Such changes weighed heavily on the men and women whose skills were exclusively engaged in tending the famous looms of Lancashire or digging in the Welsh mines. Few American workers face anything comparable because most American industries have a large home market, strengthened by tariff fences, such new influences as advertising, and tight connections with distributive outlets. American industries are also organized to provide transition benefits.

In the advanced countries, many traditional jobs in industries making staple goods and mass consumer goods for export are, however, doomed. Furthermore, unless they establish foreign subsidiaries, the United States and Europe lose also their invisible exports—the earnings from abroad provided by the royalties on their patents and their foreign profits. Without these earnings, American labor would have to pay higher taxes for offshore defense—or foreign aid would have to be reduced with political consequences affecting defense. Work previously done in the United States for foreign countries is now being done in those countries, and this shift is the main goal of foreign economic development. The strongest motivation for development in the less advanced countries is hope for full employment. The prosperity that developing countries are determined to have is modeled after that of the United States—particularly a high, and still rising, standard of living of American labor.

The future welfare of American labor depends on smoother, quicker transition to new products for home consumption and on foreign trade in industrial specialties. These goals can be achieved through American participation in foreign industrialization. American subsidiaries abroad are large importers of equipment and components from the United States, and they have a natural bias toward products with which they are familiar. The United States lead in these areas can be maintained by well-directed effort.

International enterprise receives warm and practical encouragement from the leading western governments. The Paley Committee's Report to the President indicated one reason why when it reported that one-third of the minerals considered strategically important to the United States are only obtainable abroad. It also noted that indigenous capital and technology for extracting these minerals might not be adequate. The advantages of United States control were discreetly left to be read between the lines. Tax concessions and other government assistance were, however, recommended, and were subsequently provided for American companies in the extractive field in foreign countries.

Benefits to the Investing Country

In industry generally, foreign operations add to the financial resources of a country, as British history shows, not only in the two wars with Germany but as far back as the Napoleonic wars. Today Britain, the Netherlands, and Switzerland need all the revenue they can get from the foreign subsidiaries of international firms domiciled inside their borders, in order to finance imports of food and materials essential to maintenance of their population, domestic industry, and their export industries. The United States has a surplus of physical exports, as well as large and growing invisible exports in the form of profitable investment in foreign subsidiaries. These sources of income are outweighed, however, partly by new foreign investments but mainly by foreign aid, both military and economic. There have been similar disbursements by Britain, mainly in the former colonies, despite Britain's difficulties in financing essential imports.

The financial resources for making gifts and loans—British subsidies to foreign rulers in the nineteenth century, as well as current American foreign aid—have enhanced the influence of the advanced western nations. The means for obtaining this influence may be the chief benefit their governments have recognized from international enterprise. A deeper insight shows, however, that foreign subsidiaries also exert more direct influence. They help improve conditions in less advanced countries, supplementing and eventually reducing the need for government gifts and loans. The fundamental objective of foreign aid is to enable the less developed countries to become self-supporting at rising levels. Reinvestment of earnings is therefore more advantageous than repatriation that would go to taxes to finance foreign aid. Their own industry must eventually support all these countries, but this can include joint ventures. International enterprise can help industries get started sooner and grow faster, while at the same time increasing local participation.

Benefits to Developing Countries

International subsidiaries benefit the countries where they locate by affording participation in the American, British, Dutch, German, and Swiss "way of life." The chance to own a motor vehicle has probably won more support for western economic ways than all the ideological activity of all the western governments. American and British-Dutch companies have built the service stations. Governments have improved the roads, using American loans, engineers, and bulldozers. The vehicles that have been most significant in this change have been, however, the Lambretta and Vespa motor scooters from Italy and the Volkswagen from Germany. In southern Europe and parts of Latin America, they have provided the same impetus to development that the original Ford provided in the United States. The so-called uncommitted nations are areas that lack modern roads, service stations, and cars—Indonesia, for example, and large parts of Africa.

The benefits of international enterprise to the countries where foreign subsidiaries are established need to be considered in relation to the governments of those countries, their workers, industrialists, investors, professional classes, and consumers. The common starting-point is the contribution of industrialization, including manufacturing within a country of as much as possible of its requirements, to economic development in foreign countries. Professor Hirschman has shown how local manufacture works by stating that "domestic availability" has become recognized as an "effective spur to further development" because "importing requires special skills . . . importing is subject to special balance-of-payments uncertainties . . . and the fact that a certain product is produced domestically is likely to result in efforts on the part of the producers to propagate its further uses." (Hirschman, 1958, p. 100.)

Industrialization is a fairly new objective in many parts of the world. The previous alternative was to concentrate on natural advantages, to grow cotton and tobacco in the southern United States for export to Britain, to grow pulpwood in Canada and sugar in Cuba for export to the United States, to grow beef in Argentina, coffee in Brazil, wool in Australia, rubber in Malaya. Why should Brazil, India, and now the province of Quebec, which is just downstream from Buffalo, want their own steel mills?

Obviously, some countries will continue to have surpluses of particular commodities that it will profit them to export and that other countries need to import. It would be absurd for Venezuela to try to consume all its oil. There could be advantages, however, in developing petrochemical industries—to avoid using intermediary countries for processing—in order to supply the needs of the growing Central and South American markets. Each stage of processing, whether for home market or export, offers opportunities for employment of labor and capital.

Manufacturing has generally provided higher wages, more continuous employment, more office and management positions, more demand for professional services, and steadier returns to the investor than the fluctuations and speculation in commodity markets allow primary producers to offer. In the future, these differences seem likely to increase. More processing of products reduces further the percentage of the final price that goes to the primary materials. Furthermore, the stages of processing and distribution of finished goods are being coordinated more closely by the use of computers. The steady flow from one stage to the next reduces inventories. Commodity inventories still collect, however, in pools at the source, and the producer pays the carrying charges.

Economic development is equated with industrialization. Industrialization is recognized as beneficial to employment, investment, the professional classes, and national governments. Governments benefit by the contributions of improved employment to political stability and by increased tax revenue. Professor Hirschman has added that "efficient public administrators, admittedly so much needed, can perhaps best be trained in the arts of management by being first exposed to the powerful teaching aids which are standard equipment in any industrial production process." (P. 155.)

The people who gain from industrialization as employees and investors are also, of course, consumers, and their consumer interests may seem at first to be adversely affected. The products of their national industries may be more expensive than imports. There will usually be one country, at least, that can manufacture anything more cheaply—and that country has often been Japan. The early stages of industrialization and manufacturing on a scale to serve small markets used to be equated with high costs. These last two propositions are now in doubt. A recently equipped factory will incorporate the latest improvements. As to scale, a volume that permits automation cuts the kind of labor bill that arises at the Ford plants at River Rouge, Detroit, or Dagenham, England. Labor morale and efficiency are often better in medium-sized plants. Large-scale operations make occasional unavoidable mistakes—like the Edsel car—extremely expensive.

Consumers pay more for domestically manufactured products in some cases because there is a monopoly profit provided by patents or excessive tariff protection. This system is, however, one way for a country to form the necessary capital for further industrialization. A large number of new multi-product plants built by foreign subsidiaries have been financed out of the profits of previous single-product assembly or packaging lines. There are many such factors to be considered when comparing the domestic price and the cheap foreign competition which Japan and others have offered from time to time.

The role of the international firm in the spread of industrialization provides benefits that have, on balance, appeared great enough to stimulate favorable policies toward foreign subsidiaries among most noncommunist governments, including moderate socialist regimes in Britain, India, New Zealand, and the Scandinavian countries. The chief benefit is commonly agreed to be the provision of capital. Direct acquaintance with the actual operations of international firms suggests, however, that transfers of money are of relatively minor significance. This suggestion is confirmed by the figures now being obtained on investment and profit factors in balances of payments. United States profit inflow exceeded private investment outflow throughout the 1950's.

The international firm can afford to wait for dividends while its plant is being built and its sales are being developed. It has credit that can mobilize local capital, especially in the form of bank loans. It can send in blueprints, machines, and teams of technicians. It has patents and trademarks. Its great contribution is know-how. Brazil can obtain a complex modern pharmaceuticals industry in a very few years. "Brazil now meets 95 per cent of its drug requirements as the result of investments from abroad." (Benveniste, 1961, p. 49.) Incidentally, the medical profession cannot grow as fast, which leaves scope for a good deal of self-medication. The country has, however, saved the long drawn-out research required in developing and testing new drugs. The cost to Brazil is the acceptance of foreign domination of this vital industry, meaning continuing high profits to the foreign owners.

Prior claims have been made for social improvements—public facilities like roads, schools, hospitals, and such state projects as "land reform"—on the theoretical capital invested by international firms. Much of the capital used by these firms—their patents, know-how, and credit, for example—would not be available for such uses, any more than a chemist could operate a power shovel. Even the finance is different. It is usually short-term and callable, rather than the long-term bonded debt required for housing and public works. International firms do indeed, as Professor Hirschman has remarked, "set up last industries first" (Hirschman, 1958, p. 111), notably consumer goods, but these industries can provide development incentives, reduce imports, and create employment.

This last national benefit, industrial employment, is extremely urgent because mechanization of agriculture is rapidly displacing large numbers of people. Displacement of agricultural labor will continue to spread because it is an essential element in improving agricultural productivity, inseparably related to other improvements like better seed and stock and better pest control. Investment in modernization of agriculture does not warrant any absolute priority and indeed must be kept in balance with other industries that can absorb labor. Indigenous manufacturing of implements and chemicals and modern food processing are highly effective means of increasing agricultural yield.

The international firms that distribute farm machinery, fertilizers, and insecticides also use sales methods that are effective in introducing improved agricultural methods. Professor Hansen has emphasized the need for education in underdeveloped countries, citing his experience in India, to clear the way for industrialization by breaking the hold of primitive traditions. (Hansen, 1960, p. 158.) In this connection, it is pertinent to remember that little more than a generation ago, farmers were still a stronghold of tradition in America.

The national governments of less developed countries may well expect greater benefits from some foreign subsidiaries than others, according to their respective influences on the balance of payments, a familiar and recurrent problem in Britain as well well as in Brazil and, since 1960, even in the United States. Those firms that can displace imports confer obvious benefits.

Since there is such wide demand for American manufactures, American-owned subsidiaries are often preferable.

Of course, such industries may increase imports of materials or components. The weakness of the Canadian automobile industry, as recorded in the report of the Royal Commission on the Automotive Industry as late as 1961, lies in its failure to develop enough Canadian suppliers of parts. The policy has been to import, in order to offer the same gadgets and slight model changes that are featured in the American advertising. There is also a possibility that extra profit has been earned from special discounts and allowances in the purchase of parts. A classic description of the strategic position of the supplier of parts was given by Alfred Marshall in his paragraph on joint products. (Marshall, 1930, p. 385.)

Developing economies receive extra benefits from companies that are prepared to go beyond supplying the national market and to export some of the products they make. Countries that encourage foreign subsidiaries incur the charge of remitted dividends, and foreign firms themselves cannot be indifferent toward earning the necessary foreign exchange. Foreign investment in extractive industries is usually made with a view to exports, which has led national governments to encourage them by concessions of land, subsidies for transport (railways and harbors), and generous continuing allowances for depletion of assets. But the further these companies go in processing the ores, oil, timber, and so forth in the countries where they extract them, the greater the benefits to those countries. Firms that are mainly processors but that maintain a certain local color and flavor in their products can also gain exports. Libby exports from Italy canned tomatoes that suit the British market better than the American type. In another category, Ford cars designed and built in Britain have a large sale in export markets.

The wide spread of industrialization and domestic manufacturing to meet domestic requirements makes exporting more complicated, while, at the same time, it is very important for countries that want to import industrial equipment and materials. A few really scarce commodities are being exported in increasing quantities. Other export opportunities are provided by manufactured specialties—Japanese cameras, Swiss cherry jam, Eskimo carvings, French pictures of Brigitte Bardot, as well as traditional British woolens, German chemicals, Italian silks, and Spanish sherry.

Traditional markets fade, however, in the bright light of present industrial knowledge, which creates so many innovations and substitutions. Nimble adaptability among manufacturers, rather than price cutting by commodity producers, is the best way to earn foreign exchange in the future. The Germans have had that adaptability, and they have made the German mark a strong currency. When they rebuilt their molds and assembly lines after the war, it was easy to provide for the extra feature on the product—maybe no more than a splash of color or a few words in Spanish and Italian—that would win the Venezuelan and other foreign markets. The manufacturing subsidiary that exports, as does British Ford, is unfortunately a novelty. It can, however, be an example. Another such example is profitable British Hoover, which branched out on its own with a "compact" or "economy" electric washing machine and gained wide export sales.

A new criterion of the value of a firm, from the standpoint of national governments, is the continuity of its investment for development. As yet, this criterion is little understood by either firms or governments. International firms are far ahead of the average indigenous company in planning for development, organizationally and financially. They usually reinvest full depreciation, often augmented by a proportion of profits. They use their access to new money to increase their investments. Business savings through undistributed profits and depreciation allowances are increasing in importance. They represented 53.7 per cent of the total investment in Canada in 1953-55. (Royal Commission on Canada's Economic Prospects, 1957, p. 81.)

The figures for Canada on sources of gross domestic capital formation, given in the United Nations *Yearbook of National Accounts 1960* show savings of private corporations plus provisions for the consumption of fixed capital—depreciation—by private corporations, as 64 per cent of the total, less the national deficit. For Australia, one of the few other countries that provide this information, the corresponding figure was 68 per cent.

These high rates are paralleled by the high percentages of industry controlled by international firms in Australia and Canada. It may seem natural that when an oil industry, for example, has been created, some of the capital, including depletion allowances, should be invested in new sources, probably in another country. But that kind of withdrawal of capital has disturbing monetary effects, especially when movements in a number of substantial industries coincide.

The basis for corporate planning and investment for development has been the profitability of the firm as a whole, without commitment or sense of obligation toward particular subsidiaries—or awareness of the effects of investment changes on the economies of the countries where the subsidiaries operate. On the contrary, there has been a consensus in international business that after a subsidiary has had the use of funds to help it get started, it should pass the bottle. It should let other branches in other countries have their turns and should also make financial contributions. Profits and excess depreciation allowances over immediate replacement requirements are commonly transferred to other countries that are still in earlier stages of development. Dividend withdrawals from Canada rose steeply in 1959 and 1960, as did the category of payments that includes charges for royalties and services (Dominion Bureau of Statistics, 1962, p. 66), and these withdrawals rose again in 1961. With respect to manufacturing particularly the Dominion Bureau of Statistics noticed that in 1960 "there was evident a somewhat higher repayment of capital from continuing direct foreign investments in Canada." (P. 32.) The insistence of international investors on rights to repatriate capital as well as profits accords with policies of using an international firm's capital as a revolving fund, first in one country and then in another.

National governments and their central banks are now alert to the necessity of counteracting the effects of "hot money" movements, short-term investments, but they have not yet come to grips with the problem of variations in the rate of long-term investment. As to the companies that cause some of these variations, they have not yet recognized the consequences. Their attention may need only to be directed by public discussion to the advantages they will gain from using their power to support continuous growth, especially in the considerable number of countries where they are becoming dominant. Otherwise, governments may find real reasons to distinguish between withdrawal privileges accorded to profits and those to capital. There is this much to be said for nineteenth-century British investment abroad: The bond issues to which they subscribed were for fixed terms, often with renewal options, and entirely without provision for suddenly withdrawing capital. Such a provision is included, however, in the strangely named United States treaties of "Friendship, Commerce and Navigation."

Beside the direct economic benefits of international enterprise, there are broader social considerations for national governments. Contrary to Marx, the spread of modern western industrialization need not reduce the great majority to a proletariat. Instead of producing a revolutionary situation, integrated industrial development weaves into a firm fabric of interlocking interests a wide variety of occupations and classes. Domestic manufacturing directly employs a variety of skills and talents. It upgrades labor by on-the-job training, and it offers opportunity incentives and, increasingly, financial assistance for higher education. It exerts what Professor Hirschman calls "linkage effects" with suppliers and distributors. These links afford opportunities for small independent businesses as demonstrated by General Electric in Brazil and Sears in Mexico. The effects also reach the professional classes. Even the local artist may be astonished to receive commissions for murals and landscapes for boardrooms. International firms attain their international position by introducing new products, which may also provide these ancillary effects.

The public in most countries has welcomed the growth of international enterprise because of the new products and the better jobs it provides. Owners of land and of some native companies have been happy to sell their property. The heads of native companies usually obtain good terms of sale for themselves, which compensate them for the loss of hereditary control. Modern education and the variety of careers it opens have reduced interest in carrying on family businesses. In smaller countries, more indigenous firms have been offered for sale as more industry has been internationalized. There is competitive pressure, but there is also recognition of the need for greatly increased resources to achieve modern technological progress, and this need extends to distribution as well as to production.

Not the least of the benefits offered by international corporate activity in this crowded, pushing world is a contribution to international understanding and cooperation. Substantial numbers of intelligent and energetic people of many nationalities work together in the international companies. They are influential. They share knowledge and experience. All international companies automatically contribute to an increase in travel and to the exchange of ideas, not necessarily limited to immediate business affairs. These people share an objective that goes beyond their own branches and their own countries: the prosperity of the international firm. Some companies stress this objective by paying bonuses to staff in all foreign branches on the basis of total profits of the international firm.

The operations of international companies embrace many countries and social classes. Centralized net profits are fractional in relation to the total capital, including know-how and credit, that they mobilize and deploy and in relation to the amount and quality of employment they provide—even when these profits represent exceptionally high returns on the original cash investment. Furthermore, the influence of international firms is dynamic, contributing to growth, particularly where growth is most urgent and specifically by the spread of know-how.

There is a limit to the benefits to countries that accept foreign subsidiaries, however, and probably to their future receptiveness, if the benefits are entirely material and exclude other development. People value their traditions and languages and the other factors that compose their distinctive cultures. Concern for their survival may rise in reaction to increasing international uniformity and increasing difficulty in maintaining a sense of personal identity. People all over the world demand freedom to determine their own policies on political and social questions and also on economics and business. These desires have not yet been harmonized with the organization and control through which international firms currently provide other benefits.

17

PROBLEMS AND PROSPECTS

A REAL step forward in any form of activity is apt to appear to open up more problems than it has solved. The climber sees new peaks. International organization of business has risen rapidly. New problems arise. Some are already acknowledged by progressive companies and provide the basis for new roads to progress. There are other problems that may stimulate the search for improvements as soon as they are recognized, but the searchlight of public discussion must first be focused on them.

One of the most difficult problems today is the suspicion abroad that the new international enterprise is the old imperial-colonial master in a new disguise. Frank and enlightened discussion is essential for correcting this impression, though frankness may be painful to some. In July, 1961, Pan-American Airlines, one of the foremost examples of international enterprise, was displaced in the management of Panair do Brasil. "We are able to do things better with our own hands," was the reason given by Brazilian businessman Celso Rocha Miranda. In reporting this change, *Time* (July 14, 1961, p. 80) used the adjective "nationalistic", which has acquired a derogatory connotation. Pan-American was, however, authorized by the United States Civil Aeronautics Board to continue control over Costa Rica's national flag airline, over objections that it was monopolistic, on the grounds that "if our national objective of maintaining U.S. leadership in international civil aviation is to be realized, there must be no diminution of U.S. influence in foreign aviation activities, especially in the Western hemisphere." (*The New York Times,* February 1, 1962, p. 3.)

If international business is an instrument of national policies for obtaining influence in foreign activities, nationalistic reactions are going to be difficult to avoid. Actually Pan-American has made contributions to international air transport that have served the interests of the people of many nations. The narrow views attributed to Miranda of Brazil on the one hand and the C.A.B. on the other are part of the problem of improving the prospects for international business.

Some of the recognized problems or complications of international business enterprise are on the way to being solved. The problems that most concern investors, officials of corporations, and the men who control the funds of investment trusts are the financial risks. The most alarming of these risks—because no business remedy seems apparent—is the risk of serious political disturbances. In the past, this risk has included Nazism, Fascism, and the Falangism that so seriously damaged the economy of Spain. Communism as in Cuba, or worse still, regional or general war are the risks today.

Governments are now insuring their firms against losses from political disturbances. There is, however, a better insurance against the risk of political disturbance, and international enterprise can provide it. This safeguard is simply more economic growth in the less developed countries, especially continuous growth. Nothing else equals prosperity for promoting political stability. People with vested interests in good jobs under union contracts providing seniority and pensions, businessmen with supply contracts and distribution franchises, and professional people on retainer—as well as the rentier class—want steady growth and oppose revolutions. The governments of the most economically advanced countries have recognized this fact by providing tax incentives for foreign profits and guarantees against foreign losses to encourage their companies to establish foreign subsidiaries, the American provisions for "Western Hemisphere" corporations, for example.

Another known business risk involves the extreme nature of

the business cycle in the less developed countries. Some of its causes are known and can be gradually brought under control. Among them are the wide fluctuations in commodity prices compared to those of manufactured products and the lack of "built-in stabilizers," like unemployment insurance, to which so much economic importance is now attached. The best means of controlling fluctuations is integrated industrialization in a modern framework of social legislation. This system reduces dependence on exports of unstable commodities. It is also important for the administration as well as the financing of unemployment insurance, which helps to maintain the internal market.

Another influence on business activity involving international firms is the fluctuations that occur in the stocks of raw materials, goods-in-process, and finished products, despite recent streamlining of production in the advanced countries. The importance of trade inventories is only beginning to be appreciated as an influence on the rate of investment, which is the critical factor in Keynesian analysis of the business cycle. Keynes himself devoted one short paragraph to inventories. (Keynes, 1936, p. 332.) Inventory figures were not available in the past.

The large amounts of investment that can be absorbed by inventories, over and above the fixed capital in plant and machinery, are being increasingly recognized, in part because of improved methods of inventory control. The attention given to stocks throughout the complete productive and distributive process has also revealed variations in the amounts of this kind of investment that can take place from time to time.

Beside inventory variations in the principal industrial raw materials, there are fluctuations in retail stocks, which have been exemplified for subscribers to the Nielsen research service by food and drug products. These fluctuations have clearly been related, in a significant number of cases, to trade attitudes on future prospects for prices and volume of sales. These attitudes in turn affect manufacturers' attitudes toward the purchase of materials.

Attitudes are influenced by doubts about business prospects arising from uneven rates of growth, even in the advanced countries, and these rates may in turn be affected by those attitudes in a vicious circle. The buying policies of companies, particularly international companies that control substantial portions of the commerce of developing countries, can affect both quantity and profit margins of their own sales by influencing the rate of investment. The implication is that it may be more profitable for such firms to buy with a view to helping keep inventory investment steady, than to follow the traditional policy of holding off on a falling market and building up stocks in a rising market.

Currency control is another known hazard of foreign operations. Even countries like Britain and France have seemed to pay for every forward step with a foreign-exchange crisis. In others, like Mexico and Canada, these crises have been less frequent and more severe. When they occur, the profits earned in local currency are reduced when they are converted for remitting, or in extreme situations remission may be restricted or profits may be controlled by government intervention.

To avoid this difficulty, international firms must assume more responsibility for earning, not merely profits but also the foreign exchange for such profits as they wish to remit. Exports, however, do not fit in with the current policies of many international firms. "International enterprise" has usually meant domestic manufacture for the domestic market only. Products have been completely standardized. These policies are not adequate for the maintenance of international growth, especially if international firms are to control increasing shares of national production. They will have to encourage exports by subsidiaries. This policy will have to extend beyond raw materials from the extractive industries into manufactures, to provide developing countries with higher returns and increased employment. An important parallel policy for international companies to consider is more active saving of foreign exchange by developing indigenous sources for materials and components.

Still another risk in foreign investment is the limitation of profits imposed by foreign governments. This limitation has been imposed more than once in Britain on profits of all companies, domestic and foreign. It has arisen from foreign-exchange crises, and it usually has been partly a political move to gain support for limitation of inflationary wage increases. The answer to this problem lies in more exports and fewer imports as noted above.

A financial risk that is an accounting nightmare was illustrated in Mexico in 1954, Israel in 1961, and Canada in 1962, and shows up annually in Brazil. This risk is currency devaluation. The accountants write down the current assets and occasionally even the total assets of foreign subsidiaries in such situations, and as a result the debits can exceed the annual profits. Foreign subsidiaries are often already earning abnormal profits in those countries, which can be realized if they are remitted promptly. The earning power of Brazilian subsidiaries in foreign currencies continued to be high when this procedure was followed. Spasmodic changes in economic activity must be recognized, however, as a financial risk. They are beyond the control of the governments and monetary authorities of all but the largest and most self-sufficient economic systems. When international firms come to exert a high leverage on an economy, they incur responsibilities for, as well as profit interests in, helping to maintain continuous growth by continuous reinvestment in new productive facilities.

There are a number of recognized problems or complications in international operations that are internal and administrative. The previously quoted memorandum from the Hutton brokerage firm to investors emphasizes "well-managed companies" and "far-sighted managements." A far-flung business has problems of information and control. Increasing decentralization, which will continue, enlarges these problems. It is elementary, although not yet generally recognized, that information should flow from the branches to the head office in regular written reports. The right kind of people have to be found to prepare them at one end and to read and digest them at the other. Adequate information is often a complete solution to the problem of control.

Providing such information exerts a salutary discipline on branch managers. It keeps them conscious of responsibility, not merely to an overseas director personally, but to the firm, many members of which may read their written reports. It forces them to clarify their facts and policies. Clear writing requires clear thinking. This organizational machinery or business system is not popular with the present generation of field officers, many of whom have risen from the ranks on the basis of practical experience and without much formal learning. Some of the business schools are not doing as much as they can to meet the need for executives, line as well as staff, who are skilled in communication. "Problem-solving" and especially "decision-making" can be emphasized at the expense of literary skill. There is also a general impression that the business school is a short-cut to executive power that provides escape from the scholastic drudgery of reading and writing. This view is not in accord with the requirements of complex international operations.

A more palatable remedy for lack of information and control is travel by home executives abroad and by foreign staff to the head office. The advantages of this method are extended, however, in time, as well as throughout the organization, by written reports. The educational advantages to foreign staff can be significantly broadened by visits to more than one country. Opportunities to see subsidiaries in other countries and to see general economic progress in Italy, Japan, and Mexico, for example, allay suspicions that participation in the ultimate benefits of international business is restricted by nationality or language.

Personnel for international business have been considered a problem. Sending them out from home raises questions about languages and social adaptability of the men and of their wives, and there are difficulties about nontransferability of pensions (particularly contributions to local government schemes), home leave, and seniority on return to the home company. For line management and for accounting, marketing, and production technicians at the national level, as well as for machine operators and salesmen, there is a simple solution: to employ citizens of the country where the subsidiary is being established. Natives, including British employees of American companies in the United Kingdom and American employees of Swiss companies in the United States, may lack the familiarity with the procedures of a particular firm that can be expected of employees in the home country. They can learn, however, and so can Africans, Asians, and even idiosyncratic Australians. They may have been brought up with the implements of agriculture rather than with tools and figures. The backwoodsmen of Tennessee, for one example, and housewives, for another, became munitions workers during the war, and many have stayed on in industry, holding their own with graduates of the older apprenticeship system. On-the-job training has become a highly successful technique. It is often combined with training in business-supported technical schools.

Methods are also available for training managers, usually in cooperation with the universities. There is often an original shortage of managerial skills for any industry that is new to a country. The United States imported its first rocket engineers from Germany after the war. The training of native staff may be a problem for international enterprise in some areas, but the problem is not insuperable. Indianization of subsidiaries by international firms, right up to the top levels of management, has proved entirely practical, and similar Africanization is proceeding.

A more delicate situation exists with respect to the social attitudes that local staff may have. Some of these attitudes may seem incompatible with good business. There is, for example, strong pressure to do favors for relatives and friends, sometimes at the expense of the firm, in many less-developed communities. Similar situations are accepted, however, because they are familiar, among the Boston Irish, and among Rotarians. The need for tact and firmness is greater in foreign situations, but one way to provide this is to delegate the responsibility to other natives.

The pivotal international personnel are the supervisory and advisory staffs. Successful companies have recruited them from their own nationals who have had experience in the operating management of foreign subsidiaries. Opening to foreigners this path to advancement and influence is a step toward international representation in top management of international firms.

The Need for Greater Integration
of Foreign Nationals

Problems that are not commonly recognized by international business present serious dangers. One such problem is the fact that international companies are not yet international from any point of view but their own. The control of international firms is concentrated in so few countries that the United States, for example, occupies a dominant world position. This is partly earned and partly an accident of bigness, but in any case it is directly contrary to American democratic philosophy. Some of the policies and actions of the United States government have been intended to guard against the danger that big American companies may dominate weak foreign governments. The unilateral attempts of the Antitrust Division of the Department of Justice and the Federal Trade Commission to prevent American firms from behaving monopolistically abroad have backfired, however. By attacking agreements between American and foreign firms, they have stimulated the formation of wholly-owned subsidiaries. Only the stronger American firms are in a position to go abroad on this basis. The American firms also have advantages of credit and know-how compared with local firms. The result is that they have less competition, either American or native, in smaller foreign countries than at home.

American tax laws and regulations increase the pressure for exclusively American operations abroad and place obstacles in the path of international participation. They allow tax privileges to foreign subsidiaries of American companies—Western Hemisphere corporations, for example—but only if they are wholly American-owned (interpreted as 95 per cent or more, to allow for shares given to the incorporating lawyers).

Native participation in ownership of industry must be actively encouraged, for economic as well as political reasons. This is agreed. But the effect of American law and regulations is to discriminate in favor of wholly-owned subsidiaries and against joint participation in American companies with investors in developing countries in exploiting materials and markets in those countries. The technology needed is of course American, but the technology is useless without foreign materials and markets. Furthermore, some of that American technology was originally borrowed, and foreign countries do contribute toward the cost of searching for improvements by paying royalties to American companies. Most international firms originating in other advanced countries are equally exclusive, without the excuse of antitrust policies or tax regulations. They have formed wholly-owned subsidiaries with the simple purpose of monopolizing the high profits obtainable from their patents, trademarks, and other know-how and their higher credit.

A basic policy of encouraging international participation has recently been described by the managing director of the Rio Tinto company, Val Duncan, who writes, "just as the idea of an Empire ruled from London has faded away, so has gone the idea of business interests in London having a right to control and manage the industry and commerce of Commonwealth countries. Instead, I find the idea of partnership applying not only to the development of natural resources but indeed to all industrial activities. . . . Countries are nowadays inclined to resent their inability to invest in their own industry. . . . I believe we shall see in the coming years a great extension of local minority investment in enterprises whose majority shareholdings are held elsewhere." (Duncan, 1960, p. xxii.)

Native participation in top management is also desirable and necessary. Senior officials of the subsidiaries of international firms occupy key positions with great social influence as well as economic power. Opportunity to reach the top of the local subsidiary is essential, but that alone is insufficient. There must be evidence that international firms recognize contributions to their earnings at the highest levels. Air travel would allow directors from abroad to attend parent-company board meetings. A man from Paris could fly to New York as easily and as often as a man from San Francisco. Americans freely attend meetings of their subsidiary boards in London and elsewhere. The obstacle is psychological and nationalistic. W. R. Grace & Co. has, however, taken the lead. "The Managing Director of the entire Peruvian operations, who is also a corporate vice-president of the parent company, is a Peruvian." (Burgess and Harbison, 1954, p. 8.) It is exceptional for a Peruvian to be a corporate vice-president of the parent American company. Many international firms use foreign managers in foreign countries, but they leave them there.

International firms tend to centralize research in their home companies and countries. Modern research brings together company laboratories and the universities; without this association with industry, science in the universities risks becoming sterile. This problem of centralization is difficult and serious for international business and for governments. Its long-term effects may be to widen the gap between the leading countries and the others. It could also be one of the main reasons why already "there are signs that the rich countries are growing richer and the poor nations, if not poorer absolutely, at any rate poorer relatively. The gap is progressively growing." (Hansen, 1960, p. 165.) National efforts will be made in the less developed countries to counteract this tendency, and they may be detrimental to international enterprise. It would be simple for foreign governments to disallow as business expenses any and all remittances for research, royalties, and management advice and to make them subject to profits taxes to help finance more domestic research.

The international patent system also needs re-examination. It is already being criticized for the restrictive characteristics and high prices in the manufacture and distribution of medicines. Some countries are already supplementing laws on compulsory use of patents with requirements that research to support claims for new products must be confirmed by studies made nationally. Such requirements offer only a partial and restrictive solution to the problem of encouraging more domestic research.

When international firms recognize the full breadth of their interests and responsibilities, they will widen their research through their foreign subsidiaries, in cooperation with national universities and government laboratories. If they procrastinate, more countries may view the rapid growth of pharmaceutical manufactures, for example, in countries that have never adhered to the International Patent Convention on health products as an incentive to withdraw. Member countries now obtain some new technology, but only at the convenience of international firms and subject to policy considerations of the larger national governments—as illustrated by United States restrictions on the release of information about atomic energy. Some countries are already aware of the contributions of industry to the research facilities and staff required to keep abreast of scientific development, and they are determined to take whatever steps are necessary to obtain equivalent contributions to science in their countries.

There are complaints that foreign branches use their branch status as an excuse not to make donations to welfare and education. The managers of some subsidiary companies argue that donations of the shareholders' money can be properly authorized only by the direct representatives of the shareholders on their parent boards of directors, not by subsidiary officers. That argument is legal sophistry. The subsidiary or branch is enfranchised by the local government, and it has community and social responsibilities of the same kind that are now generally recognized by the parent companies in their home countries. International firms can help their adopted countries by leadership, as well as by money, contributing good management to hospitals, orphanages, youth centers, and so forth. They can also introduce progressive treatment for the blind, the mentally retarded, and other groups, who can be helped toward better lives for themselves and can become less of a drag on the economy.

Social welfare may require social reform. International enterprise dare not, in its own interest, associate itself with reaction or standpat conservatism. Firms that manufacture internationally and such international distributors as Safeway, Sears, and Woolworth thrive on the growth of the mass market. They have a particular interest in the improvement of popular living standards. They are a powerful force for social evolution.

To achieve the best results, international firms must ally themselves consciously and actively with forces of reform. Myrdal has warned that investment without reform means reversion to colonialism. Galbraith has analyzed how social reform influences not only markets but also production. "Until the share of the ordinary man in the product is increased, his incentive to increase production—to adopt better methods of cultivation, for example—is slight or nil. The people of the so-called backward countries have frequently heard from their presumptively more advanced mentors in the economically more advanced lands that they should be patient about social reform. . . . Reform is not something that can be made to wait on productive advance. It may be a prerequisite to such advance." (Galbraith, 1958, p. 95.)

A more recent complaint is that the proportion of foreign investment in a country can grow too large. The critical issue is the effects on the rate of investment of a large amount of international control of a country's industry, specifically on the investment of depreciation allowances that are now granted by many governments on a scale that makes them an important form of saving. International firms are more likely to shift investment from one country to another than are domestic firms that do not have such a variety of opportunities. What they see as useful international mobility can become, in particular countries, at least dangerous instability.

International firms have been guided, also, by the consensus that, after a period of growth, a dormant period normally follows. They have shifted the weight of their investment from country to country accordingly. Such prophecies fulfill themselves. Slackened investment curtails growth. International business currently aggravates such ebbs and flows of investment. Firms in New York, London, Rotterdam, and Zurich are in communication with one another. Their directors meet in clubs and at bank lunches. They share views and tend to act in concert. But this communication also makes it possible for them to act constructively, once the full effects of international investment policy are appreciated.

Recognition of the drastic effects of disinvestment on business profits and on the value of fixed investments must lead to more self-discipline on movements of reserve funds from one foreign subsidiary to another, if international firms are to increase or even maintain their present shares in national economies. Insis-

tence on rights to repatriate capital by business and by the
United States government, at the instigation of business, are
ultimately self-defeating. The objective of business is profits,
not liquidity, and continuous reinvestment is conducive to and
probably a condition of profits.

The material improvement that is so widely desired has been
provided in many cases by international firms. Continued improvement can be greatly assisted by their activities. Professor
Hansen has stated that "continued growth requires an improvement mechanism." (Hansen, 1960, p. 191.) In the interests of
the firm, considerable progress toward the creation of an improvement mechanism has been achieved. It includes continuous
reinvestment and continuous research for new and improved
products and processes. These procedures are not simple, however, in practice, requiring great skill and experience, which are
largely vested at present in international business organizations.
This fact gives international firms great influence and power.
Berle has said that "great manufacturing corporations in the
main still enjoy much of their economic power without exterior
control." (Berle, 1959, p. 107.)

The desire for material improvement is accompanied in many
parts of the world by the demand for political self-determination.
This determination expresses itself in nationalism. Berle predicts
that "all societies will demand organization of power sufficient
to realize the economic potential. The issue is whether they will
also demand restraint and guidance of that power sufficient to
permit the self-determination of men," (P. 158.)

There is not really a question that self-determination will be
achieved. The people will endeavor to assert their sovereignty.
They cannot remain dependent, politically or economically,
without losing their self-respect. There has been no stronger
example in history than Cuba, so close to the United States in
every way, representing such a tragedy of ignorance. Not only
were the Cuban peasants misled in their ignorance, but American investors in Cuban plantations, mines, and factories were
also blinded by ignorance. They were simply unaware of the
political and social effects of their business activities. Duncan
has remarked, "One wonders whether things might not have

been a little easier if, instead of owning nearly all their interests in Cuba 100 per cent, Americans had given the opportunity on a broad scale to Cubans to invest in these enterprises." (Duncan, 1960, p. xxiii.)

Many countries face problems in restraining their own nationalism. International firms face problems in avoiding regulation and ejection in more and more countries. There is a need to demonstrate that there can be and will be no political interference because of the safeguards accepted, or even proposed, by international firms. International companies have some of the secrets of an "improvement mechanism." They will, however, have to use them multinationally and jointly with indigenous enterprise, and they will have to do so publicly to prevent rising nationalism from taking over.

Failure by national governments and international companies to cope with issues of political and economic authority and domination can wreck economic progress. These issues are the heart of the biggest single problem affecting the future of international enterprise. Business is autocratic and hierarchical in its internal organizational structure and restrictive in its sharing of profits and research. On an international scale, it therefore seems imperialistic and colonialistic. Sharing can be increased, although the form of internal organization can be modified only gradually to avoid loss of efficiency.

There is a way around the problem of authority—a way long familiar in political organization, where it has been tested by experience. It is not unfamiliar in the relations between businesses and the governments of their home countries. Berle says that "the American system is accountable," and "the real tribunal is . . . university professors, journalists, politicians" (Berle, 1959, p. 113), presumably because these people can furnish the information on which the public forms its opinions.

To Berle's list should be added a group who are considered both professionals and businessmen, the certified public accountants. Their province was described fifty years ago by Dickinson of Price Waterhouse as "to devise and propagate methods by which all the essential facts in industry gradually become the property of the community." (Quoted in DeMond,

1951, p. 63.) Responsibility to the public is maintained in politics between elections very largely by publicity. Responsibility in business is being increased in the advanced countries by the same means. Berle points out that "in many areas [of domestic business activity] actions or results apparently permissible under the rules of technical law are not acceptable according to the standards of the public consensus. This is the reality of economic democracy in the United States." (Berle, 1959, p. 113.) Publicity could help ensure responsibility in other countries. The conditions are that the facts be made available and that the groups that "become the forum of accountability for the holding and use of economic power . . . are able to communicate their views." (P. 113.)

Reform and evolution must come. Will they be accepted voluntarily? Will international companies and the governments of the advanced countries lift their vision to include economic growth together with political responsibility in the less developed countries? Myrdal has suggested that "the underdeveloped countries . . . have continuously to push their interests. . . . The effort from this side is necessary for progress towards equality of opportunity; for, as I have stressed, it would be illusory to expect that the advanced nations would accommodate them out of their goodwill." (Myrdal, 1956, p. 321.) Myrdal's pessimism, however, does not allow for the self-interest of international firms that are now widely committed to economic development. Some of them are already advancing, in ownership and management, as well as in service to suppliers and customers, toward true internationalism. They can form a useful addition to the number of institutions that promote common interests among nations.

18

AMERICAN INTERESTS IN

INTERNATIONAL ENTERPRISE

PHYSICAL international trade has been too small a proportion of total, American commerce to impress the general public. American labor is definitely hostile toward business done abroad through foreign manufacturing subsidiaries. Even in Britain, living from day to day on imports, the position was not much different until the recurrent balance-of-payments crises began. The practice was adopted of marking products "this is for export" to educate and stimulate workers, staff and public. There is still a question about the sufficiency of public education in Britain. Reverse reactions can occur. Why should foreigners receive the first and best of everything the British produce? Foreign buyers have continued to find British suppliers phlegmatic, and British economic development is sluggish. Similar exhortations to Americans to produce more and cheaper for export arouse no enthusiasm and solve no problems.

The code-stencilled crates of physical exports can be seen in factory shipping bays and on railway flatcars moving toward seaboard, but sales from branch factories in Bombay and Saõ Paulo are only figures on paper. They have been seen, until recently, only by the foreign departments of the companies involved. The United States government did not see them or know about them or appear to care about them, much less the general public. No detailed sales figures were collected. Financial transfers outward in investment and inward in remitted profits were recorded, but economists have difficulty, without statistics on sales and profits (whether or not remitted), in making adequate assessments of the amount and importance of this new kind of business.

In 1962, the government of the United States issued a call for information on all foreign companies in which there is an American interest of 10 per cent or more. This call is a most important forward step, provided that reciprocal arrangements are made with other countries, that the information is made public, and that the facts are used to improve policies rather than to support preconceptions.

This call for information was made, unfortunately, at the same time as proposals to tax the profits of foreign subsidiaries of American companies, except in exempt areas, at the source where earned and time when earned, rather than when remitted to the parent company in the United States. These proposals were postponed, fortunately, because they could produce complications. Many businessmen argue that operations of foreign subsidiaries are properly private and no business of the United States government. This view is even stronger in the Netherlands and Switzerland, and the United States Treasury would face difficulties in trying to collect or even trace profits of foreign operations that pass through those countries. Thorny questions of sovereignty surround this subject, and American interests will not be served by ignoring the interests, rights, and principles of other peoples. When the United States government asks for information, American businessmen are certain to comply, but if Swiss or other foreign citizens are also shareholders of the foreign subsidiaries involved, they can go to their own courts and obtain injunctions to prevent information from being sent out of their countries.

One of the first requirements of realistic policies on international business is recognition of a new legal situation—overlapping jurisdictions. American citizens or corporations owned by American citizens are granted the rights of citizens in foreign countries, permitting them to own property and to do business there. These subsidiaries owe allegiance to the governments that charter them. Assertions of overriding authority by American courts, on the plea of the Federal Trade Commission or other United States government organs, defeat their purpose. Such moves alienate foreign governments. The alternative is negotiations leading to international conventions, for which the necessary groundwork is more public information and discussion. Presumably, stimulation of such discussion is one of the long-range purposes of the new Department of Commerce action in requiring reports on foreign investments.

Beside the international legal complications, there is also a certain reticence among businessmen themselves, which is attributable to an understandable doubt about the capacity of public and government to comprehend the complexities of modern business. Similar attitudes are prevalent among medical doctors and atomic scientists. The public is affected, and therefore it, or at least its representatives, must be sufficiently educated to protect its interests. No phase of business activity is strictly private anymore. Its effects spread too widely.

Foreign operations are a fringe activity in relation to the total of American business, but businessmen are well aware that extra sales after overheads have been met are the most profitable. Extra sales are obtainable overseas. The substantial percentages of profits earned by foreign subsidiaries of a significant number of United States companies were reported in earlier sections of this book. Market extension through foreign operations contributes to profits, and firms that make profits are those most likely to expand, both at home and abroad. The fringe area is therefore decisive. International business is a real new frontier for American companies.

Isolationism is a theoretical possibility in business, as well as in international political relations. It is an alternative to the risks and complications of doing business in foreign countries. Industries can be organized within nations, and their international activities can be confined to export and import. This arrangement provides a neat system in which every national economy is clearly defined. It makes foreign trade more manageable by national governments, and it also simplifies matters for the monetary and fiscal agents responsible for balancing international payments. Complicated money movements to make private investments abroad, bring dividends home, or transfer reserves from one country to another can be avoided. Direct loans and repayments from government to government are much simpler. This national organization of trade is administratively attractive. While it may appeal to officials, it clearly involves a complete reversal of the recent trend.

The argument of comparative advantage, which is so often used to bolster national policies that emphasize physical international trade, is a neat textbook syllogism. So many qualifications are required to apply it to any real situation, however, that in practice it is of doubtful value and even misleading. The United States has not accepted this law in its import policy.

The intentions behind policies and programs for encouraging physical international trade are, of course, the opposite of isolationist. Fortunately they are also quite compatible with the continuation and extension of direct private investment in foreign manufacturing and distribution. This investment is, indeed, the most hopeful basis for long-term increases in exports. The danger in national export promotion is oversimplification and overemphasis at the expense of subsidiary operations abroad. The latter do not yet receive the attention and assistance they deserve.

There has been a failure to appreciate the extent to which industry has already been internationalized, the contributions to development that it makes, and the developing countries' need for economic integration. Sales from American subsidiaries not only exceed physical exports substantially, but they are also growing much faster. Good margins on these sales make a large contribution to the profits of the American companies concerned and also to the United States balance of payments. Except in the years 1960 and 1961, when there was a rush of new foreign investment, the remitted profits have exceeded the outlays for expansion of American business abroad. M. J. Rathbone, president of Standard Oil of New Jersey, said in a speech to the Economic Club of Detroit on April 9, 1962, that "in the past decade dividends remitted to this country [the United States] from foreign business operations have exceeded the capital outflow by some $7,000,000,000." This figure is remarkable. It means that American foreign businesses established earlier are making so much profit that they have been able to provide all the recent investments aimed at future earnings, while still sending profits home. No similar situation has occurred since the days when emigrants from Europe were able to earn enough to send money home, while building businesses for themselves. Of course, that only happened in America.

The failure to appreciate the contributions of international business to development applies only to its amount and its special quality. There is agreement in the United States and in many of the countries seeking development that private enterprise is the mainspring of the economic organization they are seeking to foster. That is, there is agreement in principle. There is considerable confusion, however, about how to persuade more private firms to expand and start new subsidiaries. The crux of the problem is that private enterprise is essentially voluntary, and even the mighty United States government cannot compel companies to incorporate themselves and start taking the risks of making electric motors in Venezuela.

Often in desperation to get some business started, the government offers grants and loans. These can be made directly or from funds vested in international development banks. They go into projects suitable for this kind of aid—public works and so-called basic industries, a favorite being cement plants. These projects are very useful, but they are no substitute, economically, socially, or politically, for consumer-goods industries. Furthermore, government assistance has been accompanied by priorities for the kinds of investment that are suitable for governments or financial institutions, and they have omitted or relegated to some "other" category many kinds of manufacturing, distribution, and service establishments that make up an integrated economy. As a result, the development plans merely assume that these establishments will appear. They figuratively clear, drain, and plow a field—and even supply the seeds—but leave planting, harvesting, and processing the crop to take care of themselves.

International companies have demonstrated that they can do much to fill these gaps.

The quality of the investments made abroad by American companies is unique. It is quite different from that of government loans. Companies, rather than governments (except in some branches of agriculture), have the new products, the machines, the production and distribution methods that are wanted and needed by other countries. Many firms are the exclusive custodians and sole sources of these advantages, thanks to patents or practical experience. Transfusions of capital are no substitute for this type of investment. Money alone cannot buy this know-how. Some companies have willingly and profitably invested it abroad, and more could do so.

Purely quantitative trade expansion fails also to stimulate the kind of development that many countries need and demand. They want to be emancipated from the vagaries of commodity exports. More trade is not enough, if it does not further that independence. They also want the variety of occupations and the improved working conditions that are enjoyed by the citizens of industrialized countries. They want industrialization and, as the Mexican economist Victor Urquidi said, they want "industrialization in depth." Such industrialization can be quickly provided through direct private foreign investment that also stimulates the rise of suppliers, distributors, and services from the native soil.

It is too late to turn back to industrial isolationism, the organization of industry exclusively on national lines and within national limits. The American commitment to the advantages of international business is already too great. It has developed rapidly for most American companies since World War II, a short period compared with other historical developments of similar importance. The colonial form of organization of production and distribution evolved through centuries, not decades.

The commitment of the United States to this new form of international economic organization is already deep and extensive. There are a few companies originating from other countries, notably Nestlé, Philips, and Unilever, that have gone as far as any United States company, but the American aggregate is incomparably greater. It is too late to change the direction of this development. Many recent United States investments are only beginning to bear fruit in terms of both profits and local production for developing countries. Many are still pioneers that can benefit from being followed by suppliers and buyers. India and Latin America are depending on large and continuing increases in integrated industrialization. Early attainment of self-sustaining economic development, which the United States is committed to help bring about, depends heavily in many countries on importation. Although they can mobilize their own internal credit, if given expert advice on techniques, they must import some physical capital, mainly machines and components, and production and marketing know-how must also be imported. This know-how is concentrated in international firms, most of which are of American origin.

The advantages to the United States of foreign industrialization through subsidiaries of American companies are greater than figures can convey. Although the percentage of United States national income derived from foreign subsidiaries looks small, it is important to the balance of payments, the profits of many firms, and the incomes of insurance companies, pension funds, investment trusts. There is also a possibility that wide access to new ideas, obtainable from international research and product development, may augment the capital fund of innovations that is a factor in the rate of development of domestic American industry.

The political and cultural influence of the United States in the world is also greatly affected by American subsidiaries abroad. These companies are transplants of free enterprise, which strengthen the western form of economic and social organization against communism—assuming that they are responsibly managed. They actively aid the climb of large numbers of people from laboring to middle-class levels of technical and professional skill. Furthermore, an integrated economy, with great numbers and variety of factories and shops, is an obstacle to communistic centralization. There is practical difficulty in taking over and directing the diverse activities of an advanced economy, which thrives on decentralization and individual initiative. The opinion that an advanced economy is riper for socialization than a primitive society is based on a theoretical and oversimplified comparison between primitive agriculture and primitive industrialization that includes only a few large firms. The only integrated modern economy to be absorbed by communism so far has been Czechoslovakia which fell through treachery.

The advantages to the United States of foreign subsidiaries must be cultivated in the face of competition. The most experienced competitors are the British. They contributed greatly to the present form of international business organization. Old colonialist ideas have also persisted, however, and much of the British effort has been directed toward physical exports at the expense of foreign manufacturing. The British motor car industry, for example, has lagged in foreign manufacturing. Prospects of association with the European Economic Community have also distracted British attention from the opportunities to use their historic connections to participate in more rapid and integrated industrialization in the old and the new dominions. The Japanese are a new factor. Their ambitions for political empire have been successfully replaced by concentration on trade, and their necessary adaptability makes them ready to follow exports with foreign branch plants. They are even opening department-store branches in the United States to display and sell an increasing variety of their products. The next wave of foreign investment is swelling in France and Germany. Flushed with the benefits of integrated industrialization in their European Community and completely disillusioned with colonialism, they also can use growing manufacturing exports as a base from which they can expand into foreign assembly and production.

The new pattern of international investment and business operation was not planned by state or commerce departments, nor by banks or chambers of commerce. The companies that performed that metamorphosis responded only to environment. They were influenced by the prospects of profits. They acted independently. In some cases, firms discovered only afterwards —by a chance meeting in the Tamanaco Hotel in Caracas, for example—that suppliers and competitors were also becoming interested in Venezuela. Standard Oil of New Jersey went there to pump crude oil, pumping gasoline into Venezuelan cars and tractors as an afterthought. Aluminium Limited went abroad to obtain cheap electricity for manufacturing; foreign marketing of pots and pans was slowly and quite reluctantly undertaken later. Sears went to Mexico to sell American luxuries to the upper classes but found a middle-class market and local suppliers. Much more deliberate planning is now required by business, in addition to all the help that the United States government can provide, because of the rapid increase in economic planning by foreign governments.

Americans were simply responding to the exciting stimulation of extra profits in most of their foreign ventures. They kept their approach casual. In contrast, the British, the Dutch, and the Swiss depend on invisible exports to maintain their economies, and on large foreign earnings to pay their dividends. Both their governments and their companies had to seek policies that would increase foreign earnings. While not consistent or always far-sighted in this direction, they pioneered many of the institutional characteristics of the modern international enterprise. An example with some human interest is the selection, training, and rotation abroad of a managerial élite taken from the universities on personal and family, as well as academic, qualifications, similar to those required for the senior grade in the British Foreign Office and the old Indian Civil Service. British companies also pay transportation and fees for overseas employees to send their children as boarders to the British Public Schools, which have taken care of the educational problem for generations of colonial administrators.

United States subsidiaries have been welcomed in many countries, not with the intention of obtaining know-how or displacing imports, but simply as an alternative to and competition for the British and Dutch firms. In most countries, the reputation of the United States seemed to promise emancipation from colonialism. American executives are personally more informal. Also, as Europeans have remarked in their relations with the United States—specifically in the reports of the productivity teams sent here in connection with the Marshall Plan

—American businesses are far less secretive and exclusive than those controlled from other countries. They are readier to share knowledge and help others in business, including competitors. This flexibility can be a great advantage in adapting to the new national economic planning of foreign governments.

American enterprise characteristically has excelled in the commercial application and development of the foreign-subsidiary form of industrial organization, as in so many previous inventions and innovations. Americans have recognized a new principle, and they have refined and improved a new technology of investment and management. This process has reached the point where international business administration can become a part of the curriculum taught in American schools of business administration, while in other countries there is still incomplete recognition that business administration belongs on the same level with the traditional disciplines of engineering, medicine, and law.

American businessmen have been the quickest to adapt on a large scale to the new international economic conditions and specifically to the determination of all countries to seek the maximum possible degree of industrialization. The rush into foreign operations is the main reason for the investment aspect of the United States balance-of-payments problem in 1960. By contrast, Germany has accumulated sterile surpluses of foreign currencies.

Among the American contributions, there has been a very important new attitude and practice toward suppliers and distributors. The older European approach was to seize every opportunity for profitable business by making any component or providing any service that was required—that is, by vertical integration. Now companies are indeed interested in diversifying, but horizontally in parallel products, rather than in raw materials at one end and chains of retail stores at the other. This diversification is, of course, an object of domestic, as well as foreign, policy for American companies. American oil companies put their distributors of fuel oil and many of their service station operators into business for themselves, while the companies went into tires and accessories. The F.T.C.'s attitude and a desire to avoid unionization of employees in retail outlets may also have been influential causes. The results abroad, however, have been more companies, whether native independents or foreign subsidiaries, and more companies add up to greater efforts to find customers and a stronger push for development.

Associated with this helpful attitude toward other businesses is a modern American policy that Robert Woodruff of Coca-Cola pinpointed when he said, "We want everybody connected with this business to make money." Coca-Cola, of course, works with a multitude of independent businesses, at home and overseas—bottle and cap manufacturers, advertising media, builders of refrigerators and delivery trucks, as well as their own franchised bottlers and distributors and the restaurant and grocery trades. The old method was to use advantages in buying power or selling strength to obtain the maximum margin of profit per sale, without recognition of the fact that sharing profits with dealers provides incentives for increased turnover which can increase the ultimate profits.

In organization, American companies have introduced the separate corporation to handle business outside of the United States—Coca-Cola and I.B.M. World Trade, for example. They have also decentralized and delegated authority, allowing area groups considerable autonomy and scope for initiative. A number of American companies have executive headquarters for all their European operations located in Paris or Brussels or elsewhere on the continent. The chief of Latin American operations for Sterling Products made his headquarters for many years in Montevideo. These arrangements do not provide complete autonomy for national operating companies, but they are a step in that direction.

United States interests in international enterprise may not have been the first, but they are now by far the largest of any nation in the world. The interests are those of the United States as an economy and a body politic, as well as those of a great number of American companies and their employees and shareholders. The proportion of the United States economy directly involved is small, but the absolute investment and its influence are large. Furthermore, the social organization of the United States relies largely on free activity among individuals and companies, and belief in this principle gives the United States an interest in the adoption of free enterprise elsewhere.

There is plenty of room for further growth of American international firms. Study of the distribution of United States subsidiaries reveals that many American companies have still reached only regional levels in their foreign activities. Sears, for example, operates only in Latin America and Canada at the time of this writing. It has, however, expressed interest in expanding into Europe. In principle, there is nothing to prevent it from successfully introducing its purchasing and distribution methods in some of the countries of Africa also. The foreign subsidiary networks of such strong companies as General Foods and Procter & Gamble are still obviously incomplete. Campbell operates in far fewer countries than Heinz. Some companies have branches only in Europe, many more only in Canada. Opportunities already exist in Australia and several countries in Latin America, and more may open up soon in Africa.

There are many American companies with distinctive products and methods that do not yet have any foreign business. The Department of Commerce has estimated that less than 5 per cent of all American companies participate in export trade. Since all companies with foreign branches are also likely to have some export business, the percentage of companies with foreign branches must be still smaller. Many American companies are, of course, only regional within the United States. They may, however, find room for expansion in less developed and less competitive foreign markets more easily than at home. The natural first step in foreign development by these companies is to begin exporting to try out foreign markets. The most progress will be attained, however, if exporting is regarded only as a transitional stage.

Full use of the opportunities abroad requires adoption of an internationalization policy by the official organs of American business and by the United States government. This policy would extend the assistance and encouragement now given to the transitional stage of exporting to the further development of local manufacturing abroad. A policy of internationalization would also lead to the formulation of planned programs—by joint action of business and government and by groups of companies that coordinate their operations. These programs would supersede the unsystematic methods of the past, which overlooked many opportunities and missed many of the savings of time and cost obtainable from synchronized activities.

A policy of internationalization that would meet conditions now taking shape in the developing countries would also include clarification of taxation policy, Federal Trade Commission policy, business policy toward publication of information, business policy toward sharing advisory services, and general policy on tariffs and industrial protection.

Any tax discrimination or other fiscal measures aimed at discouraging the growth of productive foreign subsidiaries is based on ignorance of the value to the United States and other countries of the new international form of business organization. Moreover, such tax policies ignore the inevitability of this development. They can only delay the United States contribution, or else hand over to Europe and Japan the opportunity to supply know-how in this way.

The increasing numbers of American companies adopting the enlightened practice of taking foreign partners through joint ventures, licensing arrangements, and similar devices are in danger of antitrust proceedings—unless there is a clarification of policy through legislation or the courts. Such companies are making agreements with other companies that are often exclusive and could be called restrictive. United States methods of maintaining domestic economic growth through competition do not accomplish the same purpose in the new international situation. The kind of competition that the United States encourages among its domestic companies becomes, in some foreign markets, a fight between the two or three firms in each industry that are big enough to go abroad on their own. In this fight, the bystanders—the little native firms—get hurt. Competition among American giants increases their combined share of foreign markets and is thus contributory to monopolistic conditions in those markets. The detergents business in Venezuela, for example, is monopolized by two legally competitive American giants. Also the sovereign governments of other countries have the right to decide whether or not their interests warrant one or more companies in a new industrial field—and to allow an exclusive agreement between a domestic company and one American company, without having Washington's ideas of desirable competition forced on them.

Company policies on publication of information are already far more open in the United States than anywhere else. Extension of these policies to foreign operations would be easy. It would also be the simplest, cheapest, and soundest protection against charges of economic imperialism. It would help to refute them or, where they have substance, it would contribute to arousing public pressure for reforms. Information also performs a positive task by aiding the progress of ancillary firms, American and foreign, that enrich the patterns of industrialization in developing countries. The desirable increase of information can take established and familiar forms: detailed annual reports for foreign subsidiaries, country by country, and detailed histories and case studies.

The cooperative policy that American companies often pursue in the exchange of experience and advice meets a particular need of newcomers to international business, the need for advisory services—on trademarks, for example—that are found in the large and successful international firms. Wider foreign activities by more American companies require appropriate staff. Line executives for making operating decisions are often available in a foreign country, but advisory services must supply information, guidance, and specialized know-how. Sharing of experienced staff services is possible through loans from the leading companies or through the consulting firms that are now forming pools of men with international skill and experience.

One constructive objective, in the face of the United States determination to protect its standards and of other countries to industrialize, is to alter tariffs to obtain the freest possible trade in new products, machines, and specialized components, which are the means of industrial progress. Most countries recognize the need for machines and components. A trial period for imports of new products would serve the important purpose of encouraging companies to test foreign markets with a view to domestic manufacture there. This plan would require a subtle change of attitude among customs officials, both American and foreign, whose reactions toward any new or different idea have long been obstructive. A welcome in the United States for distinctive new products from other countries would help meet their need to earn foreign exchange by exports, and might contribute innovations for subsequent American production.

No nation in human history has ever had a broader or more generous conception of its international interests than the United States. This conception showed in the great relief campaigns after the First World War, in which Herbert Hoover became a national symbol, and after World War II in the Marshall Plan and subsequent foreign aid. American interests have also included the development and continuing prosperity of other countries by and for their own people. Aid, however, consists of loans of capital and gifts of technical assistance—not a permanent tithe on American income. Successful foreign assistance stimulates economic activities to supplement the assistance and eventually make it unnecessary. These economic activities include indigenous industry, which subsidiaries of international firms provide both quickly and efficiently. This service to American interests warrants the most careful attention to public information, foreign participation in management and ownership, and any other adaptations that improve relations between foreign countries and international business enterprise.

BIBLIOGRAPHY

Aitken, Hugh G. J., *American Capital and Canadian Resources,* Harvard University Press, Cambridge, Mass., 1961.

Amuzegar, Jahangir, "Foreign Technical Assistance: Sense and Nonsense," *Social Research,* Autumn, 1959, p. 253.

Balfour Committee, *British Industry and Trade,* Her Majesty's Stationery Office, London, 1929.

Benoit, Emile, "The Balance of Payments Payoff of Direct Foreign Investments," *Michigan Business Review,* University of Michigan, July, 1962, p. 9.

Benveniste, G., et al., *Trade and Investment Prospects for Japan in Five Latin-American Countries,* Stanford Research Institute, Menlo Park, 1961.

Berle, Adolph A., *Power without Property,* Harcourt, Brace & World, New York, 1959.

Berliner, J. S., *Soviet Economic Aid,* Frederick A. Praeger, New York, 1958.

Board of Trade Journal, "United Kingdom Direct Investment Overseas," October 6, 1961, p. 715.

Brewster, Kingman, Jr., *Law and United States Business in Canada,* National Planning Association, Washington, D.C., 1960.

Brownell, Herbert, *American Business in World Trade,* National Industrial Conference Board, New York, May 16, 1962.

Bugas, John, *1961 Annual Meeting of Shareholders,* Ford Motor Co., Detroit, May 18, 1961.

Burgess, E. W., and Harbison, F. H., *Casa Grace in Peru,* National Planning Association, New York, 1954.

275

Business Week, "Mexico Tightens Grip on U.S. Companies," March 4, 1961, p. 84.

Cabot, Thomas D., et al., *Cooperation for Progress in Latin America,* Committee for Economic Development, New York, 1961.

Coyne, J. E., "Living within our Means," Bank of Canada, Ottawa, 1960.

Cutler, F., "Financing U.S. Direct Foreign Investment," *Survey of Current Business,* U.S. Department of Commerce, Washington, D.C., September, 1962, p. 17.

David, D. K., *A Plan for Waging the Economic War,* Committee for Economic Development, New York, 1958.

DeMond, E. W., *Price Waterhouse in America,* Price Waterhouse, New York, 1951.

Dominion Bureau of Statistics, *The Canadian Balance of International Payments, 1959,* Queen's Printer, Ottawa, 1961.

————, *The Canadian Balance of International Payments, 1960,* Queen's Printer, Ottawa, 1962.

Donner, F. G., "The Worldwide Corporation in a Modern Economy," General Motors Corporation, New York, 1962.

Dowd, L. P. (ed.), *International Business,* University of Michigan Press, Ann Arbor, 1960.

Duncan, Val, "Meeting the Industrial Challenge," *Investors Chronicle Commonwealth Survey,* November 18, 1960, p. xxi.

Edwards, Corwin, *A Cartel Policy for the United Nations,* Columbia University Press, New York, 1945.

Ehrenberg, Richard (trans. Lucas, H. M.), *Capital and Finance in the Age of the Renaissance,* Jonathan Cape, London, 1928.

Fayerweather, J., *Management of International Operations,* McGraw-Hill, New York, 1960.

Fenn, D. H., *Management Guide to Overseas Operations,* McGraw-Hill, New York, 1957.

Fortune, "The Unilever Story," December, 1947; January, 1948; February, 1948.

Frey, A. W., *Advertising,* Ronald Press, New York, 1961.

Funston, G. Keith, "The Private Role in Foreign Aid," *Saturday Review,* January 12, 1963, p. 48.

Galbraith, J. K., *The Affluent Society,* Houghton Mifflin, Boston, 1958.

Gairdner & Company, Limited, "Exquisite Form Brassieres (Canada) Limited," Toronto, January 9, 1961.

Geiger, Theodore, *The General Electric Company in Brazil,* National Planning Association, New York, 1961.

Globe & Mail, Toronto, November 16, 1960, p. 7; June 28, 1961, p. 19; July 4, 1961, p. 19.

Gordon, Donald, "Question Marks for the 'Sixties," Canada National Railways, Montreal, November 14, 1960.

Halasz, Nicholas, *Nobel*, Orion, New York, 1959.

Hamberg, Daniel, "Less Noise, More Research," *Challenge*, May, 1961, p. 16.

Hamlin, D. L. B. (ed.), *The Latin Americans*, University of Toronto Press, Toronto, 1960.

Hansen, Alvin H., *Economic Issues of the 1960's*, McGraw-Hill, New York, 1960.

Harbison, F., and Myers, C. A., *Management in the Industrial World*, McGraw-Hill, New York, 1959.

Harrod, R. F., *Life of John Maynard Keynes*, Macmillan, London, 1951.

Henry, Harry, *Motivation Research*, Crosby Lockwood, London, 1958.

Hirschman, A. O., *The Strategy of Economic Development*, Yale University Press, New Haven, 1958.

Howard, F., Debates, House of Commons, Canada, Session 1960-61, May 27, 1961, Volume 5, p. 5486, Queen's Printer, Ottawa, 1961.

Hutton, E. F., and Company, *Market and Business Survey*, E. F. Hutton and Company, New York, December, 1960.

Jenkins, Shirley, *American Economic Policy toward the Philippines*, Stanford University Press, Stanford, 1954.

Kahn, E. J., Jr., *The Big Drink: The Story of Coca-Cola*, Random House, New York, 1960.

Katz, E., and Lazarsfeld, P. F., *Personal Influence*, The Free Press of Glencoe, New York, 1955.

Keele, C. A., "The Rising Bill for Drugs," *Sunday Times*, London, August 28, 1960, p. 27.

Keynes, J. M., *General Theory of Employment, Interest, and Money*, Harcourt, Brace & World, New York, 1936.

Lebhar, G. M., *Chain Stores in America*, Chain Store Publishing Corporation, New York, 1960.

Marshall, Alfred, *Principles of Economics*, Macmillan, London, 1930.

Marshall, H., and Taylor, K., *Canadian-American Industry*, Yale University Press, New Haven, 1936.

Millikan, M. F., and Rostow, W. W., *A Proposal: Key to an Effective Foreign Policy*, Harper & Row, New York, 1957.

Moody's Industrial Manual, New York, 1960.

278   Bibliography

Myrdal, Gunnar, *An International Economy*, Harper & Row, New
    York, 1956.
Neale, A. D., *The Antitrust Laws of the United States of America*,
    Cambridge University Press, New York, 1960.
New York Times, March 13, 1962, p. 11; April 24, 1962, p. 54;
    May 26, 1962, p. 27.
Nove, A., *The Soviet Economy*, Frederick A. Praeger, New York, 1961.
Penrose, E. T., *The Economics of the International Patent System*,
    Johns Hopkins University Press, Baltimore, 1951.
Pizer, S., "Expansion in U.S. Investments Abroad," *Survey of Current
    Business*, August, 1962, p. 17.
———, and Cutler, F., *U.S. Business Investments in Foreign Coun-
    tries*, Department of Commerce, Washington, D.C., 1960.
President's Materials Policy Commission, *Resources for Freedom*,
    U.S. Government Printing Office, Washington, D.C., 1952.
Printer's Ink, January 6, 1961, p. 16.
Rathbone, M. J., "Address to Economic Club of Detroit," Standard
    Oil Company (New Jersey), New York, 1962.
Rostow, W. W., *The Process of Economic Growth*, Oxford University
    Press, Oxford, 1953.
———, *The Stages of Economic Growth*, Cambridge University
    Press, New York, 1960.
Royal Commission on the Automotive Industry, *Report*, Queen's
    Printer, Ottawa, 1961.
Royal Commission on Canada's Economic Prospects, *Report*, Queen's
    Printer, Ottawa, 1957.
Royal Commission on Publications, *Report*, Queen's Printer, Ottawa,
    1961.
Senate Committee on Manpower and Employment, *Report*, Queen's
    Printer, Ottawa, 1961.
Sheehan, Robert, "I.B.M. Abroad," *Fortune*, November, 1960, p. 166.
Smith, Adam, *The Wealth of Nations*, Everyman ed., Dent, London,
    1910.
Strouse, Norman H., "Selling Advertising Abroad," *Advertising Age*,
    June 12, 1961, p. 87.
Taylor, W. C., Lindeman, J., and Lopez, V., *The Creole Petroleum
    Corp. in Venezuela*, National Planning Association, New York,
    1955.
Time, July 14, 1961, p. 80.
United Nations, *World Economic Survey 1959*, New York, 1960.

United Nations, *World Economic Survey 1961*, New York, 1962.
————, *Yearbook of National Accounts 1960*, New York, 1961.
United States Commissioner of Patents, *Annual Report 1960*, U.S. Government Printing Office, Washington, D.C., 1961.
Williams, B. R., *International Report on Factors of Investment Behaviour*, OECD, Paris, 1962.
Wood, Richardson, and Keyser, Virginia, *Sears Roebuck de Mexico, S.A.*, National Planning Association, New York, 1953.

INDEX

281